WITHDRAWN

The Religion of the Heart

The Religion of the Heart

A Study of European Religious Life in the Seventeenth and Eighteenth Centuries

Ted A. Campbell

University of South Carolina Press

Copyright © 1991 University of South Carolina

Published in Columbia, South Carolina, by the
University of South Carolina Press

Manufactured in the United States of America

Library of Congress Cataloging-in-Publication Data

Campbell, Ted.
    The religion of the heart : a study of European religious life in
the seventeenth and eighteenth centuries / Ted A. Campbell.
        p.   cm.
    Includes bibliographical references and index.
    ISBN 0-87249-746-1 (alk. paper)
    1. Spirituality—Europe—History—17th century.   2. Spirituality—
Europe—History—18th century.   3. Europe—Religion.   4. Europe—
Religion—18th century.   I. Title.
    BR440.C35   1991
    274'.07—dc20   91-6913

Contents

Illustrations

Preface

The reader should know that I have been committed to many institutions. I write, in the first place, as a Methodist elder charged with the responsibility of preparing women and men for ministry. I also write as a representative of a movement of Evangelical Christians who want to relate Evangelicalism to its deeper roots in Christian tradition. I write, furthermore, as a member of a University faculty, committed to critical, cross-cultural inquiry and understanding.

The Religion of the Heart reflects concerns that have arisen from each of these commitments. In preparation for Christian ministry, the history and tradition of the Church in the last half millennium is conventionally represented as dominated, on the distant end, by the doctrinal and practical issues surrounding the Protestant Reformation, and on this end, by the crisis of understanding brought about by the Enlightenment. I want to suggest that what I shall call "the religion of the heart" was a significant part of the Church's tradition and history in this period, and is now a significant part of global Christianity.

In the Evangelical movement's quest for its own roots, two poles are often represented. On the one hand, those concerned with the distinctiveness of Evangelical identity have stressed the movement's roots in the Reformation and Pietistic movements. On the other hand, those with broader ecumenical concerns have stressed the ancient and medieval traditions of Catholicism and Eastern Orthodoxy. *The Religion of the Heart* tries to show that the Protestant pietistic and revivalistic movements out of which modern Evangelicalism grew were themselves part of a broad European cultural movement that included Catholics, Eastern Christians, and European Jews as well.

The mention of a Jewish form of the "religion of the heart" reflects a third commitment that has shaped this book, namely, the commitment to understand the "religion of the heart" movements and their latter-day descendants as a cross-cultural phenomenon. To this end, I have explicitly utilized a methodology drawn from the comparative study of religious traditions. I am aware of the objection

ix

that because we exist and work within our own "language games" or "cultural-linguistic systems," the broad, cross-cultural understanding that I seek here is quite difficult; nevertheless it is one of the objects of *The Religion of the Heart*.

I must acknowledge my indebtedness to many persons and institutions who have assisted me in the research and writing of *The Religion of the Heart*. The three women with whom I live (Dale, Elizabeth, and Lydia) have offered me the gifts of time, patience, encouragement, and occasional rebuke and exhortation. The Bishop and Cabinet of the Texas Annual Conference of the United Methodist Church have made it possible for me to serve on the faculty of Duke Divinity School as a minister in special appointment beyond the local church. The Divinity School faculty, in turn, have encouraged this project, and the Divinity School allowed me the privilege of a junior sabbatical leave in the fall of 1989 to complete the first draft of the book. Several individual faculty members in the Divinity School and the Department of Religion have read chapter drafts, and have made helpful comments and suggestions. They may breathe somewhat more easily now, no longer having to dodge an intense colleague in the halls who always has a chapter draft in hand, ready to spring on them. I owe a special debt of gratitude to students in my seminars on "Continental and British Roots of Evangelicalism," who were forced to listen to bits and pieces of written chapters rather than lectures, and whose individual research projects have contributed to my store of knowledge about the religion of the heart movements. My graduate assistant, Richard A. Jenkins, has diligently worked for the last three years on this project, assisting with bibliographical work and also offering critical reflection: I am very much indebted to him for his contributions.

The Religion of the Heart is dedicated to the memory of Verda Odessa Williams Campbell (1900–1983), my paternal grandmother, and to the memory of Lockwood Printess Cammack, Sr. (1892–1972), my maternal grandfather. These two collaborated in writing an article on the history of St. Luke's Methodist Church in Beaumont, Texas,* and so became my familial predecessors as historians of the religion of the heart.

The Religion of the Heart

Chapter One

Introduction

It is Sunday evening in an Oxfordshire village. Members of a small Methodist congregation have gathered for worship in the evening, because a circuit preacher was not available in the morning. Their service consists of about five hymns with prayers and readings between them. The sermon (between the third and fourth hymns) is given by a lay preacher from Oxford. The church building they meet in was once a barn, but was converted for the Methodist "Society" over a hundred years ago, and its one-rank pipe organ is the focus of attention. The congregation consists largely of rural and working-class folk, some of them Labour Party socialists, most of them elderly. Theirs is an old and perhaps declining movement, but when they sing "O For a Thousand Tongues" to the tune "Lydia," one can still hear the strains of their youthful devotion.

At about the same time as the Oxfordshire Methodists are meeting, an Assemblies of God congregation in Texas is concluding its morning service. Theirs is the fastest growing religious denomination in North America, and their service shows the signs of youthful vigor. They have no hymnals, but sing short choruses printed in the morning bulletin. At the end of the service, believers come forward for prayers with the elders of the congregation. Their worship is restrained and ordered: there is a specific time for speaking in unknown tongues, and it is done very discreetly. A far cry from the lower-middle-class, isolated Pentecostalism of the recent past, they represent an upwardly mobile constituency, and are largely part of the politically active American religious right.

These religious communities, however diverse, are the contemporary offspring of seventeenth and eighteenth century European movements for a "religion of the heart,"[1] and they are representative of a broader range of contemporary religious life that traces its spirituality to those ages. Alongside the Oxfordshire Methodists and Texas Pentecostals, one might consider Catholic societies in Chicago promoting devotion to the sacred heart of Jesus, left-wing activist

1

base communities of the Pentecostal Methodist Church in Chile, the "invitation" given by Jesse Jackson at the conclusion of a political rally, or the ecstatic dance of Hasidic men in their Brooklyn community. The religion of the heart movements were critical in the development of North American culture because of their influence on the First and Second Great Awakenings. When Africans were brought to North America as slaves, they encountered the religion of the heart movements, and blended them with their native spiritualities. Pentecostalism, a twentieth-century descendant of the religion of the heart movements, has spread rapidly among the developing countries of the third world, and in many cases has merged with native cultural traditions. These devotional or pietistic movements, moreover, had broad and lasting influences on European and American literature, music, art, and even politics. The contemporary fruits of the "religion of the heart" movements, then, are everywhere apparent.

It is not altogether surprising that the modern descendants of these movements should be so diverse, since the movements themselves emerged throughout Europe and Britain against the background of quite diverse cultural traditions. In the seventeenth century, movements for affective devotion appeared in French and Spanish Catholicism in the form of Jansenism and Quietism, and in the rise of devotion to the sacred heart of Jesus. Before and during the English Revolution, concerns for heartfelt religious experience arose not only among the Quakers and other sectarian groups, but also among more conventional Puritans as well. Pietism, among Continental Protestants in the late seventeenth and eighteenth centuries, developed its own forms of affective devotion, as did the Evangelical Revival of eighteenth-century Britain and the First Great Awakening in the British colonies of North America. Far afield, in Russian sectarian movements of the seventeenth and eighteenth centuries, and in the Hasidic Judaism of the Baal Shem Tov, similar concerns for affective piety appeared.

What then was the distinctive element of the "religion of the heart" movements? Although they generally maintained traditional Christian or Jewish beliefs about ultimate or religious values, they diverged from earlier forms of Jewish and Christian religious life in their understanding of how the separation between the divine and the human is to be overcome. Put differently, we might say that they differed in their way of *approaching* the religious ultimate. Concurring with older religious traditions in their belief that human beings in their "natural" state are separated from God, the religion of the heart movements maintained that this separation is overcome in affective ("heartfelt") experience: typically, in experiences of repentance (sorrow over sin) and faith (personal trust in God), but sometimes in more vivid experiences of personal illumination. The key element in their understanding of religious life, then, was their insistence that the "heart," denoting the will and affections (or "dispositions"), is the central point of contact between God and humankind.

Having this central concern with affective devotion, the religion of the heart movements began to diverge from older patterns of religious life. While not denying that sacraments are useful means of grace, they insisted that the sacraments are ineffective without appropriate inward affections. While not denying that communal moral discipline is central to religious life, they insisted that it should flow from the religious affections, or at least that it should lead persons to the affective experience of God. While not denying that meditative practices, common in mystical traditions, were helpful in leading to affective devotion, they dismissed the suggestion that ascetic discipline is necessary to the experience of God. Theirs would be a "mysticism" (if it can be called that), not of monks and nuns in cloisters, but of the rising bourgeois classes of the northern European cities. Affective experience became the center of the religious life, so that sacraments, moral discipline, and meditative techniques were relegated to the status of means to a greater end, namely, the personal and affective experience of God.

Despite the prominent role of the religion of the heart movements in Western (and now global) culture, the predispositions of critical historians of the last century and a half have not favored these movements. For advocates of the Enlightenment, the religion of the heart movements represented a vulgar form of popular superstition and "enthusiasm" (the latter with decidedly negative connotations). For liberal Christians, the religion of the heart movements were an anti-communal, grossly individualistic perversion of religious belief. For religious conservatives of the early nineteenth century, such as the proponents of the "New Lutheranism," or the Tractarian Movement, the religion of the heart movements had distorted and diluted their national and denominational traditions. Historians representing the various descendants of the religion of the heart movements tended to be naively triumphalistic, and usually focused on their own particular predecessors. Even recent Evangelical historians have emphasized more the Reformation roots of Evangelicalism than its seventeenth- and eighteenth-century precedents.

Moreover, although a good deal of historical scholarship has been devoted to each of these religious movements, their interrelatedness has not been broadly explored. One exceptional book offering a survey of some pietistic movements of this period is R. A. Knox's *Enthusiasm: A Chapter in the History of Religion with Special Reference to the Seventeenth and Eighteenth Centuries*, published in 1950.[2] The result of more than thirty years' labor, Knox's work examines claims to special inspiration ("enthusiasm") from the New Testament through the nineteenth century, but, as the subtitle suggests, Knox devoted most of the work to a consideration of the religion of the heart movements in the seventeenth and eighteenth centuries. He considered, in particular, the Quakers, Jansenism, Quietism, the "French Prophets," the Moravians, and the Evangelical Revival.

Knox claimed in the dedication of his book that although he had set out to portray "a rogue's gallery, an awful warning against illuminism," he had warmed up to the enthusiasts in the course of his research.[3] However sincere this shift may have been, Knox continued to regard the enthusiasts as a threat to the unity of the Church because of their rejection of its authority and tradition. At his best, he regarded them as alien; at his worst, he was openly hostile towards them. For what reason would he neglect to consider the Catholic advocates of devotion to the sacred heart (amongst whom claims to illumination were very common) along with Jansenism and Quietism, other than the fact that devotion to the sacred heart turned out to be approved by Church authorities, whereas Jansenism and Quietism were not?[4] Knox's book, then, despite its usefulness, essentially reiterated the early-nineteenth-century conservative reaction against the religion of the heart movements. Oddly enough—for a book focusing on seventeenth- and eighteenth-century "enthusiasm"—it failed to deal with Pietism at any length, and was very little concerned with working out the cultural relationships between the movements, pointing out only as curious coincidences such facts as Antoinette Bourignon's acceptance among Scottish Presbyterians, or John Wesley's editions of her writings.[5]

In more recent scholarship (since the early 1960s), specific relationships between Pietism and the Evangelical Revival in Great Britain have been examined by F. Ernest Stoeffler, Martin Schmidt, Karl Zehrer, and Geoffrey F. Nuttall,[6] the influence of Continental spiritualities on early Methodism has been examined by Jean Orcibal,[7] and parallels between Christian pietistic movements and early Hasidism have been examined by Bernard Weinryb, Joseph P. Schultz, and Alan Lewis Berger.[8] Moreover, a considerable number of scholarly editions and translations of primary texts, and monographs on specific movements, have appeared in this period, and current interest in the history of Christian spirituality has spurred on the production of even more works relevant to the study of the religion of the heart movements.[9]

A contemporary writer, in the course of examining the parallels between Hasidism and Western revivalistic movements, has commented,

> . . . German Pietism, English Methodism, Russian Sectarianism, and Jewish Hasidism share three characteristics: religious excitation, a strong social conscience, and a powerful undercurrent of nationalist sentiment. Scholars have long recognized the existence of parallel movements of religious revival, but with the exception of Methodism and Pietism little has been done to examine the common developments and the links between these movements.[10]

Although the point about "nationalist sentiment" does not emerge in our research as a consistent theme, this book does hope to offer a narrative of the seventeenth- and eighteenth-century religion of the heart movements, interpreting primarily their own understandings of religious life, and focusing on parallels in religious life between them. It examines affective devotion as the consistent thread that unites these various movements, and in doing so it must consider not only how the movements directly influenced each other (such as the Pietists' direct influence on John Wesley), but also how the movements simply paralleled each other in religious life, leadership, and social structures. In this manner, it understands the religion of the heart movements as the mutual co-arising of a nexus of religious ideas in varied European cultural contexts.

Background: Forms of Religious Life in Western Christianity

For such a broad perspective as this work seeks, we need a set of interpretive categories that enable us to see general parallels between forms of religious life without distorting the particularity of specific cultural and historical movements. On the one hand, there is the need to see religious movements as such, that is, as movements vitally concerned with ultimate values, without reducing them to psychological, social, or more broadly cultural phenomena. On the other hand, there is the need to avoid a kind of monism that sees all religious life as inherently similar. The latter was especially the case with nineteenth century studies of "comparative religions," in which a frequent agendum was the attempt to prove that all religions are, "fundamentally" or "at the bottom," the same, despite outward appearances to the contrary. The same problem has arisen in more recent historical studies of religion in which attempts have been made to make diverse religious traditions fit rather narrow unifying categories, such as "the experience of the numinous" (Rudolf Otto) or the all-embracing category of religious myth (Joseph Campbell).

A more appropriate perspective for viewing the religion of the heart movements in a broad perspective would see religion in the broadest sense as constituted by a concern with ultimate values or "ultimate transformation," but would also recognize the highly varied and highly specific ways in which historical communities go about living according to their ultimate values. According to this approach, forms of religious life (ways of approaching the ultimate) will be identified across religious and cultural traditions, without presuming that ultimate values themselves are the same in these traditions. This approach assumes the pursuit of ultimate values as the defining characteristic of religious life in general, but does not presume that a specific form of religious belief or practice (such as belief in God, the unifying phenomenon of myth, or a specific kind of religious experience) will be found among all historical religious traditions. Moreover, large religious traditions, such as Hinduism or Christianity, will be seen as embracing many different forms of religious life within themselves.

The religion of the heart movements emerged as a distinctive form of religious life in Europe in the seventeenth century, but they emerged out of an intricate nexus of forms of religious life, sometimes appearing as the distortion or aberration of other forms of religious life, rather than the direct descendant of earlier pietistic movements. It is important, then, to consider the variety of forms of religious life in Western culture at the beginning of the seventeenth century, not only to understand the direct connections which the religion of the heart movements had with earlier forms of religious life, but also to see in a clearer context the wider background against which they emerged. In what follows, four distinctive forms of religious life will be identified, the last of which may be seen as the most direct precedent for the religion of the heart movements.[11]

The Sacraments and the Word

One widely recognizable form of religious life approaches the ultimate by way of specific persons, places, seasons, objects, and sacred stories (or "myths"); we might say, it finds particular points in the space-time continuum where the ultimate is revealed. This form of religious life characterizes not only preliterate peoples who conceive of sacred power as residing in certain acts, persons, and objects, but also older historical traditions. The fire sacrifices of the Vedic religion, the stress on ritual performance in the priestly writings of the Hebrew scriptures, and the ritual recitation of the Shingon sect of Japanese Buddhists hold in common the belief that the ultimate is approached in specific moments, rites, persons, places, and objects in the material world which become the doors through which the sacred is encountered.[12]

The religious life of the Western middle ages, the distant background of the religion of the heart movements, was a "sacramental" form of religious life (to use the Western Church's own distinctive term). The religious ultimate was revealed as a specific human being, Jesus Christ. In continuity with Christ was a sacred community, the Church, which continued the event of incarnation as "the body of Christ." Within this community, the grace of Christ was experienced through sacred acts (the sacraments of baptism, confirmation, the mass, penance, holy orders, matrimony, and last anointing), sacred persons (priests, bishops, and members of religious orders), sacred seasons (the annual cycle of the Christian year, with fixed commemorations of specific saints), sacred objects (relics), and sacred places (cathedrals, churches, shrines). The notion of sacrament, then, was not a theological abstraction or an auxiliary point of doctrine in the religious life of the late middle ages and of the Catholic tradition after the middle ages; it was at the very heart of religious life, expressing the means by which the separation of God and humankind was overcome.

By the time the religion of the heart movements emerged, the Protestant Reformation had already brought about a degree of reaction against this sacramental form of religious life, but Protestants differed amongst themselves as to how much of the sacramental system and its theology were to be retained. For the various Anabaptist movements, a thorough rejection was required: God could not be limited to specific times, persons, objects, or places, including the dominical sacraments themselves. "Magisterial" Churches (Anglican, Lutheran and Reformed), however, retained much of the older sacramental spirituality and theology. Anglicans and Lutherans would continue to speak of baptism as conferring the grace of regeneration (the new birth in Christ), and Calvinists saw baptism as at least the sign of the grace by which the elect are reborn. Similarly, Anglicans and Lutherans would insist on the "real presence" of Christ in (or under, or with) the eucharistic elements, and Reformed Christians would understand the Lord's Supper as communicating the presence of

Christ to those who received it with true faith, or at least as a symbol and reminder of Christ's presence. In their own ways, each of the Magisterial Reformation traditions retained the sense that there are acts instituted by Christ and intended by God to be the usual means by which human beings come into contact with divine grace.

What the Protestant Reformers did was to shift the emphasis from the "sacramental" mode of religious life to the "mythical," that is, they shifted the emphasis (in varying degrees) from a stress on sacred persons, places, objects, and acts to a stress on the sacred words which form the distinctive Christian "myth."[13] The religious ultimate was shown, first in the Eternal Word incarnate in Christ, then in the revealed Word of Scripture, but also in the Church's faithful proclamation of the Word. Because of their emphasis on the sacred story, the translation and reading of the Scriptures, preaching, and the understanding of the sacraments as themselves teaching or recalling the sacred myth became central to Protestant religious life.

It is particularly important, in understanding the religion of the heart movements, to note that in conflict with Roman Catholics (and in controversies amongst themselves), Protestants had become intensely concerned with the definition of correct doctrine by the beginning of the seventeenth century. This led to a "scholastic" enterprise of formulating and expositing Christian doctrine, a *Verkonfessionalisierung*, or hardening of confessional boundaries, against which the Protestant pietistic movements would react. "True Christianity," Johann Arndt wrote against the Protestant scholastic teachers in the first decade of the seventeenth century, "consists not in words or external show, but in living faith."[14]

Moral Rigorism and the Problem of Moralism

Another general form of religious life understands ultimate value as a universal "rightness" of things, and attempts to enable men and women to approach this ultimate (a divine law or eternal principle of rightness) by living rightly. For Confucians, the way to the ultimate lay in adherence to unchanging moral principles expressed in the ideals of respect for humanity and devotion to the family; for Taoists, by contrast, the way to the religious ultimate lay in constant sensitivity to the mysterious and ever-changing force pervading the universe. For Rabbinic Judaism and *Sunni* Islam, the way to sanctity lay in right behavior guided by a divinely given law, interpreted by an authorized religious community.[15]

In some cases, the religion of the heart movements grew out of a late medieval Christian tradition stressing rigorous moral life, flowing from the conversion of the will by the example of Christ. As popularized by the Brethren of the Common Life in fourteenth-century Holland, moral rigorism was pursued not only by persons in religious orders, but by committed laity as well. The *Devotio Moderna* ("modern devotion"), as their spirituality was called, was popularized in such works as Thomas à Kempis's *Imitation of Christ*, and involved an elaborate program of self-examination, confession, and the making of personal resolutions under the guidance of a spiritual director.

Despite its attractive spirituality, the *Devotio Moderna* became attached to a particular theology (sometimes associated with "nominalist" teachers) that held good works to be a prerequisite for the grace of justification. It was this nominalist theology that led Martin Luther and other reformers to reject the moral rigorism of the *Devotio Moderna* as incompatible with the doctrine of justification by faith alone. Despite the fact that Calvin and the Churches patterned after his Geneva community began to incorporate elements of moral rigorism,[16] Protestants in general remained wary of any program of moral reformation, suspecting that a theology of works-righteousness lay behind it. Protestant pietistic movements, such as the Evangelical Revival in England, often emerged in a reaction against what they perceived as "moralism."

Catholic pietistic movements also reflected similar concerns to avoid moralism. In the background of Jansenism, in particular, it is important to understand that in the last decade of the sixteenth century, Catholicism was torn on the critical Reformation issue of human nature and grace, with Jesuits and Dominicans taking opposing views. The Jesuits took, in general, what might be described as a more "optimistic" view. As expressed in a work by the Jesuit Luis de Molina (in 1688), human beings have freedom to accept or reject Christ's grace, and God grants grace on the basis of his foreknowledge of those who would make this free choice. The Dominicans, championed by Domingo Báñez, insisted on a more traditional Augustinian theology, according to which God not only foreknows those who will be elect, but actually determines who they will be.

The Dominicans attacked the Jesuits, identifying their teaching on grace as "Molinism," and associating it specifically with the errors of Pelagius. The Jesuits returned the favor by accusing the Dominicans of "Calvinism." In 1597 Pope Clement VIII appointed a "Congregation on the Help [*Auxiliis*] of Divine Grace" to investigate the charges and countercharges. Refusing to ratify an initial finding that Molina should be condemned, the controversy was carried on for ten years until 1607, when Pope Paul V simply decreed that the

Dominicans should not be accused of Calvinism, and Jesuits should not be accused of Pelagianism.[17]

The controversy *de Auxiliis* (as it was called, from the Congregation *de Auxiliis* appointed to investigate it) shows that Catholicism as well as Protestantism found the relationship between human moral effort and the divine "aid" (*auxilia*) given in the sacraments and in the proclaimed Word to be a crucial issue in the sixteenth century. Not just theologies, but alternative forms of religious life had come into overt conflict throughout Western Christianity in this period. The situation was complex, because almost no one understood the sacraments, the proclamation of the Word, and a program of moral discipline to be *incompatible* with each other; but on the other hand, the question of the *relationship* between these forms of religious life was a question of ultimate consequence for many Western Christians. Moreover, the issues raised by the controversy *de Auxiliis*, so similar to those raised by the Protestant Reformers, suggest that there was in this period a widespread religious anxiety, a search for security in one's relationship to God. The religion of the heart movements would emerge in many cases as a reaction against—or even as a subtle redirection of—the moralistic tendencies of the age, and as an attempt to respond positively to the religious anxieties of the age.

The Ascetic Mystical Tradition

A third recognizable form of religious life maintains that the religious ultimate is approached by a progressive course of ascetic discipline, initiation into secret learning, and meditative practices leading to union with the ultimate. This approach is most typically called "mysticism," although the term is problematic, since in a wider sense "mysticism" can denote any form of religious life that focuses on a direct or unmediated divine-human encounter. (On this broader definition, both our third and fourth forms of religious life would be described as "mysticism.")[18] Ascetic mystical teachings emerged simultaneously in the fifth century B.C.E. in the Vedanta traditions of Hinduism (the "way of knowledge" or *jñāna-mārga*), in Buddhism, and in Jainism. In late Mediterranean antiquity, techniques of *ascesis* ("discipline") and mystical meditation had become prominent in Hellenistic religious traditions that influenced ancient Judaism and Christianity.

Although teachings on mystical ascent had been advocated by Christians since ancient times, in the late medieval, Western Church the mystical tradition had developed as an extension of the tradition of moral rigorism. At the same time as the moral-rigorist program took its characteristic form in the *Devotio Moderna* movement, mystical teachings flourished in the Dominican communities of the Rhineland. At the time of the Catholic Reformation, the mystical tradition was again revived, in this case by members of the Carmelite Order. Mysticism also appeared in Protestant churches. Luther himself had been influenced early in his career by his reading of the works of Tauler and the *Theologia Germanica,* and edited the first printed edition of the latter. Although Luther vehemently rejected asceticism and did not in the end advocate a theology of mystical ascent, it is thought that his reading of mystical works at a crucial point in his theological development may have spurred on his rejection of the tradition of moral rigorism. Throughout the seventeenth and eighteenth centuries Calvinists (such as Francis Rous) and Lutherans (such as Jakob Böhme) advocated ascetic mystical teachings.

The religion of the heart movements of seventeenth- and eighteenth-century Europe were indebted, on the one hand, to medieval mystical teachings, and yet ascetic mysticism remained in those ages a constant threat to these movements, on the other. Quietism, in particular, is thought to have had precedents in the eccentric mystical teachers and communities that appeared in sixteenth-century Spain, some of which were identified as *Alumbrados* (or *Illuminati,* the "enlightened ones"). These teachers are known from the records of their trials at the hands of the Spanish Inquisition, which questioned and acquitted numbers of people regarding over-rigorous discipline, such as John of Ávila, a popular preacher in the region. Others were condemned, however, and records show that those condemned were often advocates of mental prayer, or were persons who shunned meditation on the humanity of Christ. Still, since the Alumbrados left no records of their own, it is difficult to judge in what particulars the methods they advocated may have actually differed from more orthodox mystical practices.

Advocates of Divine Love

Most relevant for the study of the religion of the heart movements is a fourth consistently identifiable form of religious life that stresses personal encounter with the divine through affective experience. In this form of religious life, the ultimate value is conceived of in highly *personal* terms, that is, the ultimate is a person (God, or a particular god) who has emotions, passions, and affections. This form of religious life may be described as "mysticism" in a broad sense, but replaces ascetic discipline and hidden knowledge among a religious elite with an insistence that the experience of God is immediately available to all persons through affective experience.[19] The religion of the heart movements of the seventeenth and eighteenth centuries correspond most naturally to this broad form of religious life, and there were some cases in which they emerged directly from earlier traditions stressing immediate religious experience.

The concurrence of an emphasis on heartfelt religious experience with a highly personal understanding of God and a stress on common persons' access to God is relatively common in religious history. The Hindu tradition of *bhakti-mārga*, "the way of devotion," which developed in the first two centuries before the Common Era, stressed "devotion" (*bhakti*) as one means to end the cycle of birth, death, and rebirth. Similarly, the thirteenth-century C.E. Japanese Buddhist sect of *jodo shinshu*, the "True Pure Land Sect," reacted against the ritualism and mysticism of earlier Japanese Buddhism (the Shingon and Tendai sects in particular) and insisted that the grace of the Bodhisattva Amida could alone bring men and women to a new birth in Amida's "pure land" whence they would be led to *nirvana* or fulfillment.

In Western Christianity, two distinct traditions that stressed affective, popular piety lay in the background of the religion of the heart movements. One was a tradition of apocalyptic speculation, often associated with claims of personal illumination. Apocalyptic teachers had appeared throughout the middle ages in the Western Church,[20] and during the Reformation age appeared in the most radical branches of the Reformation. Revolutionary Anabaptists identified themselves with popular movements for reform, and claimed immediate divine revelations, according to which the end times predicted in Daniel and the Revelation were quickly approaching. The violent overthrow of the city of Münster in 1533 by revolutionary groups, and the consequent siege and recovery of the city by Lutheran forces, largely discredited the apocalyptic teachers in the sixteenth century, although they were to emerge again at the time of the English Revolution.

A quieter religious tradition focusing on popular, personal devotion was represented in the Reformation age among Catholics by the development of Oratories and new religious orders in Italy early in the sixteenth century. Grounding themselves in the work of Franciscans and others who had preached itinerantly and fostered devotion among the common people, the sixteenth-century Italian movements tended to attract laypersons as well as those in religious orders, and focused on the cultivation of love for God and for all humanity. The "Oratory of Divine Love," for instance, a religious society consisting of thirty-six lay men and four priests, had been formed at Genoa in 1514. The idea of the Oratory spread throughout Italian cities, with the result that by the middle of the century, Oratories of Divine Love existed throughout Italy. In these societies, laity and clergy together committed themselves to a common program of prayer, fasting, frequent communion, and charitable work among the poor.

New religious orders of the early sixteenth century took up similar work. Reformers within the Franciscan order, at about the same time, formed a new order stressing strict adherence to the primitive Franciscan rule, including the work among the poor and itinerant preaching that had characterized the earliest Franciscans. These came to be known as Capuchins, for the distinctive pointed cowl they wore. Even more prominent were the orders of "Oratorians" (not necessarily connected with the Oratories of Divine Love) which were organized late in the sixteenth century and early in the seventeenth century. The Oratorians, in Italy and later in France, sponsored a program of prayer and itinerant preaching, and sought to make confessors and spiritual directors widely available to the public.

At the beginning of the seventeenth century, this tradition advocating the cultivation of divine love on the part of the laity found a prominent spokesperson in Bishop François de Sales of Geneva (1567–1622). Born of an aristocratic family, de Sales had been educated by the Jesuits, but belonged to no religious order. After his work in winning the area of France south of Lake Geneva back to the Catholic fold from Calvinism, he became Bishop of Geneva in 1602, and continued to act as a confessor and spiritual director. His *Introduction to the Devout Life* (1609) and *Treatise on the Love of God* (1616) laid out a program by which secular women and men could pursue the goal of spiritual perfection, and became widely read devotional treatises.

* * *

At the beginning of the seventeenth century, with the Protestant Reformation just in the past, Christianity in Western Europe was an intricate network of Catholic and Protestant Churches, with underlying spiritual traditions often crossing formal denominational boundaries. It was not just that there were Catholics, Anabaptists, Lutherans, Calvinists, and Anglicans in their own churches, but older Catholic traditions, like the teaching of mystical ascent, had come to be expressed by Lutherans and Calvinists. The tradition of careful self-examination under a spiritual director was taken up by English Puritans, like William Ames, who was teaching in The Hague. The tradition of preaching divine affection among the laity was carried on at the same time by François de Sales in Geneva, preaching to ex-Calvinists. The religion of the heart movements represented not only the continuation of the older tradition of the preaching of divine love, but also the subtle transformation of sacramental, rigorist, and mystical traditions, so that the whole, intricate religious background came to play in the development of new religious movements in the seventeenth century.

Foreground: The New Historical Context

The religion of the heart movements emerged from this religious background in a new set of historical circumstances—what I shall call its "foreground"—in the seventeenth and eighteenth centuries. The seventeenth century, in particular, must be remembered as a period of extended Christian bloodshed on the European Continent and in the British Isles. Conflicts between Protestants and Catholics had already raged for almost a century, with religious persecutions of Christians by Christians a long familiar reality. In England, Catholics burned Protestants during the reign of Queen Mary (1553–1558), then had the favor returned under her half-sister Elizabeth I (1558–1603). In France, the "St. Bartholomew's Day Massacre" of 1572 was but one instance of long and barbaric conflicts between Catholics and Huguenots in the late sixteenth century. These religious conflicts were fueled by the nearly universal supposition that a political state could tolerate only one form of religion.

The religious wars in Europe became even more widespread late in the second decade of the seventeenth century, in the Thirty Years War (1618–1648). The war began as a small uprising of Protestants in Prague, but spread to the Palatinate (the German territories along the Rhine) and eventually to most of Europe. The Holy Roman Empire, consisting of Spain, Austria, and other states, represented the Catholic side, and was dominated in this period by the Hapsburg family. On the other side were the Protestant states of Germany, Holland, England, and Sweden. France entered the conflict very late, and provided the resources necessary to secure a stalemate, with only slight Protestant gains. France, it is important to note, came in on the Protestant side: French Catholicism in this period ("Gallicanism") claimed juridical independence from the see of Rome, much as Anglicans claimed, and so could ally itself with the Protestant forces.

The Thirty Years War had significant effects on the development of movements for a "religion of the heart." France emerged as the leading political state in Europe under the leadership of Cardinal Richelieu, with its church largely independent of both Protestantism and of Roman Catholicism. The United Provinces (the present Netherlands) emerged as a Protestant center of trade and a haven affording religious toleration. It is not surprising, then, that many spiritual movements of the middle and later seventeenth centuries should arise in or derive from the Christianity of Northern France and the United Provinces. Although conventional estimates of the destruction wrought by the war have been exaggerated, the war did leave many parts of Europe in disrepair, and many areas were depopulated both by the war itself and by migrations from smaller towns.[21]

The causes of the Thirty Years War were more than theological: historians have pointed to critical distinctions between the economies, styles of government, and cultures of southern and northern Europe. From a cultural perspective, however, these non-theological causes are of little comfort, since the popular mind *conceived* of the war as a struggle over Christian teachings and practices, whatever the underlying causes may have been.[22]

The English Revolution was also an inter-Christian bloodbath, but in this case chiefly between rival members of the same national Church. Again, one can point to non-theological causes: the Puritans largely represented Parliament and the rising mercantile classes of London and the southern coastal cities; the "Anglicans" represented the Crown and the older feudal economy of the northern shires. In contemporary understanding, however, the struggle was also a conflict between those members of the Church of England who were satisfied with the *via media* that had been forged in the age of Elizabeth I, and those who wanted to "purify" the national Church along more obviously Protestant (specifically Calvinistic) lines.[23]

The outcome of the English Revolution, politically and ecclesiastically, remained unclear for some time. After an initial period of success by the Puritan forces, Charles II was restored to the throne (1660) and Anglicanism established again as the sole religion of the state, with "Dissenting" worship forbidden. Twenty-eight years later, Parliament invited a foreign prince (William of Orange) to invade England, and shortly thereafter passed an Act of Toleration (1689) granting a limited degree of freedom of worship to dissenting Protestants. At the same time, an influential group of Anglican and moderate Puritan divines advocated a "Broad" Church Establishment in which Dissenters would be included, although their plans were not realized.

The English Church and nation, then, remained unstable throughout the seventeenth century.[24]

Overt social and cultural conflicts provide a likely setting for new religious movements; perhaps even more so when religious values are prominently at stake in them.[25] In the cases of the Thirty Years War in Europe and the English Revolution, cultural conflicts simmering in the late sixteenth century boiled over into full-scale warfare in the seventeenth century. Several cultural shifts began to occur in this period, and they provide the immediate background to the development of movements for a religion of the heart.

In the first place, the wars of religion brought with them a sense of frustration, uncertainty, and futility. The wars in Europe and in England had accomplished very little, and religion could be blamed for the human suffering they brought about. German literature of the period during and after the Thirty Years War, including the novels of Hans Jakob Christoffel von Grimmelshausen, reflects a sense of frustration and anger over the War. Eighteenth-century writers could look back with some distance, but still recognized the futility of warfare. The warfare of previous generations seemed incongruous with Christian faith:

> There is a still more horrid reproach to the Christian name, yea, to the name of man, to all reason and humanity. There is war in the world! war between men! war between Christians! I mean, between those that bear the name of Christ, and profess to "walk as he also walked." Now who can reconcile war, I will not say to religion, but to any degree of reason or common sense?[26]

It followed that since Christian "parties" had wreaked the havoc of war, many after would seek a "party-less" (*unparteiische*) Christianity.

In the second place, the cultural conflicts of the late sixteenth and early seventeenth centuries led to a questioning of traditional authorities, and a consequent search for surer sources of knowledge. The seventeenth century began with the invention of the microscope and the telescope, and saw the development of experimental scientific methods. From Francis Bacon and René Descartes through G. W. Leibniz and John Locke, seventeenth-century philosophy was preoccupied with epistemology, that is, with the quest for the surest basis of human knowledge. Their questioning of traditional sources of knowledge would usher in the Enlightenment of the eighteenth century.

Although the religion of the heart movements have been portrayed as reactionary in clinging to older forms of belief and refusing to face the challenges of modern epistemologies, the fact is that these movements would themselves reflect much of the same passion for finding certitude as the philosophers of their age did. They could hardly see the critical nuance, but their own stress on the authority of inward assurance reflected a shift towards experience as the basis of knowledge. Some advocates of the religion of the heart developed epistemologies explicitly derived from that of John Locke, holding that religious experience provides basic data on which the mind may operate.

A third cultural motif that emerged between the seventeenth and eighteenth centuries was the conspicuous theme of "classical revival." Almost all despised the middle ages, whose Gothic architecture was decried as "the pointed style." Classical studies replaced the scholastic traditions of the universities, and classical culture provided models for literature and architecture. By the beginning of the eighteenth century the transition to Greek and Roman models of architecture was well underway. There was also a religious version of classical revival at the same time, indicated by the conspicuous rise in publications of ancient Christian texts, and historical studies of ancient Christianity in the period. Various programs for return to the pristine, primitive conditions of the Church were advocated, and religious reformers frequently would unconsciously write their own visions of Christianity into the past in their search for ancient precedents.[27] The various religion of the heart movements would claim that their versions of Christianity or Judaism were in fact a revival of true primitive Christianity, or of the pristine faith of Isreal.

*   *   *

Protestant and Catholic Reformations, proliferation of spiritual teachings, the warfare of Christian states, the rise of the middle classes, frustration and anxiety, distrust of traditional authorities, and classical revival—all of these factors lay in the background of the religion of the heart movements of the seventeenth and eighteenth centuries. But despite their historical backgrounds and foregrounds, historical events are also shaped by distinctive persons, movements, accidents, and providences. The rest of this book considers how the religion of the heart movements actually emerged against the background and foreground sketched in this chapter.

Chapter Two

Catholic Religious Movements of the Baroque Age

There emerged in seventeenth-century France, Spain, and Italy several distinctive religious movements, all of them subtly altered versions of older Catholic devotional traditions in the direction of a "religion of the heart." *Jansenism* grew out of the tradition of moral-rigorist spirituality, but insisted that the point of rigor was not the detail of one's confession, nor the performance of specific penitential acts, but was rather the cultivation of proper inward dispositions— true penitence, and true love for God. *Quietism* grew out of the tradition of mystical spirituality, but soon became a mysticism of the bourgeoisie, stripped of its traditional setting in monastic life. Though they differed widely from each other (and frequently attacked each other), both Jansenism and Quietism indicate the tendencies of Catholic spirituality that were active during, and immediately after, the Thirty Years War. Moreover, the remarkable revival of devotion to the sacred heart of Jesus, which grew out of the medieval tradition of devotion to the wounds of Christ, indicates the depth to which affective devotion had influenced the mainstream of Catholicism in this period. These Catholic movements emerged at the same time that Protestant movements for heartfelt devotion were developing in England and the United Provinces, and together with them represent the first stirrings of the religion of the heart movements.

The Jansenists

Jansenism originated in a Cistercian convent about eighteen miles southwest of Paris which had been founded in 1204 c.e.[1] In 1602 a new Abbess was appointed to Port-Royal, as the convent was called: she was Jacqueline Marie Arnauld, who at her confirmation had taken the name Angélique. She was ten years old (but almost eleven) when she became Abbess of Port-Royal. In 1608 Angélique Arnauld underwent a religious conversion after hearing a sermon by

18

Jacqueline (Mère Angélique) Arnauld

An engraving by Pieter van Schuppen (1623–1702) after a portait by Phillippe de Champagne (1602–1674); in Lillian Rea, *The Enthusiasts of Port-Royal* (London: Methuen and Co., Ltd., 1912), opposite p. 34.

an itinerant Capuchin. She began a reform of the convent, insisting on strict prohibition of private property, forbidding sisters to leave the convent, maintaining the daily office with regularity, and enforcing uniformity of dress, frequent fasting and abstinence, and silence, all of which were part of the strict Cistercian regimen.[2]

By 1625, the reforms of Port-Royal had attracted enough novices that the sisters were forced to abandon their old convent temporarily, and moved to a new house in Paris, Port-Royal de Paris. Two years later, with the assent of their bishop, the sisters of Port-Royal were formally removed from the Cistercian observance and were allowed to form their own *Ordre du Saint Sacrement* ("Order of the Holy Sacrament"). They took as their distinctive habit a plain white robe with a very large, red cross emblazoned on it. Up to this point, the story of Port-Royal parallels the stories of so many religious orders, which began with the strict observance of an older rule, and eventually became separate.

But in 1633 Port-Royal de Paris acquired a new spiritual director at the invitation of Angélique Arnauld, a director who would propel the convent into considerable controversy. He was Jean Duvergier de Hauranne, more commonly referred to as Saint-Cyran (or "the Abbé de Saint-Cyran") for the monastery over which he had been made titular Abbot in 1620. Saint-Cyran, like Angélique Arnauld was intent on the reform of the religious life, and in 1637 some of his disciples, men and women, returned to the older convent, now called Port-Royal des Champs, to live as hermits (or *solitaires*). In the next year, however, Saint-Cyran was imprisoned at Vincennes by order of Cardinal Richelieu, and died shortly after his release in 1643.

What prompted Richelieu to pursue and imprison Saint-Cyran is unclear; what is clear is that Saint-Cyran had identified himself as a vigorous opponent of the Jesuits in their theology of human nature and in their practices of penance and attrition.[3] In his days as a student at Paris and then at Bayonne, Saint-Cyran had befriended a Flemish theologian named Cornelius Otto Jansen. Together, they had devised a program for the reform of the Church, to which they referred enigmatically as "Pilmot" (the meaning of which has never been demonstrated). It is clear that the theology and practices of the Jesuits were the specific targets of Saint-Cyran's and Jansen's reform program. But Jansen, recently made Bishop of Ypres in what was then the Spanish Netherlands (now Belgium), died during the first year of Saint-Cyran's imprisonment at Vincennes (1639).

Two years after Jansen's death, with Saint-Cyran still in prison, a massive book written by Jansen was published. Entitled *Augustinus*, it purported to be a systematic exposition of the theology of grace as taught by Augustine of Hippo. Jansen claimed to have read the whole of Augustine's writings ten times, and the anti-Pelagian writings thirty times, while writing it. The latter is particularly important, since the work attempts to show that contemporary Jesuit theology regarding human nature, penance, and attrition was Semipelagian.

In 1649 the theological faculty of Louvain, influenced by the Jesuits, condemned five propositions supposedly drawn from Jansen's *Augustinus*. These were as follows:

(1) that some commandments of God are impossible even for "just" (i.e., justified) persons if they lack the specific grace that would enable them to keep them;

(2) that in the state of fallen nature, no resistance can be made to divine grace working within a person;

(3) that human merit and demerit require only a freedom from "compulsion," not a freedom from "necessity";

(4) that it is Semipelagian (and so heretical) to maintain that human beings can resist the work of prevenient grace; and

(5) that it is Semipelagian (and so heretical) to say that Christ died or shed his blood for all human beings.[4]

The same propositions were formally condemned in 1653 by the bull *Cum Occasione* of Pope Innocent X. Whether or not they actually reflect the thought of Cornelius Jansen (or of Augustine of Hippo, for that matter), they reflect most clearly how Jansen's thought was perceived in the Church. He was understood as undermining the Tridentine understanding of grace, and his work appeared not simply Augustinian, but actually Calvinistic to the Jesuits. With the controversy *de Auxiliis* barely in the past, Jansen's work raised again the spectre of Catholicism divided on the same issues which had rent the Church during the age of the Reformation.

A second and related issue with which Saint-Cyran and Jansen were concerned was the question of the purity of a man's or woman's intention in approaching the sacraments of penance and the eucharist. Saint-Cyran had rejected the notion, popular among the Jesuits, that a simple *attrition*, even one rooted in concern for one's own salvation, was a sufficient grounds for the administration of penance. The Jesuits argued that if there was a strong *probability* that a person was penitent, absolution ought to be granted: it was for this reason that their doctrine of penance came to be referred to as "Probabilism." Saint-Cyran wanted to insist on a more elaborate *contrition*, involving an examination for sincerity of intention, as the only appropriate grounds for granting absolution.[5] The contritionist program was well-suited to the rigorist religious community at Port-Royal to which Saint-Cyran was attached, and was understood as a natural concomitant of the Augustinian anthropology that Jansen and Saint-Cyran advocated. This combination of a sternly Augustinian theology with a rigorous approach to moral life (paralleling in some respects the theology and ethos of Calvinism) is distinctive of Jansenism, and stands in a clear contrast to earlier Catholic forms of religious life in which rigorous morality had been associated with the Nominalist theology, or was abandoned in favor of an attritionist approach.

In the decades that followed Saint-Cyran's death, Port-Royal became the rallying point for those French Catholics—Jansenists, we should now call them—who advocated both the anthropology and the penitential theology of Jansen and Saint-Cyran. By 1643 both Jansen and Saint-Cyran were dead, and by 1653 the Jesuits had secured a papal condemnation of Jansenist teachings (or, what they at least thought were Jansenist teachings); but the struggle over Jansenism was only just beginning.

In the next period in the history of Port-Royal and of Jansenism two prominent figures stand out, the first of whom was Antoine Arnauld, Angélique Arnauld's youngest brother. Antoine became a *solitaire* at Port-Royal des Champs immediately after he was ordained priest in 1641. A scholarly and reclusive figure, Antoine published in the year of Saint-Cyran's death a popular book, *De la fréquente Communion* (1643), which stressed the need for thorough preparation for receiving the sacrament, and especially the development of the right interior dispositions. A year later, he published the first of two works entitled *Apologie de M. Jansenius* (1644). Having taken up the tradition of Jansen and Saint-Cyran on both the issues of the human need for grace and the need for rigorous preparation for the eucharist and penance, Antoine Arnauld was attacked by the Jesuits. In 1656 he was formally censured by the faculty of the Sorbonne and his doctorate from that institution was removed.

Antoine Arnauld developed a critical ploy in his response to the bull *Cum Occasione,* which had condemned the five supposedly Jansenist tenets. Catholics, he reasoned, should agree with the condemnation of the five tenets; but they should not agree with the historical claim that Jansen actually taught them. The Bishop of Rome, he argued further, is infallible in his "right" (*droit*) to pass on theological matters, and rightly demands submission in these matters, but he is not infallible in matters of historical "fact" (*fait*), where he cannot demand submission. The Pope had erred, then, in *fait*, and so, the argument ran, Jansen's teachings had not really been condemned.

By the time Antoine Arnauld had been censured by the Sorbonne, he was joined in the defense of the Jansenist cause by one of the most formidable intellectual figures of his age, Blaise Pascal (1623–1662). Noted in the first place as a mathematician and scientist, Pascal had taken an interest in the life of Port-Royal from 1646 when his sister Jacqueline entered as a novice. He had considered becoming a *solitaire* himself. Although he did not take up the religious life, Pascal had a vivid religious experience on 23 November 1654, his "night of fire." On this date, he wrote the following words (referred to as his "memorial"), which he later rewrote and wore from that time as a kind of phylactery:

> The year of grace 1654
> Monday 23, November, feast of St. Clement, Pope and
> Martyr, and of others in the Martyrology.
> Eve of Saint Chrysogonus, Martyr and others.
> From about half past ten in the evening until half
> past midnight.
> Fire
> 'God of Abraham, God of Isaac, God of Jacob,' not of
> philosophers and scholars.
> Certainty, certainty, heartfelt, joy, peace.
> God of Jesus Christ.
> God of Jesus Christ.
> *My God and your God.*
> 'Thy God shall be my God.'[6]

In the next year Pascal began composing his *Lettres écrites à un Provincial* (commonly called the "Provincial Letters") in defense of Jansenism. These were published beginning in 1656, following Antoine Arnauld's condemnation by the Sorbonne. In the "Provincial Letters," Pascal used biting satire to attack Molinism as teaching a sufficient grace which is "sufficient without sufficing"[7] (that is, the Jesuits claimed only the term "sufficient grace," but voided it of meaning). Similarly, he excoriated Probabilism as teaching that one's sins could be forgiven without love for God.[8] For Pascal, religion without affective devotion was unthinkable: it was, after all, "certitude" and "joy" and "*sentiment*" that he himself had found on the night of fire.

Pascal's support signals the growing popularity of the Jansenist cause in the 1650s, even among laypersons as well as members of the religious orders. But with the Thirty Years War and the Peace of

L'an de grace 1654.
Lundy 23. Nov. jour de S. Clement
Pape et m. et autres au martirologe Romain
veille de S. Crysogone m. et autres &c.
Depuis environ dix heures et demi du soir
jusques environ minuit et demi

——— FEU. ———

Dieu d'Abraham. Dieu d'Isaac. Dieu de Jacob
non des philosophes et scavans.
certitude joye certitude sentiment veue joye
Dieu de Jesus Christ.
Deum meum et Deum vestrum.
Jeh. 20. 17.
Ton Dieu sera mon Dieu. Ruth.
oubly du monde et de tout hormis DIEU
Il ne se trouve que par les voyes enseignées
dans l'Euangile. grandeur de l'ame humaine.
Pere juste, le monde ne t'a point
connu, mais je t'ay connu. Jeh. 17.
Joye Joye Joye et pleurs de joye
Je m'en suis separé
Dereliquerunt me fontem
mon Dieu me quitterez vous
que je n'en sois pas separé eternellement.
Cette est la vie eternelle qu'ils te connoissent
seul vray Dieu et celuy que tu as enuoyé
Jesus Christ
Jesus Christ
je m'en suis separé je l'ay fui renoncé crucifié
que je n'en sois jamais separé
il ne se conserve que par les voyes enseignées
dans l'Euangile.
Renonciation Totale et douce
soumission totale a Jesus Christ et a mon Directeur.
eternellemt. en joye pour un jour d'exercice sur la terre.
non obliuiscar sermones tuos. amen.

Pascal's "Memorial"

Manuscript in the Bibliothèque Nationale, Paris; reproduced from a facsimile in Société des Amis de Port-Royal, *Trincentenaire du Mémorial de Blaise Pascal* (Paris: Presses de l'Imprimerie "La Ruche," 1954).

Westphalia behind them, the French government and Church moved to quell the religious controversy. Pope Alexander VII in 1656 dismissed Arnauld's distinction of *droit* and *fait*, and demanded that supporters of the Jansenist cause sign a Formulary of Submission.[9] The Formulary was presented to the sisters and others at Port-Royal in 1661; they largely refused to sign it. After lengthy negotiation, the Jansenists finally agreed to the Formulary in 1668, but then only on the understanding that they were affirming the Pope's *droit* in condemning the five tenets, and not his claim of historical *fait* in holding that Jansen had taught them. This led to a decade of relative quiet, "The Peace of the Church." At this point, the two houses of Port-Royal were divided, with the more conservative sisters who had signed the Formulary before 1668 taking Port-Royal de Paris, and the Jansenist majority retaining Port-Royal des Champs. In the period between 1668 and 1679, Port-Royal des Champs flourished, and in this period the sisters collected the private notebooks of Blaise Pascal and published them as his *Pensées*. Meanwhile, the Jansenist cause found wider support, in particular from the orders of Oratorians and Maurists.

The "Peace of the Church" came to an end in 1679 when Church officials, now alarmed at the growth of the movement, forbade Port-Royal des Champs from taking any new novices or receiving any boarders. Antoine Arnauld fled with a relatively new leader, Pasquier Quesnel, to the United Provinces, where Jansenist sympathies were strong. The renewed persecution of the Jansenists should be seen as consistent with the growing power of the French state under Louis XIV, and with a more widespread pattern of religious persecution in France (the Edict of Nantes, which had allowed Huguenots to worship publicly, was revoked in 1685).

Controversy emerged again in 1693 with the publication of Quesnel's *Nouveau Testament en francais, avec des Réflexions morales sur chaque Verset* ("New Testament in French, with Moral Reflections on Each Verse"), which again affirmed Jansenist principles against Molinism and Probabilism. Quesnel was imprisoned in France in 1703, but escaped and made his way back to Holland. Despite the popularity of his work, it was condemned by a brief of Pope Clement XI in 1708, and then definitively condemned as Jansenist in the bull *Unigenitus Dei Filius* (1713).[10] In the year of the *Unigenitus*, the remaining persons at Port-Royal des Champs were dispersed, and the buildings there were torn down and then burned.

This was not the end of Jansenism, however. Although Quesnel himself agreed to the condemnation and received the last anointing (although requesting a future council to reconsider), many persons, especially in the Low Countries, did not. The Church there was divided between those who accepted the condemnations ("Acceptants") and those who "appealed" for a Council to reconsider the issue ("Appellants"). In 1723 Dutch Appellants elected a schismatic Bishop of Utrecht, and the Jansenist Church there remains independent until this day.

It was in the wake of the Appellant controversy that Jansenism produced its most spectacular religious phenomena: the "convulsionaries" of Saint-Médard. Saint-Médard was a cemetery in Paris where, in 1727, a Jansenist deacon known for his austerities had been buried. A year later, when a monument was erected over his grave, a worker testified that the body in the grave had not deteriorated. This was interpreted as a miraculous sign, and soon pilgrims flocked to Saint-Médard. There followed numerous reports of cures from illnesses, often accompanied by convulsionary behavior. Men and women danced in the Spirit, some claimed to speak in unknown tongues, and women claimed not only the prophetic office, but also the priesthood, celebrating the eucharist, baptizing, and hearing confessions.[11]

If this was not enough, some of the participants asked bystanders to give them "relief" (secour) from the torments they were undergoing. The "relief" they requested took the form of bodily punishment: some asked to be kicked or walked on, some to be beaten, some to be cut with swords, some even asked to be crucified.[12] Eventually the government moved to forbid the secours, but throughout the eighteenth century there were some Jansenist circles in France where miracles, convulsionary phenomena, and the use of the secours were regarded as signs of divine favor.[13]

If the convulsionary and related phenomena represented the "underside" of Jansenism in the eighteenth century, there was another continuing side of the movement, also clandestine, but considerably more influential and respectable. Throughout most of the eighteenth century, Jansenism remained the most vigorous religious opposition in France. Though legally forbidden, its continuing existence is well attested through its clandestine weekly newspaper, Nouvelles Ecclésiastiques ("Ecclesiastical News"), published beginning in 1728. Its editor, Jacques Fontaine de la Roche, developed an elaborate system of codes that enabled contributors, printers, and editors to collaborate while successfully avoiding arrest by civil authorities.[14] The Nouvelles Ecclésiastiques was distributed throughout France, and is known to have been read by bishops and other high-ranking church officials as well as parish clergy and members of religious orders.

There are two other relatively clear indications of the extent of Jansenist influence in France in the early eighteenth century. One is the number of clergy who formally called for an investigation into the bull *Unigenitus* upon its promulgation in 1715, the other is the number of clergy who supported the Jansenist Bishop Soanen of Senez when deposed from his see in 1727. Of the several thousand clergy involved in each of these two cases, it is clearly that they were preponderantly from the northern areas of France (except for Brittany), with a very large accumulation in Paris (not surprisingly, where *Nouvelles Ecclésiastiques* was published). Moreover, these cases show that Jansenist support had come to be especially concentrated in the area around Paris by 1727.[15]

Given Jansenism's wide appeal as a religious movement, we must ask how it can be understood as a "religion of the heart"? This is a critical question, since there is a very specific sense in which the Jansenists were *opposed* to "affective devotion," and that is the sense in which "affective devotion" denotes the mystical tradition taught by the Jesuits in the seventeenth century.[16] Despite their vivid religious experiences, such as Pascal's "night of fire," the Jansenists did not uniformly stress a direct, personal experience of God, that is, an experience in which the person of God is the direct object of human experience. Some did, such as the convulsionaries, but more conventional Jansenists, writing after the time of the English Revolution, would look with horror upon the Quakers and other "visionary" sects who claimed immediate divine revelation.[17]

There is another sense, however, in which almost all Jansenists reflected a transition towards affective or heartfelt religion, and that lies in their consistent teaching that the experiences of sincere contrition and love for God are conditions for receiving the grace of the sacraments, and the surest evidences of divine grace. The "heart" was a central category for Jansenist spiritual writers, who distinguished it from the intellect. The heart, they maintained, is the center of the affections, and is the root or principle of personhood. The heart stands in contrast to the intellect, which is merely the "surface" of human personality.[18]

This shift in religious intentionality can be seen in the Jansenists' attitude toward the sacraments. The Jansenists, from Cornelius Jansen on, insisted that without interior contrition, the sacrament of penance was worthless.[19] Unlike the medieval nominalist theologians against whom Luther and Calvin had reacted, the Jansenists stressed not only the necessity of a complete confession in which a human being could accomplish all within her power before divine grace would be given, but also the interior motivation, itself a divinely given gift. Thus the Jansenists developed a new form of the contritionist spirituality, one tied intimately to the Augustinian theology that had, ironically, been the theological grounds for the *rejection* of contritionism by the Protestant Reformers.

Antoine Arnauld's work *De la fréquente Communion* ("On Frequent Communion") provides an insight into the shift in religious life that the Jansenists brought about. The book is directed against Probabilism, and is an extended argument against "frequent communion," that is, against what Arnauld perceived as the Jesuits' prostitution of the mass (and the sacrament of penance) by admitting persons to the eucharist, and granting absolution, to those who had not given evidence of a complete, inward contrition. The work is by no means an attack on the sacramental system itself; its consistent presupposition is that penance and the mass are the divinely ordained means by which Christians receive forgiveness for post-baptismal sins.[20] But *De la fréquente Communion* presents a critical nuance in sacramental theology: the grace of the sacraments is contingent on the *affective devotion* of those who receive them. Arnauld argues that it is not only appropriate but necessary for devotees to abstain from the mass during periods when they do not sense an interior disposition of sincere sorrow over sin and deep love for God. Similarly, it is the duty of the priest to examine candidates for the sacraments carefully, and to defer absolution or refuse the eucharist to those who are not affectively prepared.

This attitude toward sacramental grace relied upon a clear conceptual distinction between "acts of the will," which were associated with the affections (the "heart") and mere thoughts, which were not. Arnauld explained these distinctions in this manner:

> Contrition and love for God are actions of the will, and actions of the will are not merely thoughts, but rather are movements, inclinations, and (so to speak) "bents" of the heart towards an object . . . So what does it mean to love God, or to have true contrition over one's sin? Let each one consult his heart, and if there is found there any strong affection at all, whether of a husband towards his wife, or of a father towards his child, or of a lover towards his beloved, then let him examine these movements and he will easily perceive what it means to love God.[21]

This critical distinction between "thoughts" and "affections" is central to Arnauld's and the Jansenists' conception of the religious life, and lies at the basis of the phenomena, however varied, of the religion "of the heart." For Arnauld, the critical point was that if penitence lay merely in one's thoughts, it was only "imaginary" (that is his term), not real, penitence. For his contemporary Pascal, too, this meant the rejection of any penitential theology (to be specific, Probabilism) that did not insist on interior penitence and true love for God.

This same tendency to make the grace of the sacraments conditional upon one's affective state was applied by Jansenists not only to penance and the eucharist, but to ordination as well. Saint-Cyran asserted that without an internal calling ("interior vocation"), ordination confers only "ecclesiastical power," but not divine grace.[22]

Here in particular—in their insistence on affective devotion in various particular forms as a condition for the sacraments—the Jansenist challenge to conventional forms of religious life is most apparent. It was difficult for religious leaders to find specific theological assertions on which they could hang this change in religious ethos: one gains the impression that the various charges against the Jansenists, now cataloged in the Denzinger *Enchiridion*, resulted from a sense that somehow the conventional bases of religious life were threatened, yet without having a clear or consistent propositional basis on which such charges could be made. In their propositional claims, the Jansenists could call upon Augustine and Aquinas, and (as Blaise Pascal never let the Jesuits forget) contemporary Dominican theologians.

It was possible, though, for one form of religious life to change subtly into a different one, without an explicit disavowal of earlier orthodoxy. It was also possible for one spirituality to change subtly into another, without an explicit disavowal of earlier spiritual techniques. In this case, the Jansenists stood by the propositions of patristic, conciliar, and at least Dominican theology, and they never lost the moral rigorism they had inherited from the *Devotio Moderna*. Nevertheless, the divine grace by which alone humans may be saved had become conditioned upon interior religious dispositions, which themselves could only be the gift of grace. Moreover, the moral rigor of the Jansenists was expressed not so much in conventional "casuistry," but in examination of conscience for true penitence and love for God. In this way, Jansenism can be understood as the straining of a new religious culture to emerge from the womb of the Catholic Reformation.

The Quietists

Whereas Jansenism had developed from the medieval traditions stressing moral rigor, "Quietism" developed from the older traditions of mystical devotion. With earlier Christian mysticism the Quietists held many points in common, but diverged from the common pattern in their view of the highest states of the contemplative life and in their opening of the mystical tradition to the middle classes of Europe. In common with traditional mystical teachings, the Quietists accepted the pattern of religious life characterized by a "conversion" to a religious vocation, followed by a life of disciplined devotion under the guidance of a spiritual director, and also accepted a common pattern of growth in the spiritual life, sharing with the Discalced Carmelites, in particular, the view that in more advanced stages of this growth the soul could be elevated by God into a *prayer of infused contemplation*, that is, a state of contemplation given by God and not accomplished by the effort of the believer.

Where the Quietists differed from the earlier Catholic traditions concerning meditative prayer was in their claim that in the highest states of meditation all human effort is a hindrance to the soul. In the state of "infused contemplation," they maintained, the human soul is completely passive or "quiet," resting in God, and all activity is a hindrance: even the use of the sacraments, meditation on the humanity of Christ, perhaps even resistance to temptations.

It is difficult to tell the point at which the mystical tradition of Teresa of Ávila and John of the Cross began to show these quietistic tendencies, but many point to the *Alumbrados* of sixteenth-century Spain as progenitors of the movement. Again, however, the problem is that so little is known about the *Alumbrados* that the association of them with seventeenth-century Quietism is at best conjectural.

More immediately relevant than the *Alumbrados*, especially for the development of the religion of the heart movements, is the Flemish mystical teacher, Antoinette Bourignon (1616–1680). Born in Lille in Flanders, near the frontier between France and the Spanish Netherlands, Bourignon entered a Carmelite convent at the age of eighteen (against the wishes of her family), and began to experience divine revelations of her role as a reformer of the church. She left the convent at Lille in 1667, and moved to the thriving city of Amsterdam. From this point, she undertook a career of religious writing and teaching, frequently traveling about northern Europe, and welcoming into her home members of all Christian churches who desired to hear her teachings.

Bourignon displayed some Jansenistic tendencies, especially in her sharp rejection of attrition and consequently her insistence on complete contrition. However, she also rejected the harsh Augustinianism of the Jansenists, and insisted that all persons, by a special work of grace, can turn to God and be saved. Her work is most like that of the later Quietists, in that it represents a popularization of the Carmelite tradition of mystical spirituality: Bourignon and the Quietists shared the conviction that the highest state of contemplation is one in which the soul no longer needs sacraments, or indeed any outward observances. Unlike the Quietists, however, Bourignon insisted that the highest contemplative state is not completely "quiet" or passive, but is an active state of love for God, expressed outwardly in acts of charity. Bourignon, then, represents a somewhat eccentric example of the distortion of mystical theology, but her "distortion" is critical, since it was clearly in the direction of affective and popular piety.

If Bourignon is difficult to classify, one of the earliest clear teachers of the quietistic doctrine of meditative prayer was Miguel de Molinos, a Spanish-born scholar who went to Rome to teach in 1663. Molinos's *Guida spirituale* ("Spiritual Guide"), published in 1675, was a popular exposition of the techniques of mystical prayer, and has been judged orthodox by most Catholic theologians who have examined it.[23] In Molinos's letters of direction, however, he advocated secret teachings which by the mid-1680s brought him censure. According to his accusers (the letters themselves have not been preserved), the private letters taught that the state of perfection to which all Christians should aspire is a state of constant union with God. Moreover, the accusers claim, Molinos held that in this state all external observances, including resistance to temptation, were a hindrance to the soul. The claim is made further that Molinos taught that the soul progresses in three recognizable stages: in the first stage, the soul is devoted to the Church; in the next, the soul is devoted to Jesus who is described as *deiformis non deus* ("in the form of God, but not God"); and finally the soul progresses to pure contemplation of God, and is at this point superior to the Church and to Jesus. Finally, the accusation ran, Molinos maintained that the state of pure contemplation involves a complete annihilation of the human will.[24]

Molinos was imprisoned in 1685, and in 1687 the bull *Coelestis Pastor* formally refuted several propositions drawn from his teachings.[25] Molinos recanted on all the points, maintaining an enigmatic silence and refusal to debate, even on charges of immorality for which he was sentenced to life imprisonment.

Along with Molinos were condemned two other theologians, François Malaval and Pier Matteo Petrucci. Malaval's *Pratique facile pour élever l'âme à la contemplation* (published in two parts in 1664 and

1669) was condemned, although subsequent Catholic theologians have been unable to find in it the quietistic errors of which Molinos was accused. Perhaps most importantly, Malaval refused to condemn Molinos, and so was understood as supporting him. Petrucci had been made a Cardinal in the year before *Coelestis Pastor* was promulgated, but fifty-four propositions from his works were condemned in the bull, among them being his claims that our spirits ought to aspire to the *divinity* of Christ, and so become higher than Christ's humanity, that the soul which has abandoned itself to God does not ask whether it loves God, and that all activity (even love) during contemplation is a hindrance. Petrucci, like Molinos, retracted his condemned propositions, and in his public writings after 1687 never denied that he had taught the things of which he was accused.

By 1687, then, at the time of the promulgation of *Coelestis Pastor*, Quietism had emerged in Spain and Italy, and despite the controversies over whether those accused of teaching its doctrines in fact taught them (much like the accusations against Cornelius Jansen), the Church had recognized quietistic teachings as a threat to orthodoxy. But by 1687, another figure had emerged who was to symbolize in the popular mind the quietistic doctrine.

Jeanne Marie Bouvier de la Mothe was born in the year of the peace of Westphalia (1648).[26] She was married to Jacques Guyon, (and hence is conventionally referred to as "Madame Guyon"). After her husband died in 1676, she decided to enter a life of religious devotion, although she attached herself to no order. She read Molinos's *Guida spirituale* and attached herself to a Barnabite friar and spiritual director, François Lacombe.

In 1681 Jeanne Marie Guyon and Father Lacombe embarked on a five-year crusade in southern France and northern Italy, teaching their methods of meditation. At the end of this period, in fact, in the very year in which *Coelestis Pastor* was promulgated, she and Lacombe were arrested and charged with both heresy and immorality. The accusation of immorality should not, perhaps, be taken seriously: it was not pursued, and may well reflect a combination in the popular mind of the quietistic doctrine that the soul does not resist temptation in the highest contemplative states, and the simple observation that she and Lacombe traveled together. After her release in the next year, she became a celebrity, prominent in aristocratic circles and even at the royal court.

Jeanne Marie Guyon's teachings were attacked again in 1694 in a doctrinal letter from Archbishop Jacques Bossuet. Bossuet, Archbishop of Paris, was the leading theologian of Gallicanism. As a result

Jeanne Marie Guyon

Engraving by Dunker (possibly Balthasar Anton Dunker, 1746–1807); in Jeanne Marie Bouvieres de la Mothe Guyon, *La Vie de Madame J. M. B. de la Mothe-Guyon* (Paris: Librairies Associés, 1791), frontispiece.

of the letter, Guyon demanded a theological conference to clear her. The conference assembled at Issy (near Paris) in the next year. Thirty-four articles were drawn up, condemning especially the notions that the soul is indifferent to its own salvation in the highest meditative states, and the notion that all explicit acts of faith ought to be suppressed in that state. The articles, however, were worded in an ambiguous enough manner that Bossuet and Guyon were both able to sign them. Despite her submission, she angered Bossuet again by her teaching in Paris the next year, and was imprisoned from then until 1702. She spent the remaining fifteen years of her life in relative quiet in Blois, where she died in 1717.

Jeanne Marie Guyon wrote in a manner that does not lend itself to clear explication (at least, I suppose, to those who have not attained her level of mystical prayer). Nevertheless, the exaggerations of her thought are everywhere apparent, when considered alongside Teresa of Ávila, Juan de la Cruz, and other conventional mystical teachers. She did not hesitate to speak of the "indifference" and even "annihilation" of the soul which has come to pure, passive contemplation: such a soul ceases to be a "river" or "stream" unto itself and is lost in the "ocean" of divinity.[27] She was sensitive to the accusation that this indifference implied even an indifference to sin, but maintained that although the soul in such a state vehemently hates sin, nevertheless it must be entirely indifferent in the highest degrees of contemplation: such a soul is

> without action, without desire, without inclination, without choice, without impatience, seeing things only as God sees them, and judging them only with God's judgment.[28]

Moreover, the soul in this state has no need of "means," since it has found the true "end."[29] Not surprisingly, the sacraments play no significant role in her most popular works, *Moyen Court* (or *Short and Easy Method of Prayer*) and *Spiritual Torrents*. She presumed that the seeker reading her works had already come to "the first cleansing which confession and contrition have effected."[30]

What also comes through rather clearly in Jeanne Marie Guyon's writings is her anti-intellectualism and appeal to common people. True enough, she envisioned a kind of spiritual elite, as mystical authors had often done. She distinguished three sorts of Christians: those who lead an active life of benevolence and simple piety, those who are partly given to the passive way of contemplation, but who are enough of the world that they can lead others, and those few who are led (as "rushing torrents") directly to God and who are so engrossed in contemplation of the divine that they have no time for other pursuits.[31] Most Christians belong to the first class, and they cannot (and should not) aspire to "meditation" (which for Guyon is the lowest step on the way to pure contemplation).[32] The second and third classes are consistently described as being progressively "higher" and more blessed than the first. Nevertheless, she insisted that these classifications had nothing to do with worldly distinctions, especially educational ones. Her method was, she claimed, "suited to all, to the dull and ignorant as well as the acute and learned."[33] Men and women must be led to live "less in the intellect and more in the affections"[34] and she decried the "greater part" of humankind who "pride themselves on science and wisdom."[35] Like her predecessor Antoinette Bourignon, then, Jeanne Marie Guyon taught a mystical way in which common folk could claim a place among the spiritual elite. Traditional ascetic mysticism had stressed the discipline of the mind, the body, and the will; with Guyon, the mind and the body slip into the background, and the discipline of the will or affections became central. For women and men living in the cities of northern Europe, the discipline of the will was far more easily contemplated than the discipline of the mind or the body.

At the conference of Issy, Guyon's cause had been defended by a distant relation and prominent ecclesiastical leader, François de Salignac de la Mothe Fénelon. Fénelon had been acquainted with Guyon since the time of her first imprisonment in 1688. He had been at one time a tutor to Louis XIV's grandson, then was made Archbishop of Cambrai in the year of the conference at Issy (1695).

Like Guyon, Fénelon had signed the Articles of Issy, but within two years he too ran afoul of Bossuet. The occasion (in 1697) was the publication of his *Explication des Maximes des Saints*, forty-five articles on true and false spirituality. Bossuet immediately attacked the book as teaching the doctrines condemned at Issy and in *Coelestis Pastor,* and in the same year succeeded in having Fénelon banished from the court and exiled in Cambrai. When the Vatican formally condemned twenty-three propositions from the *Maximes des Saints* in 1699, Fénelon submitted, and from that point turned his attention to the persecution of the Jansenists.[36] Even after this, however, his writings remained popular among sophisticated and pious Catholic circles, and so in his own way he offered a way in which mysticism could be adapted to the middle classes of post-Reformation Europe.

* * *

R. A. Knox seems to have derived a certain sinister satisfaction from the fact that "de la Mothe"—the family name of Jeanne Marie

Guyon and François Fénelon—was in fact the old family name of the Arnaulds of Port-Royal.[37] By the end of the seventeenth century, however, cousins or not, Jansenists and Quietists were combating each other, and both were struggling against the more conservative religious establishment (even the Gallicans, in this case). As with the Jansenists, the Quietists found themselves faced with a lengthy series of accusations, condemned propositions, and forbidden books. Just as it was difficult for the religious establishment to condemn what outwardly appeared to be the Augustinian theology and moral-rigorist spirituality of the Jansenists, so they found it difficult to frame propositions condemning the Quietists without condemning in the same breath the more conventional mystical traditions taught by the Jesuits and the Carmelites.

Again, however, one must look beyond the propositions and consider the challenge that Quietism posed for conventional forms of religious life. The sacramental tradition had focused above all else on the incarnation as the point of contact between the divine and the human. The Quietists, though consistently affirming orthodox formulations about Christ's humanity and deity, seemed to abrogate the centrality of the incarnation in their suggestion that there is a meditative state in which one can be indifferent to the humanity of Christ. The sacramental tradition had revolved around the sacraments as the moments in which individual Christians come into contact with divine grace. The Quietists never formally denied the importance of the sacraments, but again, their mystical teaching suggested that the sacraments were appropriate for a lower form of religious life, beyond which the advocates of pure contemplation had advanced. For those who saw sacramental acts as the center of religious life, then, both Jansenism and Quietism had to be seen as severe aberrations. The conflict was over ways of approaching ultimate reality.

Devotion to the Sacred Heart of Jesus

Although Jansenism and Quietism both influenced popular Catholic spiritualities in the Baroque age, they were perceived as moving so far from the mainstream of Catholic doctrinal and spiritual teaching that they were formally condemned. Yet, there were other forms of spirituality that emerged in Catholic circles in the same period which had more lasting and institutional effects on popular devotion in the Roman Church. Perhaps most remarkable, considering movements for a "religion of the heart," was the rise in this period of devotion to the sacred heart of Jesus, which was understood as representing the divine love for all of humankind, the human love of Jesus, and the love for God which is infused into the believer.

There was a long-standing tradition through the middle ages of focusing devotions on the suffering of Christ, with the bodily wounds of Christ (the nail marks in his hands and feet, the wound in his side, and the wounds of the thorns on his forehead) becoming particularly prominent from the thirteenth century. Devotion paid to the "broken heart" of Jesus was added to these by Bonaventure and other spiritual writers. This tradition was taken up in the *Devotio Moderna* and by mystical teachers of the Catholic Reformation.

In the seventeenth century, devotion to the sacred heart of Jesus underwent a notable rise in prominence, largely the result of cooperative efforts of Jesuits and their allies. François de Sales had advocated devotion to the heart of Jesus among the adherents of the Order of the Visitation of the Blessed Virgin Mary (or "Visitandines") which he founded with Jeanne Frances de Chantal (1572–1641). De Sales wrote to the latter at the founding of their order, suggesting that the heraldic representation of the order should be "a single heart pierced by two arrows, and set in a crown of thorns," a reminder of its connection with devotion to the wounds of Christ.[38]

The practice of devotion to the sacred heart of Jesus might not have attained broad acceptance by Catholics were it not for the theological explication of the practice laid out by the French Oratorian Jean Eudes (1601–1680), who eventually withdrew from the Oratory to found the Congregation of Jesus and Mary (1644; members of the Congregation were later referred to as "Eudists").[39] Eudes advocated devotion to the sacred heart of Jesus and to the immaculate heart of the Virgin Mary. He had studied previous spiritual writers on the subject, and endeavored to interpret this devotion against the background of traditional Catholic teachings about the Trinity and human salvation. Eudes insisted that as Jesus is human and divine, and united to the Trinity, devotion to any specific aspect of Jesus (i.e., to the sacred heart) becomes worship of Christ and of the whole godhead.[40] He further clarified that the love revealed in devotion to the sacred heart is the love for God lost because of human sin, and restored through the grace of Christ expressed in the sacraments.[41] He also cited specific Catholic saints who had expressed similar forms of devotion.[42] In this way Eudes provided an explanation for the practice of devotion to the sacred heart in which it could be understood as broadly harmonious with traditional Catholic theology.

Jean Eudes

Engraving (engraver's name is illegible) after a portrait (1673) by Jean Leblond (1635–1709); in *Oeuvres complètes de bienheureux Jean Eudes, Missionaire apostolique* (vol. 1, Paris: P. Lethielleux, n.d. [1906 or before]), frontispiece.

Within this orthodox framework, however, Eudes explicated a Catholicism focusing on the encounter with God through the affections. The heart of Jesus becomes the heart of the believer:

Yes, this admirable Heart is mine. It is mine because the Eternal Father has given it to me; it is mine because the Blessed Virgin has given it to me; it is mine because [Christ] himself has given it to me, not only to be my refuge and shelter in my needs, to be my oracle and my treasure, but also to be the model and rule of my life and of my actions. I wish to study this rule constantly so as to follow it faithfully.

I must consider what the Heart of Jesus hates and what it loves, in order to hate only what it hates and to love only what it loves. The only thing it hates is sin . . . I will hate nothing but sin; I will love all that Thou lovest, even my enemies.[43]

Building on this central focus on love for Christ and hatred for sin, Eudes developed a pattern for the religious life, embracing an individual's initial desire to pay devotion to the sacred heart, her humility in despising her own unworthiness to offer such devotion, and her self-sacrifice to the godhead.[44] Throughout his treatise, Eudes portrayed the heart of Jesus, and the human heart following it, as "a furnace of burning love."[45]

If Jean Eudes gave the practice of devotion to the sacred heart its theological justification, however, it was the Visitandine Marguerite Marie Alacoque (1647–1690) who drew significant public attention to the practice. Having grown up (according to her *Autobiography*) in a very unpleasant home, and having suffered frequent illnesses, Marguerite Marie was given to religious melancholy, which she described in the following terms:

What distressed me most of all, though, was my fear of offending God. There seemed to be no end to my sins—and such big ones! I was amazed that hell didn't open at my feet to swallow me up, I felt so wicked.[46]

Finally, she renewed an earlier sense of religious vocation, entered the Visitandine Convent at Paray-le-Monial in 1671, and quickly rose to prominence there.

Two years after entering Paray-le-Monial, Marguerite Marie underwent a religious experience in which she felt that Christ revealed himself directly to her:

My divine Heart is so passionately fond of the human race, and of you in particular, that it cannot keep back the pent-up flames of its burning charity any longer. They must burst out through you and reveal my Heart to the world, so as to enrich mankind with my precious treasures.[47]

In a later revelation (in June 1675), Christ instructed her to encourage Christians to observe the Friday after the octave of Corpus Christi as a feast day, focusing on devotion to the sacred heart. Though reluctant at first, she disclosed the revelation to her confessor, the Jesuit Claude de la Colombière, who supported her claims against those at Paray-le-Monial who regarded them as delusions.[48]

Through the combined efforts of Jesuits, Visitandines, Eudists, and others who supported the practice, devotion to the sacred heart of Jesus came into widespread use in Catholic countries by the beginning of the eighteenth century. Itinerant preachers, such as the Jesuit Bernard Francis de Hoyos, devoted their entire careers to promulgating devotion to the sacred heart.[49] Iconographic representations of the sacred heart emerged in this period, and typically depicted a flaming heart (much like that in the frontispiece to Jansen's *Augustinus*), with a cross affixed, or a crown of thorns above it (or around it; it is not affixed to the breast of Jesus, as in nineteenth century and later representations).[50] For almost a hundred years, however, the devotion was practiced solely in private, until 1765, when the Vatican officially recognized a mass and office (prepared by Jean Eudes) celebrating the sacred heart for use in public worship.

*   *   *

It has been observed that Baroque spirituality, like Baroque art and Baroque architecture, places such an emphasis on detail that it tends to lose a sense of balance, or a sense of the whole. In this respect, Jansenism and Quietism could be seen as grotesque mutations of moral rigorism and mysticism, respectively.[51] Similarly, devotion to the sacred heart of Jesus might be understood as a distortion of the medieval devotion to the wounds of Christ. But consider Jansenism and Quietism in the light of the century of inter-Christian warfare in which they developed. Consider the spiritualities of the Oratorians and other itinerant orders, and the work of François de Sales, as well as the development of devotion to the sacred heart of Jesus, and a different possibility emerges. That possibility is that in their own ways, each of these movements reflected a deep and widespread dissatisfaction with existing religious culture, and consequently not simply the mutation of existing religious traditions, but the gestation and birth struggles of a new religious and cultural tradition: the religion of the heart.

By the end of the seventeenth century, Antoinette Bourignon and Jeanne Marie Guyon were widely read and studied by Protestants: candidates for ordination in the Scottish Presbyterian Church were questioned as to whether they had read Bourignon (and whether they assented to her doctrine), Quakers recognized Guyon as a kindred spirit, and in northern Germany the works of both women enjoyed notable popularity.[52] By the middle of the next century, John Wesley was publishing editions of Bourignon, Fénelon, and Saint-Cyran. Nicholas Ludwig, the Graf (or Count) von Zinzendorf and organizer of the Moravians, was corresponding with a Jansenist Archbishop, and the Moravians recognized Jansenists and Quietists as part of the general movement of religious revival throughout Europe.

At the same time, the concerns expressed throughout Catholic Baroque culture for a religion of the heart—the distinction of affections and intellect, the concern for right affections as contrasted with right "opinions" and actions, the appeal to the middle classes, the leadership of women and lay teachers—these concerns came to expression in the British Isles, Holland, and Germany, and were even echoed in Polish and Russian religious movements. The next chapters will examine the concurrent development of the religion of the heart in those cultures.

Chapter Three

Affective Piety in Seventeenth-Century British Calvinism

Almost twenty years before Jean Eudes completed his treatise on devotion to the sacred heart, a book was published in London with the title, *The Heart of Christ in Heaven towards Sinners on Earth; or, a Treatise Demonstrating the Gracious Disposition and Tender Affection of Christ in His Humane Nature, now in Glory, unto His Members, under all Sorts of Infirmities, either of Sin or of Misery* (1651).[1] Despite the similarities, however, this was no work of Catholic devotion. Its author, Thomas Goodwin (1600–1679/80), was an almost exact contemporary of Jean Eudes (1601–1680), but was one of the staunchest of English Puritans, an outspoken defender of the Calvinism of the Synod of Dort, and personal chaplain to Oliver Cromwell. The title of the book alone suggests that certain religious tendencies that we have observed in Baroque Catholicism were also coming to expression in English Protestant circles.

At the same time as Jansenism, Quietism, and devotion to the sacred heart of Jesus were unfolding as vital forces within European Catholicism, a series of religious movements emerged in the British Isles, sharing the concern for affective piety we have seen in the Catholic movements. A train of English Puritans cultivated the inward religious life, exhorting sinners to the experience of repentance and holding out to believers the assurance of election. In Scots-Irish Presbyterianism at the same time, a tradition of revivalistic preaching developed from the institution of sacramental meetings. During the period of the English Revolution (1640–1660), millenarian and "enthusiastic" sects arose, the Society of Friends or "Quakers" having the most lasting effects of them all. Toward the end of the seventeenth century, the pietistic emphasis of British Calvinism came to more "reasonable" expression in the Cambridge Platonists' epistemology of religious experience and in Richard Baxter's popular and irenic restatement of the call to repentance and conversion.

There appears to have been little direct borrowing between the Catholic movements and British Calvinism in the seventeenth century. The emergence of affective piety in both contexts, then, must be due more to the impetus of common historical factors than direct influence. In some respects, the political and social fortunes of Britain in the seventeenth century resembled those of Europe. Although the English were themselves modestly involved in the Thirty Years War, their European involvements were overshadowed by the social and religious upheaval in their islands, namely, the struggles of the English Revolution (1640–1660), the Restoration of the Stuarts (1660), and the "Glorious Revolution" (1688). The European conflict had pitted Catholics against Protestants; the British conflict pitted radically Protestant Puritans against Catholic-leaning Anglicans. The northern European states in the Thirty Years War represented a nascent mercantile economy and the rising middle classes, and so did the Puritan factions of London and the southern coastal towns and cities of England during the time of the Revolution. In the background of the religion of the heart movements in Britain, it is important to recognize that although the English Revolution did not break out until 1640, the social, cultural, and explicitly religious conflicts that underlay it were apparent from the last decades of the sixteenth century.

In other respects, however, the development of the British religious movements was structured by distinctive factors. In Europe, the conflict was between Protestantism (of various sorts) and Catholicism. In Britain, the struggle was an inter-Protestant one, with all sides agreeing at least in their rejection of the supreme authority of the Bishops of Rome and in their nominal affirmation of Protestant principles. The spiritualities of British Calvinism, then, would have to develop along more or less explicitly Protestant lines, with medieval institutions and spiritual traditions veiled, if expressed at all. Gone were the monastic houses that had played such a long-standing and central role in European religious life. Gone, too, was the confessional, and its prominent role in the direct encounter between the seeker and the religious counselor.

Consider the Jansenists and the English Puritans. Both groups taught a stern, Augustinian theology that maintained total human depravity and predestination. The Jansenists, it is worth recalling, had been accused of "Calvinism" by their Jesuit opponents. Both groups, in the first half of the seventeenth century, were locked in struggles over forms of religious life; both groups developed from a kind of moral-rigorist spirituality; both groups marked a turn towards a piety centered on the affections.

And yet, despite the obvious parallels, the critical nuances were different in each case. The Jansenists struggled against the Jesuits, with Probabilism and Molinism the obvious targets of their reforms; the Puritans struggled against Anglicans who, at least at the beginning of the seventeenth century, were formally committed to a moderate, Calvinist theology; consequently, their struggle was as much over matters of liturgical forms and church polity as it was over penitential theology and the "way of salvation." The moral rigorism out of which Jansenism emerged was that of medieval monasticism, tinctured with the spirituality of the *Devotio Moderna*; the moral rigorism out of which English Puritanism developed was that of Calvin's Geneva. The affective piety of the Jansenists centered on the sacraments of penance and the mass; the affective piety of the Puritans centered on the proclamation of the Law and the Gospel.

The presuppositions of Protestant theology and practice, then, gave a different form to the affective piety that emerged among British Calvinists in the "century of revolution." And yet, this century, which saw a remarkable diversification of British religious culture, would see affective devotion expressed in as remarkably different forms as the stern piety of Perkins and Ames, the rich literary gifts of John Bunyan, the enthusiastic preaching of Scottish and Irish revivalists, the illuminations of the early Quakers, the reasoned treatises of the Cambridge Platonists, and the kindly spirited appeals of Richard Baxter. We begin, then, with the impulse towards affective piety in the English Puritans before moving on to consider the more exotic varieties of British Calvinist spirituality that emerged in the seventeenth century.

The Pietistic Impulse in English Puritanism

Puritanism emerged late in the sixteenth century as an attempt to "purify" the worship, discipline, and polity of the Church of England. Grounded in the sentiments of English Protestants who had fled to the Continent during the reign of Mary Tudor, the Puritans hoped, during the reign of Elizabeth I, to remake the English Church after the model of Continental Protestantism, perhaps especially Calvin's Geneva.[2] Although all Puritans looked to the heritage of Reformed Protestantism, they expressed their desire for purity in a number of particular areas of church and civil life. At first, they sought liturgical reforms, some rejecting the liturgical vestments traditionally worn by English clergy. Others soon after contested the inherited form of Church government, advocating a presbyterian polity against the episcopal structure of Elizabethan Anglicanism. The controversy over polity came to a head in 1572, when Puritan leaders presented an "Admonition" to Parliament insisting that episcopalianism be dismantled. They were defeated, but for at least two decades afterwards moderate Puritans pressed a positive program of reform of the English Church along more obviously Protestant lines.[3]

It is perhaps worth noting that two years before the "Admonition" was defeated, the influential Puritan divine Thomas Cartwright had been expelled from his teaching post in Cambridge. In the 1580s, moderate Puritans again attempted to compromise with Anglicanism by organizing unofficial presbyteries (referred to by the less offensive Latin term *classes*) within Anglican dioceses and pressing for official recognition of them. But the defeat of the Spanish Armada (1588) led to a resurgence of Anglican authority, and in the next few years (1588–1592) the *classis* movement was defeated, and many of its members arrested.[4] Up to this point, the forms of religious life supported by the English Puritans answered in large measure to those advocated by their Continental (and Scottish) Calvinist counterparts. The preeminent issues for them had been the definition of a public liturgical, "political" (in the sense of church polity), and doctrinal consensus. From this time Puritans became more and more alienated from the formal structures of Elizabethan Anglicanism, and many turned to Independency and Separatism. Many, in the decades after 1570, supported semi-independent "lecturers" who traveled about the country, often speaking in churches or to other gatherings at times (such as Sunday afternoons) other than the formal services of the parish churches.[5] By the early decades of the seventeenth century, Puritan preachers took up outdoor "combination preaching" or lecturing, sometimes associated with market days, and sometimes associated with days appointed for fasting, possibly culminating in the celebration of the Lord's Supper.[6]

Moreover, it was in the period after the expulsion of Cartwright, the failure of the Admonition, and the defeat of the *classis* movement, that the English Puritans' cultivation of piety became most prominent, and during the reigns of James I and Charles I they developed a distinctive literature that carefully outlined the stages of the Christian life, illustrated these stages by biographies and journals, and counseled the Christian who followed this path.[7] Puritans who pursued this concern with the life of piety have been variously identified as "Pietistic" or "Evangelical" Puritans, although they probably illustrate a tendency that characterized the whole of the Puritan movement in this period.[8]

The pietistic tendencies in English Puritanism appeared very early on in the systematic theological reflections of William Perkins and his student William Ames. Perkins (1558–1602) was a fellow of Christ's College, Cambridge, who laid out a systematic account of redemption in his *Golden Chaine* (1597). Ames (1576–1633), who had studied under Perkins at Cambridge, left England to teach in The Hague around 1610. His *Marrow of Theology* (1627) presented a more general overview of Calvinistic teaching, but, like Perkins, devoted considerable space to the out-working of human redemption by God. Both Perkins and Ames, in fact, held that the essence of theology lies in the pursuit of the Christian life. "Theologie," according to Perkins, "is the science of living blessedlie forever."[9] Similarly, Ames defined theology as *doctrina Deo vivendi*, "the doctrine or teaching of living to God."[10]

Having this central concern with theology as explicating the *life* of the religious seeker, Perkins and Ames were careful to affirm, as the foundation of their teaching on salvation, that it is God's grace alone that can effect human salvation. For Perkins, this meant adherence to the doctrine of Augustine and Calvin that only God's choice of specific men and women could bring them to salvation. Human beings, on their own, might be "free" in the sense that they could choose between options, but without the grace of election their options were all evil, and would lead to eternal death.[11] For Ames, the affirmation of this teaching was made in the particular context of an influential protest against it leveled by Jakob Harmensen (in Latin, "Arminius") and other progressive Dutch Calvinists. Where Arminus had argued that divine grace gives all human beings the possibility of accepting or rejecting salvation in Christ, Ames insisted on particular election.[12] It is worth noting that the "Arminian" controversy among Reformed Christians arose at the same time as the controversy *de Auxiliis* was coming to a head (see Chapter One), and the issues, in each case, were remarkably similar.

With their grounding in the doctrine of election, both Perkins and Ames went on to outline the stages of the Christian life as elements in the out-working of election. Following Romans 8:30 and a tradition of Calvinistic exegesis, Perkins identified four "degrees" or stages:

> "effectual calling,"
> justification,
> sanctification, and
> glorification.[13]

To these four stages, William Ames added a fifth, "adoption," between justification and sanctification.[14] Although the "order of salvation" (*ordo salutis*) was a standard component of Protestant Orthodox theological treatises, Perkins and Ames are distinguished both by the stress they laid on it as lying at the center of the theological enterprise, and more particularly by their concern with the question of how a woman or man could *know* they were elect to eternal life. Moreover, the role of the affections became prominent in their accounts of the order of salvation.

In their general delineation of this order of salvation, Perkins and Ames agreed. The first stage, "effectual calling," (also described as "conversion" by Ames) was described by them as that event in which men and women are brought to repentance and faith by means of the proclamation of the Law and the Gospel.[15] Both Perkins and Ames defined "justification" in characteristically Reformed language as the imputation of Christ's righteousness to the believer, and the believer's being "accounted" righteous before God on the basis of faith alone and for the sake of Christ.[16] They understood "sanctification" to denote the Christian's continuing death to sin ("mortification") and growth in life to Christ ("vivification").[17] "Glorification" they explained as the completion of the Christian's likeness to Christ, which begins at death and is consummated at the time of the final judgment.[18]

Both Perkins and Ames stressed the possibility that human beings can *know* of their election to eternal life, although they differed in their placement of this doctrine within their schemes. In his discussion of effectual calling, William Perkins distinguished several degrees of Christian faith. "The highest degree of faith," he wrote, "is *plerophoria, a full assurance,* which is not onely certaine and true, but also *a full perswasion* of the heart. . . ."[19] In the concluding chapter of *A Golden Chaine,* Perkins again returned to the question of the knowledge of election, and maintained that believers may know of their election both by "the Testimonie of Gods Spirit" and by the works of sanctification.[20] Where Perkins had but briefly discussed "adoption" as denoting the privileges bestowed by God on believers,[21] Ames developed the topic into a fifth section in his account of the order of salvation, interposed between "justification" and "sanctification."[22] Here Ames claimed that one of the principal benefits of adoption is "the witness of the Spirit which is given to believers" or "assurance of salvation."[23]

With Perkins and Ames, then, Puritanism made an important turn towards affective devotion: to the older Calvinist search for signs of grace revealed in the works of sanctification was added the assurance given in the experience of adoption, a divinely given sense of one's eternal election.[24] Moreover, their works display a consistent concern with the affective appropriation of grace throughout the order of salvation. "Effectual calling" involved no simple conversion experience: Perkins and Ames could describe how the heart had first to be "brused in peeces"[25] with a sense of conviction and desperation over one's own abilities before one could apprehend Christ by faith.[26] Their descriptions of assurance follow this. Both describe the struggles of the justified with remaining, indwelling sin, their strife with satanic powers, their need for grace to combat temptations, and their need for continuing repentance over post-conversion sins.[27] Perkins elaborated on the "sanctification of the affections,"[28] specifically calling the Christian to develop hope for final salvation, the fear of God, contempt for worldly things, zeal for God's glory, and "anguish of mind" for our own sins and those of others.

It is important to note that neither Perkins nor Ames despised the enterprise of scholastic theology as later "Pietists" (properly so-called) would do. In fact, both *A Golden Chaine* and *The Marrow of Theology* conform to the conventions of Protestant scholasticism. Their fundamental religious values were virtually unchanged from earlier Calvinism. What we have with Perkins and Ames, then, is an indication of a developing shift in the focus of religious life, a shift in which concerns for the out-working of election, and especially the affective appropriation of the grace of election, were moving to the foreground of theological concern. If we were to imagine Calvinism as a weighty branch on a great tree, what we might see in Perkins and Ames is a slight bending of the branch as a new wind began to blow.

The exposition of the order of salvation comprehending effectual calling, justification, sanctification, and glorification that Perkins and Ames had analyzed was then popularized by Puritan preachers and spiritual writers, and by the widespread practice of keeping diaries or journals recounting one's own spiritual experience. Thousands of these diaries were produced, though few survive, some utilizing various forms of shorthand or cipher. By mid-century diary keeping had spread from the Puritans through the population in general: perhaps the most famous in the broad range of English journaling is the diary of Samuel Pepys, whose cipher diary (beginning in 1660) was transliterated and published early in the nineteenth century. What the Puritan diaries accomplished was to make concrete the idealized order of salvation that Perkins, Ames, and others had described. Moreover, they served as a means of making clear the affections experienced by particular women and men as they traversed the order of salvation.

Thomas Goodwin, for example, whose work on the heart of Christ in heaven is noted at the beginning of this chapter, began keeping a spiritual diary shortly after his conversion, which occurred around 1620.[29] Like other Puritan diaries, Goodwin's begins with a detailed description of the events leading up to his conversion.[30] His account is shaped by the Puritan understanding of the order of salvation, and dwells on his affective appropriation of grace. His effectual calling involved the growing recognition and hatred of sin, and a growing sense of divine judgement hanging over him, even from his childhood:

> I began to have some slighter workings of the Spirit of God from the time I was six years old; I could weep for my sins whenever I did set myself to think of them, and had flashes of joy upon thoughts of the things of God. I was affected with good motions and affections of love to God and Christ, for their love revealed to man, and with grief for sin as displeasing them.[31]

As a young man, he was beset by the thought of sinful lusts, and then, upon examination, discovered the root of them to be a heart in rebellion to God. He had terrifying visions of hell, "and saw no way of escape."[32] After these struggles, Goodwin at last experienced the assurance of his election:

> . . . this speaking of God to my soul, although it was but a gentle sound, yet it made a noise over my whole heart, and filled and possessed all the faculties of my whole soul. God took me aside, and as it were privately said unto me, Do you now turn to me, and I will pardon all your sins though ever so many, as I forgave and pardoned my servant Paul, and convert you unto me, as I did Mr. Price, who was the most famous convert and example of religion in Cambridge.[33]

Goodwin's diary then went on to recount the ways in which his conversion was confirmed, both by his inward affections and by his outward actions following it. Goodwin continued the diary through his career, recounting his continuing struggle against sin and his triumphs in faith.

A modern historian who has examined Puritan diaries and journals has suggested that they functioned for the Puritans much in the same manner in which the confessional functioned in traditional Catholic spirituality, since journal and diary accounts were shared with family members and with one's minister.[34] We might suggest not only the parallel with the confessional, but also the parallel with the medieval institution of spiritual direction, since diary accounts shared with one's pastor, in particular, could serve as a basis for exhortations to conversion, to repentance (and confession) of remaining sins, to the recovery of hope, and to perseverance in the way to sanctification.

Towards the middle of the seventeenth century this concern with the out-working of election was further popularized by a proliferation of spiritual biographies of Protestant saints. The biographies and autobiographies, the latter of which grew directly out of diary and journal entries, served again as a way of teaching, by concrete example, the way of salvation. The most prolific author of biographies was Samuel Clarke, who himself composed *The Marrow of Ecclesiastical Historie* (1650) and *A General Martyrologie*, and who also worked to procure the publication of others authors' spiritual biographies.[35]

But the tradition, well established by the period of the English Revolution, of Puritan spiritual narratives, was to find its most lasting (and perhaps most influential) expression in John Bunyan's *Pilgrim's Progress*. Bunyan (1628–1688) lived out his adult life in the throes of the English Revolution and the Restoration period. He had had a vivid experience of conversion in 1653, and two years later became pastor of a Dissenting congregation in Bedfordshire. His *Grace Abounding to the Chief of Sinners* is a typical Puritan autobiography, recounting the struggles leading up to his conversion and the joys of assurance in Christ. Imprisoned during the first twelve years of the Restoration (1660–1672), Bunyan produced a number of works, including *The Pilgrim's Progress* and *The Holy War*, both of which developed the traditional images of spiritual pilgrimage and spiritual warfare. *The Pilgrim's Progress* was first published in 1678, and utilized the medieval tradition of the allegory to describe the soul's journey to the heavenly city.

The Pilgrim's Progress follows the pattern of effectual calling, justification, sanctification, and glorification. It begins with a vision of a soul under conviction of sin, terrified at the thought of hell:

> As I walked through the wilderness of this world, I lighted on a certain place, where was a den; and I laid me down in that place to sleep: and as I slept I dreamed a dream. I dreamed, and behold I saw a man clothed in rags, standing in a certain place, with his face from his own house, a book in his hand, and a great burden upon his back. I looked, and saw him open the book, and read therein; and as he read, he wept and trembled: and not being able longer to contain, he brake out with a lamentable cry; saying, "What shall I do?"[36]

The Pilgrim's burden is his sin; his book is the Bible; his cry is the cry of the soul who is effectually called. But his calling is an intricate

John Bunyan in Prison

Engraving by J. Gilbert; in John Bunyan, *The Jerusalem Sinner Saved* (London: Thomas Nelson, 1845), frontispiece.

process, which leads him through the "Slough of Despond" where many turn back, and through the "wicket gate," the narrow way that few enter. He is deterred by those who think him crazy, but is aided by "Evangelist," "Help," and "Interpreter," who guide him along the right path. At last he comes to an assurance that his sins are forgiven:

> He ran thus till he came at a place somewhat ascending; and upon that place stood a Cross, and a little below in the bottom, a sepulchre. So I saw in my dream, that just as Christian came up with the cross, his burden loosed from off his shoulders, and fell from off his back; and began to tumble, and so continued to do till it came to the mouth of the sepulchre, where it fell in, and I saw it no more.
>
> Then was Christian glad and lightsome, and said with a merry heart, "He hath given me rest, by his sorrow, and life, by his death." Then he stood still a while, to look and wonder; for it was very surprising to him that the sight of the Cross should thus ease him of his burden.[37]

Although the Pilgrim's burden was lifted in this moment of justification and assurance, his real struggle was only just commencing, and that, of course, was the struggle of sanctification. The pilgrim's affections—his hatred of sin, his love for God—must be purified. The assurance he had experienced had to be tried by further bouts of despondency and despair. More religious deceivers lay ahead, more pious friends to accompany him, more resting places where he could take (and where Bunyan could give) instruction. The narrative[38] ends when the Pilgrim and his companion, Hopeful, cross over the river of death and enter the Celestial City, where their glorification begins.

The Pilgrim's Progress was popular in Bunyan's time, and has remained so through the centuries since his age, becoming one of the most frequently printed of English books. Among English-speaking Evangelicals of every description, it was to become an honored standard. If common readers were unable to follow the rigorous logic, and the traditional references, of Perkins's and Ames's systematic treatises, they could not miss the richness of Bunyan's narrative. Moreover, perhaps because Bunyan's work was narrative and descriptive, as opposed to systematic and analytical, its theological underpinnings could be reinterpreted more easily, and consequently it could be read by Arminian as well as Calvinistic Evangelicals as faithfully recounting the pilgrim's way from this world to the next. In it, the pietistic genius of English Puritanism was transmitted to new ages and new worlds.

In their formal theology, in their personal diaries and journals, in biographies, autobiographies, and martyrologies, and in the allegory of *The Pilgrim's Progress*, the Puritans taught the way of salvation. In doing so, they had not rejected academic theology, but had added to it a concern with the out-working of election, with effectual calling, justification, sanctification, and glorification becoming not only doctrines, but path markers for the seeker. In advocating the way of salvation, they had not rejected the sacraments or the visible institutions of the Church, but had stressed the proclamation of the Word and the precise observation of the soul to find signs of grace revealed there.

And yet a significant change in forms of religious life was underway. The religion of the Puritans had become a religion of the heart. The "heart," for them, was not exactly the "heart" of medieval theologians and spiritual writers, who thought of it as comprehending both the affective (or emotive) and the intelligible aspects of human life: for the Puritans, the "heart" denoted the will and the affections, but could be contrasted with the "head," the center of the intellect. "A Heart full of Graces," said Goodwin, "is better than a Head full of Notions"; and "Notional knowledge, it makes a Man's Head giddy, but it shall never make a Man's Heart holy."[39]

For the Puritans, the religious life had come to be centered on the changed "heart"—the will and affections convicted, converted, and sanctified by the predestining grace of God. In Bunyan, this concern with the inward religious life is primary, the older quest for a reformed nation and civil order being almost nonexistent in his work. Although moderate Puritanism would have its representatives through the seventeenth century, by Bunyan's time the winds of affective devotion were fairly howling, and had flexed the branch of Calvinism noticeably, with some boughs of the branch now beginning to shake in the draft, and others at the point of splitting apart.

Scots-Irish Revivalism

In Scotland and Northern Ireland, the strains of affective devotion had become perhaps most noticeable, even from the early decades of the seventeenth century. A somewhat different form of spirituality was developing among Calvinists in the Celtic lands. Although it, too, would proclaim the way of conversion and sanctification, it tended to do so within the context of "revivals of religion," often structured around the periodic celebration of the Lord's Supper.[40]

The political conditions in which English Puritans had worked for the reform of the English Church also prevailed, with somewhat different nuances, in Scotland and Ireland. In Scotland, Calvinism in doctrine and presbyterianism in church polity had been introduced after 1560 (following the accession of Elizabeth I) as a result of the efforts of John Knox and other Reformers. It would have appeared that the hopes of English Puritans had been accomplished in Scotland by these actions, and indeed English Puritans pointed to the Scottish precedents. But when James VI of Scotland reached maturity and took control of the government in 1578, their hopes were frustrated. James's principal motivation was to succeed Elizabeth I as monarch of England (which he did upon her death in 1603), and consequently he tried to mollify English concerns by steering the Scottish Church in an obviously Anglican direction. In 1584 he secured the passage of the so-called "Black Acts" re-establishing episcopacy, but these were replaced in 1592 with the "Golden Acts" that again established presbyterianism in the state church. After his accession to the English throne (as James I) in 1603, overt opposition to his rule ceased, and episcopalianism was again established in Scotland in 1612.

In Ireland, despite the fact that Elizabeth I had established a nominally Protestant Church there following the Anglican pattern, there was little sentiment in favor of Protestantism during her reign. She established Trinity College, Dublin, in 1591, and it had come to be dominated by Calvinist teachers from Cambridge. It was James's settlement of English and Scottish Protestants in Ulster, however, that led to a significant Protestant presence on the island. Declaring invalid the ancient claims of the feudal rulers of six counties in Northern Ireland, James replaced them with English and Scottish overlords, and began to repopulate the area. It is ironic that despite James's strongly pro-Anglican leanings, he (out of necessity) permitted Scottish Presbyterian ministers to be appointed to Anglican parishes in Ulster.

It was among Scottish and Irish Presbyterians—strongly Calvinistic in their theological leanings—that a tradition of revivalistic preaching emerged. Building on a late sixteenth-century tradition of preaching associated with sacramental meetings, these revivals flourished in the 1620s and 1630s in southwestern Scotland and Northern Ireland, perhaps inspired by Presbyterian indignation over the five Articles of Perth (1618), by which James I had attempted to force on Scotland the English custom of receiving the eucharist kneeling.[41] As early as 1622, one preacher noted a deep awakening among the people at Stewarton in Ayr (in southwestern Scotland), an awakening which continued for several years thereafter.[42] By 1626, large crowds were attracted to sacramental meetings in nearby towns as well. The preacher John Livingston noted his participation in numerous sacramental gatherings at this time, where hearers were convicted of sin and converted in great numbers.[43]

Similar revivalistic preaching emerged almost simultaneously in Northern Ireland. The first noted revival of this sort among Irish Presbyterians occurred within a decade of the foundation of the Ulster Plantation in County Antrim in the area of "Six Mile Water." A relatively uneducated but licensed Scottish preacher at Carrickfergus named James Glendinning,

> began to preach diligently, and having a great voice and vehement delivery, he roused up the people; and wakened them with terrors, but not understanding well the Gospel, could not settle them nor satisfy their objections.[44]

Glendinning, that is to say, was adept at leading his congregations to the beginning of an effectual calling, but was unable to help them from that point. A better educated minister in the area, John Ridge, set up a monthly "lecture" at Antrim to deal with such inquirers. He invited three other ministers (Robert Cunningham, James Hamilton, and Robert Blair), but alas, not Glendinning, to assist him in this work. In the summer months, they would offer four sermons during the day, but only three in other seasons.[45]

The revival spread among the nearby counties, with more preachers coming over from Scotland to help in the movement. An autobiography from the period, that of Robert Blair, recounts the large and earnest congregations, inspired and extempore preaching, and awakenings and conversions among the people.[46]

By 1630 the revivalistic preaching in southwestern Scotland and Northern Ireland had become a dominant feature of Presbyterian life. In that year, a spectacular revival broke out associated with the preaching of John Livingston at a sacramental meeting in Shotts (near Stewarton), which is sometimes represented as the beginning of Scottish revivalism. The preaching of Livingston and others, outdoors in the churchyard, was protracted for several days (and nights), and many hearers were struck unconscious with emotion and reported themselves to have been truly converted as a result.[47]

The Scottish and Irish revivals were typically associated with "sacramental occasions" or "seasons"—what the poet Robert Burns would derisively call "The Holy Fair"—which grew in prominence from the 1630s and formed the consistent backdrop for recurrent Scottish revivals after that time. In fact, the tradition was carried to North America, and lasted both in Scotland and in America through the nineteenth century. Crowds were so large that the preachers were forced out of doors, setting a precedent for open-air preaching. Moreover, in their preaching of repentance in preparation for the Lord's Supper, and in their following this by stressing the sinner's justification by faith in Christ and the necessity of a sanctified life, the sacramental occasions gave a dramatic form to the "way of salvation."[48]

Political events soon disturbed the first phase of revivalistic piety in the Celtic lands. When James I's son Charles I attempted to force the use of the English Prayer Book in Scotland in 1637, riots broke out, and within a year Calvinistically inclined Church leaders had adopted a "National Convenant" (1638) again supporting presbyterian polity. In Ireland, where Protestant sympathies did not run quite so deep as in Scotland, the program of Charles I succeeded, and resulted in the removal of all Scottish Presbyterian ministers from the Anglican parishes there. This brought the revival in Ulster completely to an end.

During the English Revolution, Scotland sided at first with the (English) Parliamentary forces, its Church adopting the "Solemn League and Covenant" and the Confession, Catechism, and Directory of Public Worship passed by the Westminster Assembly in the Mid-1640s. Presbyterianism was officially established (for the first time) in Ulster during the 1640s. After the execution of Charles I, however, Puritanism was divided. Some leaders favored an Independent (or Congregational) polity, much as Cromwell himself supported. Others argued for presbyterianism, and could accept compromise with the Cromwellian forces. But others, believing that Charles I had agreed in good faith to the Solemn League and Covenant, could not approve of "regicide," and so were forced in the mid-1650s into an independent existence. With the failure of the Revolution and the Restoration of Charles II, moreover, episcopalianism was imposed again on Ireland and Scotland (1660). This, too, forced traditional Presbyterians ("Covenanters") to carry on their church life independently of the state.

It was under these conditions that the Covenanters of Scotland and Ireland took up the tradition of sacramental meetings—a tradition shaped by the revivals of the 1620s and 1630s—as the principal institutional form for their religious life. Because they refused to *conform* (that is the legal term) to Anglican worship and polity, their meetings were deemed "conventicles," and were outlawed. Consequently, the sacramental meetings of the Convenanters had to be carried on not only out of doors, but also apart from traditional churches. Moreover, the ministers who were ejected from their churches because of their nonconformity took up the role of preaching and assisting in conventicles as they itinerated throughout the countryside.[49] In this manner, they resembled the Puritan "lecturers" of the Elizabethan period, who itinerated and were privately supported.

The period of "conventicles" ended with the "Glorious Revolution" of 1688 when William and Mary came to rule the British Isles, and religious toleration was affirmed. Presbyterianism was finally established for good in Scotland in 1690, and most of the Presbyterians returned to the national church. Although Ireland remained formally Anglican, Presbyterians were free to organize congregations and presbyteries there. The Protestant religious situation in Scotland and Ireland was thus regularized from the last decade of the seventeenth century, although there were important minorities throughout the eighteenth century who saw themselves as the true inheritors of the Scottish Presbyterian tradition.[50]

As one looks beyond the seventeenth century to the eighteenth, especially keeping in mind religious developments both in the British Isles and in North America in the eighteenth century, it is remarkable to consider what had developed in Northern Ireland and Scotland during the century of revolution: by 1688 there was a long-established tradition of periodic sacramental meetings, involving enthusiastic preaching and the expectation of experiences of conviction and conversion, hosted by a semi-independent fellowship of traveling (or itinerant) preachers. The precedents for the Evangelical Revival (and American Awakenings) were well in place.

The Quakers

If the revivalism of Scotland and Ireland represents the boughs of Reformed Protestantism that were shaking in the winds of affective piety, the radical movements of the English Revolution would represent the limbs that were splitting apart. There had been, through the last decades of the sixteenth century and the early decades of the seventeenth century, a tendency towards increasing radicalization on the part of many English Calvinists. From the late 1580s some had rejected presbyterianism, preferring an "Independent," or what was later called "Congregationalist," polity. The Independents themselves were divided between those who advocated an establishment of Independency as the national Church, and others

("Separatists") who insisted that there could be no compromise with civil government. The numbers of the Independents increased steadily in the first four decades of the seventeenth century. From late in the first decade of that century, some Separatists rejected infant baptism. This occurred at first among English Separatists living in Amsterdam, but from 1612 there were Baptist congregations in England. From their roots in Amsterdam, the English Baptists brought at least a small influence of the Radical Reformation, since they had met Mennonites there.

The English Revolution, and the Civil War in particular (1642–1648), released an amazing coterie of Christian movements that developed from the more radically inclined of the Puritans. Among these groups traditional Calvinist teachings and practices were transformed in startling directions. The doctrine of original sin could become a doctrine of radical human equality; the questioning of "superstitious" sacramentalism could become a rejection of all institutional church life; the notion of an "inward testimony of the Holy Spirit" or direct assurance of pardon could become a claim of direct divine inspiration for present action; the narrative of redemption and the way of salvation could become a narrative of political and social liberation. Muggletonians, Salmonists, and Coppinists all claimed a unique inspiration from God, and rejected authorities besides their own inspiration. "Levellers" and "Diggers" (or "True Levellers") claimed a radical equality and, in the case of the Diggers, advocated a form of Christian communism.[51]

Of all the radical movements that emerged during the English Revolution, none had a more lasting effect on Christian spirituality than the Religious Society of Friends, or "Quakers." In fact, many members of other sects which had failed (or had been crushed) by the mid 1650s eventually found their way into the Society of Friends. Moreover, it would appear that George Fox himself gathered the movement in the period between 1647 and 1652 from various persons already "seeking" a new spirituality. The Quakers, then, can be taken as an instance of the more radical spiritualities that were emerging in England during the period of the Parliamentary victories in the Revolution.

It was precisely during the period of the English Civil War that George Fox's religious quest began. The son of a Leicestershire weaver, Fox was troubled in the early years of the War with religious depression, very similar to earlier Puritan descriptions of conviction. In his journal, which followed the Puritan precedent, he noted, ". . . a strong temptation to despair came upon me," and he stated further that he was "in great sorrows and troubles, and walked many nights by myself."[52] He rejected the Church of England, spent some time with Puritan pastors, then rejected their teachings because they had nothing to offer him in his travail.[53]

Finally, toward the end of the Civil War, Fox's quest was rewarded with a direct revelation:

> And when all my hopes in them and in all men were gone, so that I had nothing outwardly to help me, nor could tell what to do, then, Oh then, I heard a voice which said, "There is one, even Christ Jesus, that can speak to thy condition," and when I heard it my heart did leap for joy.[54]

Fox "saw," was "enlightened," to use his own terms, and his knowledge of Christ was "experimental," that is, of his own experience.[55]

From this point, Fox seems to have taken up the earlier Puritan model of itinerant preaching, wandering about from place to place prophecying, preaching, and gathering other seekers about him. Although he was imprisoned many times in this period (and later, during the Restoration), Fox began to attract some prominent followers. In 1652, he made the friendship of Judge Thomas and Lady Margaret Fell; Lady Margaret (whom Fox would marry after the death of her husband) was convinced of Fox's teaching. Her home—Swarthmoor—became a meeting place for early Friends, and she raised funds to support Quaker evangelists and missionaries. In the same year, Fox had seen a vision of "a great people in white raiment by a river's side coming to the Lord."[56] So that by 1652, we might say, the Quakers had the formal appearance of a religious movement. They were acknowledged as such in 1655, when Oliver Cromwell mentioned them in a proclamation.

Though severely persecuted during the Protectorate, and even more so during the Restoration, the Friends continued to gather converts, many from other radical groups. Having rejected all outward religious observances, including formal liturgies, prepared sermons, and memorized prayers, the Quakers' worship took the form of informal meetings in which any person (men or women) could speak what the Spirit had given them to say. In this respect, the Quakers represent a radical, but in a sense a logical, extreme of the "religion of the heart": with the heart as the center of religious life, all external observances, institutions, and forms became strictly secondary. Earlier Protestants rejected transubstantiation, images, episcopacy, and eventually presbyterian polity and infant baptism. With their dominant concern for the inward life, the Friends pressed the rejection of medieval sacramentalism to its logical extreme.

George Fox

Sketch after a painting by Sir Peter Lely (1618–1680); in Elizabeth Braithwaite Emmott, *A Short History of Quakerism* (*Earlier Periods*) (New York: George H. Doran Co., 1923), opposite p. 81.

It is remarkable, given their radical rejection of institutions, that the Quakers managed to survive the English Revolution, when almost all other radical groups had disappeared. This was partly due to the fact that the Quakers developed some institutions of their own that enabled the movement to survive. There was little formal organization among the Quakers at first, the movement being held together by the charismatic presence of Fox and other preachers. By the late 1660s, however, it had become customary among them to hold Monthly Meetings to take care of church business. These developed within a couple of decades into Quarterly Meetings of all the Friends in a county, and a Yearly Meeting representing the whole Society. The Act of Toleration of 1689 allowed Quakers (along with other dissenting sects) the right of public worship in England.

For all their other-worldliness, in fact, the Quakers did reflect—perhaps in an exaggerated way—many of the cultural patterns of their age. One of the most important of these was their concern with epistemological issues. This concern places them squarely within (not outside of) the recognizable parameters of seventeenth-century culture in Europe and Britain, when challenges to traditional authorities and epistemological issues came to the fore. Quakerism emerged between the times of Bacon and Locke. The concern for valid sources of the human knowledge of God is evident in Fox's own quest for knowledge of God, and his stress on the "Inner Light" that Christ gives to the individual. Another early Quaker, Isaac Pennington, put it in this manner:

> We, who are reproachfully by many called Quakers, are (for the most part) a people who have much and long sought after the Lord, and after an experimental knowledge of these truths which are testified of and related in the Holy Scriptures . . . We sought not after a new Christ, or a new Spirit, or new doctrines concerning Christ and his Spirit: but to know Christ so as to receive life from him . . .[57]

Pennington, like Fox, stressed the "experimental" (we would say, perhaps, "experiential") knowledge of Christ that is available, unmediated, to every person.

This epistemological concern is most prominent in the systematic work of the Scottish Quaker Robert Barclay, whose *Theologiae Verae Christianae Apologia* (*Apology for the True Christian Divinity*) was published in 1676, and became a standard exposition of Quaker teaching. Barclay's *Apology* reflects the "routinization" of Quaker theology, and was written at the same time as Quaker institutional structures were developing. Following a conventional theological pattern, the work lays out a series of propositions, then comments on each of them. Of Barclay's fifteen propositions, the first two have to do with religious knowledge. Proposition one, "Concerning the true Foundation of Knowledge," asserts that the *knowledge* of Christ is the object of Christian faith. Proposition two, "Concerning Immediate Revelation," then explains how a human being comes to this knowledge:

> . . . therefore the testimony of the Spirit is that alone by which the true knowledge of God hath been, is, and can only be revealed; who . . . by the revelation of the same Spirit hath manifested himself all along unto the sons of men, both patriarchs, prophets, and apostles; which revelations of God by the Spirit, whether by outward voices and appearances, dreams, or inward objective manifestations in the heart, were of old the formal object of their faith, and remain yet so to be . . .[58]

The third proposition in Barclay's book, "Concerning the Scriptures," asserts that the Scriptures are a faithful account of God's work in the past and in the future and set forth all the doctrines of Christianity, but are nevertheless ". . . a secondary rule, subordinate to the Spirit, from which they have their excellence and certainty."[59]

It is true that beginning a systematic theological treatise with a discussion of the grounds of knowledge was not original to Barclay: Calvin's *Institutes* began with a consideration of "The Knowledge of God the Creator."[60] What is radically distinctive about Barclay's book, though, is his subordination of Scripture to the immediate testimony of the Spirit. Just as the scientists and philosophers of Barclay's century had subordinated traditional authorities to experiential knowledge, so the Quakers, as represented in his work, subordinated all traditional authority (including the authority of Scripture) to "experimental" knowledge of God:

> Though then we do acknowledge the scriptures to be very heavenly and divine writings, . . . yet we may not call them the principal fountain of all truth and knowledge, nor yet the first adequate rule of faith and manners; because the principal fountain of truth must be truth itself.[61]

If the epistemology of religious experience was the ground of Quaker spirituality, the substance of their spirituality was a conception of the way by which women and men come to salvation. Again, Barclay systematized what Fox, Pennington, and others had emphasized in their more fragmentary writings. According to Barclay, Quakers teach that human beings are incapable of doing any good on their own. Christ, however, has "enlightened" every human being, giving each one a supernaturally graced ability to accept or reject the Gospel.[62] That is to say, in traditional Puritan language, "effectual calling" is, to some extent experienced by every human being. "Justification" is the righteousness which Christ gives by faith only to those who do not resist the light. Following justification is "perfection," a work of Christ's grace accomplished when human beings are "free from actual sinning and transgressing of the law of God."[63] Nevertheless, this perfection allows for further growth in the knowledge of God, and it is possible that justified persons can fall away from the grace that they have received.[64]

Though differing significantly from the English Puritans (and some would classify the Quakers as "radical Puritans"), the Quakers show signs of a common, cultural shift in religious consciousness. Fox's own life and the experience of other early Friends reflected a melancholy character that displayed itself in a kind of religious depression, and propelled individuals to find a more secure knowledge or assurance of God than traditional authorities offered. The Quakers, moreover, developed an epistemology in response to this crisis of assurance, an epistemology grounded in an individual's direct (unmediated) knowledge or experience of God. The Quakers, further, developed their understanding of the "way of salvation," which had been a central concern of pietistically inclined Puritans in the decades before them. The enterprise of the Friends, then, can be understood as a kind of "skewing" or "stretching" of traditional Calvinist tendencies under the unique conditions of the Revolution and the Civil War; to traditional Calvinists, it meant a break or crack in their branch of Christian tradition.

Reason, Toleration, and the Religion of the Heart

There were, however, some boughs of the Calvinist branch that bent less violently than did that of the Quakers under the influence of affective piety. The later years of the seventeenth century in Britain, especially after the Glorious Revolution of 1688, were dominated by the themes of reason and religious toleration. Both of these seemed to stand in sharp contrast to what appeared then as the authoritative bigotry of all sides in the English Revolution. Both themes were prominent in the works of John Locke, who stands as the preeminent British thinker of the period. And yet, even during the period of the Revolution, while radicalism was reaching its zenith, there were advocates of a more rational and tolerant piety who would set the precedents for the last decades of the seventeenth century.

It is helpful to think of the seventeenth century in Britain, in respect to its philosophical development, as being punctuated by Francis Bacon's *Novum Organum* (1620) at one end, and by Locke's *Essay concerning Human Understanding* (1690), at the other. In both cases, British philosophers showed themselves concerned with *experience* as the truest conveyor of knowledge to humankind. "Reason," at least for British philosophers, meant reflection on experience. For religious authors, especially those concerned with affective devotion, it was natural to take up the notion of *religious* experience as a grounding for the theological enterprise. We have already seen how in Perkins and Ames, Bunyan and Barclay, epistemological questions were met with a doctrine of personal assurance and illumination. In Barclay, writing in the 1670s, this epistemological concern and what we might call his "religious-empirical" response, had come to the forefront of theological inquiry. But Barclay was not alone in this enterprise.

In the period between 1638 and 1688 an influential group of Cambridge divines developed a sophisticated response to the epistemological challenges of the day, and they too would insist on the central role of religious experience in the grounding of religious claims. The "Cambridge Platonists," true to the Plantonic heritage, insisted on the independent existence of a spiritual realm. They differed sharply from traditional Platonism and from the rationalism of European thinkers (Descartes in particular) in borrowing from the philosophy and science of their age the claim that, just as knowledge of material things comes by way of the "bodily" senses, so knowledge of spiritual things comes by way of a "spiritual sense" (or "sensation").

The Cambridge Platonist John Smith (1618–1652) began his *Discourse concerning the True Way or Method of Attaining Divine Knowledge* with the proposition, "That divine things are understood rather by a spiritual sensation than a verbal description, or mere speculation."[65] This "spiritual epistemology" became the philosophical hallmark of their school.[66] Though the Cambridge Platonists could be described as part of an intellectual elite, their epistemological concerns were grounded in their piety: "To seek our divinity merely in books and writings," wrote Smith, "is to seek the living among the dead."[67] It would be fair to say, moreover, that the piety advocated by the Cambridge Platonists was closer to mysticism than what we have described as "the religion of the heart," or affective piety. Nevertheless, their *grounding* of theology in a doctrine of religious experience or "sensation" was generalized, that is, not limited to the pursuit of the mystical path. Further, the parallel between their doctrine of religious "sensation" and Barclay's notion of religious experience shows in general how affective piety could itself be called upon in addressing the pressing philosophical issues of the age.

The Cambridge Platonists reflected not only the passion for "reason" (as reflection on experience) but also the concern for religious toleration that was to develop late in the seventeenth century. The advent of William and Mary in 1688 marked an unequivocal rejection of older attempts to enforce a single religious Establishment on the British nations. Their advent was followed by an Act of Toleration in 1689 which allowed "Dissenting" Protestants freedom of worship, so long as they officially registered their chapels. "Puritanism," as the hope of "purifying" the national church, was dead; but the spiritual impetus of Puritan piety was carried on by both Anglicans and Dissenters in the ensuing decades.

Representing the old Puritan spirituality in the spirit of this new age was the pastor and theologian Richard Baxter (1615–1691). Baxter was ordained priest in 1639 by the bishop of Worcester, but rejected episcopal polity two years later when he refused to subscribe to the "etcetera" oath. He remained as pastor of the parish of Kidderminster through the Revolution, and opposed both the Solemn League and Covenant and Cromwell's theological and political views. "Ejected" from his parish in 1660, he participated in the Savoy Conference of 1661, arguing for a moderate religious Establishment that would embrace both a limited episcopacy and some elements of presbyterian government.[68] These reforms being rejected, he served as pastor of Presbyterian congregations for the remainder of his life, although he never relinquished his claim to be a faithful minister of the Church of England.

Baxter wrote both formal theological treatises, after the pattern of Perkins and Ames, and also popular sermons, tracts, and books. He began, as the old Puritans had done, with the doctrine of election, but, while holding to a doctrine of predestination, Baxter was unhappy with the traditional Calvinistic claim that Christ's death was effective only for the limited number of the elect. Baxter argued that Christ's death made a sufficient satisfaction for the sin of every human being, and that salvation is granted to every human being on the condition of her believing in Christ. Nevertheless, Baxter affirmed, God never intended or foresaw that all would accept this condition, so that the condition (of faith) is fulfilled only in those whom Christ has elected to salvation.[69] In this way, Baxter avoided Arminianism (since he did not maintain that God intended the salvation of all hu-

Rev.ᵈ Richard Baxter.

Richard Baxter

Engraving by R. Hicks; in Richard Baxter, *The Saints' Everlasting Rest* (London: Caxton Press for Henry Fisher, 1822), prior to frontispiece.

mankind), but was able to argue that the work of Christ was "for all humankind" (*pro omnibus*) in the sense that it paid the equivalent of the debt owed by all human beings.

With this somewhat altered theology of election, however, Baxter proclaimed the way of salvation along the lines of the older Puritans.[70] His autobiography, *Reliquiae baxterianae* (published posthumously in 1696), followed the well-established pattern of recounting one's conversion, then the struggles of sanctification following it. But Baxter made a distinctive contribution in his detailed account of the role of the pastor and of the community in leading the religious seeker along the order of salvation. His *Gildas Salvianus: or, the Reformed Pastor* laid out a program by which the pastor would call upon all under his care, and inquire about their spiritual condition. They were to be especially concerned to note whether the individual was converted, or not, and to try to prescribe the next steps in the way of salvation to each.[71] In his own works directed to such seekers, Baxter could give an even more elaborate series of tests for the truthfulness of one's conversion, and in these tests, the conversion of the will and affections (as well as the conversion of the mind or intellect) was central:

> The second part of the work of conversion is upon the Heart or Will, to which this change of the mind or understanding is preparative: and in this change of the heart, there are these several parts available. 1. The will is brought to like what it disliked, and to dislike what it liked before. 2. It is brought to choose what it refused; and to consent to what it would not consent to. 3. It is brought to resolve, where it was, either resolved on the contrary, or unresolved. 4. The several Affections are changed, of love and hatred, desire and aversion, delight and sorrow, hope and despair, courage and fear, and anger, and content, and discontent.[72]

The *Treatise of Conversion* and a host of other works on the subject which Baxter produced described further methods of self-examination, and examination by a pastor or community, to discern the individual's spiritual condition and prescribe the appropriate exercises for them.

Though Baxter was no "Latitudinarian" with respect to the fundamentals of Reformed theology, his works do convey a sense of reasonableness and toleration that fit the spirit of their age. Baxter's appeal to the unconverted was a winsome one: true enough to the Puritan stereotype, the terrors of hell were there, but Baxter constantly pointed the seeker towards the goal of eternal happiness, describing the joys of communion with God and *The Saints' Everlasting Rest* (almost unquestionably his most popular work).[73] Baxter may stand for us, then, as the culmination of the rich and colorful pageant of affective piety as it appeared among the British Calvinists in the century of revolution. He represents the continuation of the old branch of Calvinism, now weathered and bent in a new direction by the influence of affective devotion, but still recognizable, and firmly attached to the trunk of what Baxter knew and loved as "catholic" Christianity.

* * *

Looking over Baxter's works, and considering the long train of historical events winding through the Reformation and the history of British Calvinism that had led from the middle ages to his "enlightened" time, one is struck by how much of the medieval spiritual tradition remained. If the Puritan diary had replaced the confessional, Baxter's Reformed pastor acted very much the part of the Spiritual Director, carefully considering "cases of conscience" (Baxter used precisely that term), utilizing his best skill to analyze the needs of the seeker, setting exercises to evaluate spiritual progress, calling back the weary and backsliding, gently leading the believer to sanctification. But then, it could be objected, Baxter's Augustinianism (admittedly modified) and his stress on affective devotion most clearly differentiate his piety from that of the *Devotio Moderna*.

That is true: but it is at this point that the parallel with Jansenism is most clear. Jansenism and the affective piety of British Calvinism developed synchronously through the seventeenth century. Jansen's *Augustinus*, with its strong affirmation of the Augustinian theology of grace, was published in the year in which the English Revolution began. Blaise Pascal's "night of fire" occurred within months of Bunyan's conversion. By the end of the century, both Jansenism and English Calvinism were well-established "dissenting" communions within their respective lands. Both had begun with a tradition of moral rigorism, and had seen it subtly transformed by the emergence of affective devotion. Both Jansenism and "pietistic" Puritanism could be described as religious movements having an Augustinian understanding of human nature and grace, a long tradition of communal, moral discipline, and a growing focus on personal, affective appropriation of the grace of election. Both spawned eccentric, radical offshoots (admittedly much later, in the case of Jansenism). It is tantalizing to consider, further, that both seemed to have appealed to the bourgeois classes that had grown from the mercantile economies of northern Europe, and that both groups played an important role in the development of experimental science.

The parallels should not be pressed too far: the historical circumstances were considerably different in these movements. But consider them in relation to the broad currents of spirituality that we have seen throughout the seventeenth century: in relation to the development of a popular, affectively oriented mysticism and to the rise of devotion to the sacred heart in Spain and France, in relation to the rise of Scots-Irish revivalistic meetings, the development of Quaker spirituality, and the explication of a reasonable and tolerant piety in the Cambridge Platonists and Richard Baxter. Considered in this context, a certain pattern begins to emerge across Protestant and Catholic religious and cultural boundaries. It was not that their understanding of the religious *ultimate* had changed, but the manners in which women and men *approached* the ultimate, what we have called their forms of religious life, had begun to be altered in a similar manner in both the Catholic and the Protestant contexts.

If, then, we are to envision seventeenth-century Calvinism as the branch of a tree moved by the winds of the new impetus towards affective piety in that age, we must see Jansenism not as a part of the same branch (for in all its particulars it was quite different), but rather as another branch quite differently placed, but whose own bending motion paralleled that of the Calvinists. Quietism and devotion to the sacred heart would also be seen as distinct limbs, but displaying a similar, parallel motion, as the impetus of affective piety surged through the Christian community.

We must now return to the European Continent at the beginning of the seventeenth century to take up one more branch of this tradition of affective piety, and that of course is the branch that came to be known as "Pietism," within the Reformed and Lutheran Churches of Europe. But before making this geographical and chronological leap, it is worth considering for just a moment the affective piety of seventeenth-century British Calvinism in respect to what (we now know) lay in the future in the British Isles. Looking to the near future (the 1730s) in England, we may ponder what Richard Baxter and his followers were sometimes called in their own age: "New Methodists."[74]

Chapter Four

Pietism

In the second decade of the seventeenth century, the new state of the United Provinces (what today is the Netherlands) was a social, cultural, and religious crossroads. One would have encountered a remarkable array of religious figures there and nearby in this decade. Although Cornelius Jansen was then studying at Paris and Bayonne, he would within a decade become the bishop of Ypres, in the neighboring "Spanish Netherlands" (now Belgium). At the University of Leiden, Jacobus Arminius had recently died, but the controversy over Arminianism had become the theological focus of Dutch Calvinism. Amid the population of Amsterdam one would have found not only the first English Baptist congregation, drawn from Separatist Puritan exiles and founded by John Smyth, who died in there in 1612, but also a congregation of English Puritans soon to leave aboard the *Mayflower*. At the Hague one would have found in that decade the figure of William Ames, who brought the pietistic impulse of English Puritanism in its nascent form to the Reformed Churches of the European Continent. The state of the United Provinces, then, is the natural place to begin a consideration of European Pietism.

The United Provinces had been organized in 1589. The very existence of the nation could not be taken for granted, for since it had been established as a Protestant state, it was challenged by the power of Spain (who held the Spanish Netherlands immediately to the south), and its political independence would not be secure until the end of the Thirty Years War (1648). The young nation proved itself a powerful economic force, however, reaping the benefits of international trade. There was a certain congruence between the rising middle classes of England and the United Provinces in this period, with the *bourgeoisie* in both nations propelled by the economics of international trade and attracted to the theology of the Reformed tradition.

In the early decades of the seventeenth century, the United Provinces became not only a mercantile, but also a cultural crossroads. In addition to the influx of population, the United Provinces had supported an unusually tolerant attitude toward religious traditions. Since the time of Erasmus, in fact, the Dutch people had been known for their moderate stance, and their toleration had attracted not only Catholics and Protestants of all stripes, but considerable numbers of European Jews as well.

It was in this cultural mixing pot that the traditions of affective devotion already developing in Catholicism and in English Puritanism would begin to emerge in a distinctively European Protestant environment, and the movement that thus developed has been almost uniformly described as "Pietism."[1] But if it is clear that European Pietism emerged at first in the United Provinces, the question of the deeper origins of the movement is much disputed. Some scholars have traced its origins directly from English Puritanism by way of William Perkins and William Ames. A more cautious approach would maintain that Ames found in European Reformed Churches an environment already prepared for such a movement, perhaps already showing indications of it.[2] It is, in fact, very difficult to disentangle early Pietism from its immediate roots in Reformed and Lutheran doctrine, and its more distant roots in medieval spiritual teachings.[3]

Like the British Calvinist movements described in the last chapter, Pietism stressed personal religious experience, especially repentance (the experience of one's own unworthiness before God and of one's own need for grace) and sanctification (the experience of personal growth in holiness, involving progress towards complete or perfect fulfillment of God's intention). It spread from the Reformed Churches to the "Evangelical" (or Lutheran) Churches of Europe, and by the end of the seventeenth century had become a powerful cultural force in northern Europe, even dominating some areas (such as Prussia). Although Moravianism was one of a very few denominations that resulted from the Pietist movement, it had a broad and lasting effect of its own on European Protestantism and, in its own turn, influenced the future development of the "religion of the heart" movements in the British Isles and in North America. Somewhat more distantly, Pietism contributed to the rise of Romanticism and Protestant Liberalism.

Reformed Pietism

Pietism emerged at first among the Reformed Christians of the United Provinces, with whom there were strong ties to English Puritanism.[4] William Ames, in particular, had moved from England to Holland (part of the United Provinces) and brought the theology of English Puritanism with him. It may be remembered that Ames defined theology as *doctrina Deo vivendi*: "teaching [or doctrine] about living for God." He insisted that there is a spiritual meaning of scripture which can be known only by the regenerate. He defined "faith" in such a way as to imply conversion of the will, and maintained that faith effects our justification, adoption, sanctification, and glorification, thus following in his own way the *ordo salutis* of Romans 8:30, as William Perkins had done.[5]

Another figure who mediated the spiritual impulse of British Puritanism to Continental Reformed Churches was Willem Teellinck (1579–1629). Teellinck was a native of Holland, but had traveled in England, where he made the acquaintance of Puritan theologians and had the opportunity to live in a Puritan home. He wrote extensively—especially devotional and edificatory tracts and sermons—and his works were published in English as well as Dutch. Teellinck, like William Perkins and William Ames, was doctrinally orthodox (particularly in his adherence to traditional Calvinism against the challenge of the Remonstrants), and his writings too show tendencies towards affective devotion.

The question of "assurance of salvation" which had concerned Perkins and Ames was also a critical, practical issue for Teellinck (the term, in fact, is quoted here from Teellinck's writings). In a pair of sermons on Romans 7:24 ("Wretched man that I am! Who will deliver me from this body of death?") he expounded what he took to be the scriptural response to this issue. Proceeding by the typically Puritan method of expounding "doctrines" and then "uses" of the doctrines of scripture, Teellinck found this passage to teach as a doctrine that "The more holy a man is, the more sensible is he of his naturall corruption."[6] From this "doctrine," Teellinck derived the application (or "use") that

> by this Doctrine may every man prove, and try himselfe, whether he be a childe of God or not; in which the most part of men are wanting, suffering themselves to be deceived in the case of assurance of salvation . . .[7]

This sensitivity of one's "natural corruption" is, according to Teellinck, an "infallible Rule" by which one's spiritual state can be discerned.[8] Teellinck's point, it should be noted, was not that believers experience a specific sense of pardon, but that their "sensibility" of sin, their conviction of their own "corruption," is itself the unfailing sign of the work of grace.[9]

The Pietist tradition initiated in the United Provinces was carried on by Jadocus van Lodensteyn (1620–1677), a pastor in Utrecht two generations younger than Ames and Teellinck. Lodensteyn organized conventicles of believers and, by the middle of the seventeenth century, came to be respected as the leader of a recognizable Pietist party within the national Church. There is a sense, then, in which he may be regarded as the originator of Dutch Pietism, at least as an influential religious movement within the church.

Lodensteyn's organization of members of his congregation into small groups for the cultivation of piety was a critical move in the development of Pietism. His own teacher, the renowned Dutch theologian Gysbert Voët (Latin, "Voetius"; 1589–1676) had organized his students into similar, small groups for the careful—or "precise," to use their term—observance of the moral law. Voët's outlook has been described as "Precisianism," for his concern with the "precise" following of the moral law, and his organization of conventicles[10] seems to have been motivated more by his concern with the following of the law than with the cultivation of piety. Nevertheless, "Precisianism" and "Pietism" were not at odds, and Lodensteyn himself is sometimes described as a "Precisian" as well as a "Pietist." "Precisian," it may be observed, carried about the same range of meanings in this period as "Methodist" would at the beginning of the eighteenth century. What was distinctive about Lodensteyn's conventicles was that they were designed for the cultivation of personal religious affections (as well as the following of the moral law), and that they were used for the congregation in general (not just students) as a means of bringing reform to the Church. In Lodensteyn's conventicles, moreover, disputes over doctrinal issues were forbidden, since the focus was to be on practical Christianity.[11] In this we may see a first instance of Pietism's reaction against dogmatism, and its ecumenical concern. In this, moreover, we may begin to see how Pietism was diverging from the patterns of Puritanism and Protestant scholasticism.

In addition to his development of the conventicles, Jadocus van Lodensteyn distinguished himself as a preacher of the "way of salvation" and the reform of the Church. His passion for both is evidenced in the title of a collection of his sermons, *Spiritual Awakener, Meant for a Christendom which Lacks in Self-Denial, is Dead and Spiritless.*[12] Lodensteyn sensed what generations of Pietistic and Evangelical preachers after him would claim, namely, that Christianity in their day was "dead," "lifeless," or "spiritless," and must be brought to life by personal conversion and corporate revival. In his exposition of the way of salvation, however, Lodensteyn displayed a tendency towards quietism, both in his insistence that meditation on the scriptures and on Christ brings one to faith, and in his claim that true self-denial implies a lack of concern for one's own salvation. [13]

By the middle of the seventeenth century, and especially under the leadership of Jadocus van Lodensteyn, Pietism was a recognizable movement within the Dutch Reformed Church. Lodensteyn was joined by Jan Teellinck (d. 1663), the son of Willem Teellinck, and by another father-son pair of theologians, Theodore Gerardi à Brakel (1608–1669) and Willem à Brakel (1635–1711). With the latter two, in particular, the pietistic stress on the affections was heightened. Theodore Gerardi à Brakel, for instance, could describe three states of Christians based upon their appropriation of divine love. His son developed a theological textbook, *The True Service of God*, in which the teachings of Dutch Pietists were systematized. By the 1670s, then, when Lutheran Pietism clearly appeared with Spener's *Pia Desideria*, Dutch Pietism was already a well-established religious movement, well on its way to having formalized structures for transmitting the movement to future generations. [14]

The Dutch Reformed Church was closely allied in this period to the Reformed Churches of the Hanseatic coast of northern Germany, and many German Reformed pastors were trained in the United Provinces. One such pastor was Theodor Untereyck (1635–1693), who had studied in Holland, was converted under the influence of Lodensteyn, and had also studied mystical teachings. Untereyck organized conventicles in Bremen, where he served as head of the *Ministerium*, following the pattern set by Lodensteyn, and his wife oversaw daily meetings for women in the parish. His moves for reform were opposed by other pastors of the *Ministerium* of the city, and Untereyck himself eventually ceased to meet with his conventicles (although his wife continued to meet with hers). [15]

From the circle of Theodor Untereyck at Bremen came the German Reformed Pietist and hymn composer, Joachim Neander (1650–1680). Neander's hymns, predating those of Isaac Watts in the Reformed tradition, expressed the thirsting of the soul for God, the repose of the soul in the Savior, and the soul's aspiration to union with Christ. [16] His "Praise to the Lord, the Almighty" (German, *Lobe den Herren*) was to become a standard in Protestant worship, and others of his hymns were taken up by Reformed and Lutheran Pietists, and then by English Evangelicals. Neander set a precedent for pietistic hymnody that was soon to be followed by Gerhard Tersteegen and others.

Pietism spread from Bremen to the Reformed Churches of Northern Germany, so that by the time of Philipp Jakob Spener, a strong tradition of Pietism was already present, not only in the United Provinces, but also in the Reformed Churches of Prussia. Christians were already gathering in small groups, sermons were focusing on the way of salvation, the renewal of the Church was passionately prayed for, and new hymns were expressing the depths of affective devotion. Before we turn to Spener and the Lutheran Pietists, however, we must consider one of the more colorful offspring of Reformed Pietism.

Labadism

Theodor Untereyck and Joachim Neander, it may be noted, were suspected of heresy, and although both were cleared of the charges, the fact is that by their time Reformed Pietism had already begun to spawn some eccentric offspring. Just as the Pietistic emphases within English Puritanism came to a radical expression in George Fox and the early Quakers, so Reformed Pietism came to a radical expression, following the Thirty Years War, in the sect of Jean de Labadie (1610–1674).[17] Labadie's career itself provides a remarkable narrative of a soul's pilgrimage through the religious movements of the Baroque age, passing, as he did, from the Society of Jesus to Jansenism, from there to Reformed Protestantism, and finally to the leadership of an independent sect. In each of these transitions, Labadie's life illustrates the complex intertwining of the varied strands of the religion of the heart movements. Moreover, just as the Quakers illustrate the extreme to which affective devotion could be carried by English Puritans, so Labadism illustrates the extreme to which affective devotion could carry Continental Reformed Pietists.

Labadie's parents, from Gascony in southwestern France, were Huguenots who conformed to Roman Catholicism upon the accession of Henry IV. Thus, although Labadie grew up as a Catholic, there was a strong strain of Calvinist influence in his family. In his early teens he joined the Society of Jesus, and was quickly promoted through its lower ranks, being ordained priest in 1638. Even in his early years, Labadie experienced visions, trances, and a consistent sense of divine vocation to reform the Church. It was a time when the Society was rife with suspicions, accusations, and counter-accusations of illuminism (specifically, fear of the *Alumbrados*), and even by the time of his ordination, Labadie had begun to question whether he could carry out his vocation within the Society. A year later (in 1639), he was formally released from the Jesuits.[18]

Labadie then spent a decade in the company of Oratorians and Jansenists. (The Oratorians, it may be recalled, had generally supported the Jansenist cause against the Jesuits.) He visited Saint-Cyran while the latter was imprisoned at Vincennes, and made more than one retreat to Port-Royal des Champs during the 1640s. He appears to have supported the Jansenist cause wholeheartedly, both in its Augustinian view of human nature and the need for grace, and in its strictness in administering the Mass and penance with an eye to the affective devotion of the recipient.[19]

Labadie was pursued by Church authorities during his Jansenist period, and during one of his flights he lodged with a Huguenot family, where he read Calvin's *Institutes*. He was attracted by the congruence he perceived between Calvinism and "the Primitive Church," and so it was that at mid-century, two years after the Peace of Westphalia, Labadie made a sensational conversion to the Reformed faith. Despite the protestations of his family and Catholic peers, he was recognized in 1652 as a Reformed minister, and began a career of preaching in the Reformed Churches of France, the United Provinces, and Switzerland. At one point, at the height of the Protectorate in England, he was invited to become the pastor of a prominent, newly formed Independent congregation in London (with a letter to him written by none other than John Milton). Although the appointment in London did not work out, it illustrates how Labadie was perceived, at this juncture, as a leading spokesperson for the Reformed Churches throughout Europe and Britain.[20]

At this point Labadie joins our earlier narrative of Reformed Pietism. From 1666 Labadie spent the remainder of his career (with very few exceptions) in the United Provinces, becoming pastor of a French-speaking Reformed congregation in Middleburg in that year. Willem Teellinck himself had been the pastor of a Flemish-speaking congregation in the same city several decades before. Most importantly, while in the United Provinces, Labadie came into the contemporary circle of Jadocus van Lodensteyn (at Utrecht), and so was from this time increasingly drawn into the sphere of Reformed Pietism in the United Provinces.

While at Middleburg (from 1666 to 1669), Labadie's separatist tendencies surfaced. He embarked upon a stringent program of reform for the congregation, laying out his plan in *The Reform of the Church through the Pastorate* (1667), his best-known work. The book is important, not only because of the clear manner in which Labadie laid out his concerns for renewal in the Church, but also because it provided a model for subsequent pietistic and Evangelical tracts. It is comprised of two pastoral letters, the first of which lays out the need for a "general reform" in the Church. Labadie provided "particular evidences of a general corruption among Christians."[21] He lamented the Christians' spiritual dryness, their lack of zeal, and their failure to show the marks of sanctified lives. The letter focuses on the pastorate, beginning with such mundane problems as the ministers' lack of education, or their extreme age or youth, then goes on to analyze more critical problems: the pastors lack zeal for the reform of the Church; they lack zeal because they lack "divine anointing," which Labadie also calls "sensible grace"; and they lack divine anointing because, in the end, they lack a true, divine and interior calling (or vocation).[22] Having demonstrated the need for reform, his second letter lays out a program of eleven specific steps for the reform of the Church. Among other things, Labadie called for a universal penitence, zealous and "united" preaching for reform, the establishment of separate seminaries (that is his term) for the training of youth who have a true, interior calling to the pastorate, a renewal of the discipline of time, life, and manners, and the regulation of Church assemblies, especially those for instruction and catechesis, so that true faith could be laid before the congregations.[23]

Consistent with the program laid out in this work, Labadie proceeded to organize conventicles in his congregation (hitherto unknown in French-speaking Reformed circles), strictly fenced the Lord's Table, and preached congregational discipline and personal union with Christ. His preaching and discipline soon brought him into conflict with the congregation and local Church officials, especially after he refused to sign a Confession of Faith demanded of all pastors in the French-speaking congregations.[24]

In 1669, Labadie was dismissed from the Middleburg congregation, and from that year operated as an independent minister with a formally separate religious sect. In Amsterdam, where he lived in 1669 and 1670, he made the acquaintance of Antoinette Bourignon, and was attracted to her mystical teachings. He also met Robert Barclay, the Quaker theologian, and he met and won the respect of Jan Amos Comenius (with whom he had corresponded earlier), one of the last surviving bishops of the old Moravian *Unitas Fratrum*.[25] Labadie and his followers in Amsterdam established a communal house, where followers could be gathered, and set up their own press to disseminate religious tracts. With increasing opposition from city leaders, however (even in tolerant Amsterdam), the Labadists were forced to flee to the area around Bremen in Northern Germany. After spending two years there, Labadie died in 1674.[26]

By the end of his life, Labadie had not only come to accept mystical teachings on the way of union with Christ, but he had also rejected outward sacraments and other religious acts, and had separated his community from existing Churches. He had engaged in millenarian speculations, and even commended the Jews of Amsterdam in their attachment to the false messiah Sabbatai Tsevi.[27]

There was a congruence, perceived even within his own community, between Labadie's beliefs and those of the Quakers, and there were attempts during the last years of his life to forge an alliance with Quakers in northern Germany. These attempts failed, partially because Labadie engaged himself in a personal struggle with William Penn, then the spokesperson for the Quaker community.[28] Although their negotiations broke down, there is a striking parallel in the impetus of the two movements, since both followed a trajectory that led them further and further from a form of religious life stressing the encounter with the divine through religious acts (sacraments) and closer and closer to a form of religious life in which spiritual experience alone was the true means of encounter with the divine. Both Quakerism and Labadism, then, represent in their unique contexts the ultimate stretching of the spiritual impetus of the religion of the heart movements.

Labadie's death in 1674 marks an important point in the development of the religion of the heart movements. A year before Spener's *Pia Desideria* was published, it was both an end and a beginning. Perhaps most significantly, in Labadie's life there were intertwined together most of the strands of the religion of the heart movements we have considered up to this point. Labadie had met Saint-Cyran, had visited Port-Royal, and considered himself to be a Jansenist for about a decade. In Amsterdam he had met Antoinette Bourignon, and became something of a Quietist, at least in his attraction to mystical theology, in the latter years of his life. While a respected Reformed pastor, he had been in communication with English Puritans, and he was also part of the Reformed Pietist circle of Jadocus van Lodensteyn in the United Provinces. His meeting with Robert Barclay and his correspondence with William Penn put him in touch with the Quakers. Labadie's pilgrimage was thus a path along which he was pulled by the pervasive influence of the religion of the heart movements.

Lutheran Pietism

A year after Labadie's death, Philipp Jakob Spener's *Pia Desideria* was published (1675), and some would date the origins of Pietism, properly so-called, from this year. This view does not take Reformed Pietism into account, and can misrepresent the precedents for Pietism within the Lutheran Churches. Lutheran Pietism sprang from at least two roots. In the first place was the inheritance of Reformed Pietism, which by this time had spread to the Reformed Churches of Germany. Spener himself was even influenced by Jean de Labadie, whom he had met, and whose *Reform of the Church through the Pastorate* he had read.

In the second place, however, there was a distinctively Lutheran tradition which combined Lutheran Orthodoxy with the inheritance of medieval mystical teaching, and which was represented in the influential figure of Johann Arndt (1555–1621).[29] Heiko Oberman refers to Arndt's spirituality as "the hidden and powerful source of a tradition that moved for some time in subterranean channels, surfacing toward the later part of the seventeenth century as German Pietism."[30]

Arndt was a student of Philip Melanchthon and was roughly contemporary with William Perkins. Although he agreed with the Lutheran theologians of his age in rejecting both Catholicism and Calvinism (and in advocating Lutheranism as the true faith), he reacted against the enterprise of polemical theology, insisting that Christians should be instructed in practical, living faith, rather than doctrinal controversies. Arndt was familiar with the traditions of both Western and Eastern Christian mysticism: he was able to utilize the *German Theology* and Tauler in his work, and was also said to have memorized the fifty *Spiritual Homilies* attributed to Macarius of Egypt. Although no discernible religious movement can be associated with him, his *Four Books on True Christianity* (1606) were very widely read (as far away as Russia), and directly influenced Spener, Francke, and other Pietist leaders.

True Christianity, as its title suggests, is an exposition of what Arndt took to be the practical essence of Christian religion, and his intention was made clear in his foreword to the work. The book attempts to show, Arndt wrote,

> wherein true Christianity consists, namely, in the exhibition of a true, living faith, active in genuine godliness and the fruits of righteousness. [It also shows] how true repentance must proceed from the innermost source of the heart; how the heart, mind, and affections must be changed, so that we might be conformed to Christ and his holy Gospel; and how we must be renewed by the work of God to become new creatures.[31]

Johann Arndt

Engraving by C. Meyer; in Wilhelm Hadorn, *Geschichte des Pietismus in den schweizerischen reformierten Kirchen* (Constance and Emmishofen: Verlag von Karl Hirsch, 1901), opposite p. 10.

And again,

> Many think that theology is a mere science or rhetoric, whereas it is a living experience and practice . . . True Christianity consists, not in words or in external show, but in living faith, from which arise righteous fruits, and all manner of Christian virtues, as from Christ himself.[32]

The book carries out this exposition of true faith, with book one describing true repentance, book two illustrating true faith, and book three showing the way of perfect union with Christ.[33]

It may be fairly said, then, that *True Christianity* laid out an understanding of the way of salvation parallel to the patterns by which Lutheran and Reformed teachers had taught the *ordo salutis*.[34] At one point, Arndt laid out a three-fold understanding of the way of salvation:

> Just as our natural life has its steps, namely, childhood, manhood, and old age, so also does our spiritual and Christian life. It too, has its beginnings in repentance, by which man daily betters himself. Thereafter follows middle age, more illumination, through the contemplation of divine things, through prayer, and through suffering. By all of these the gifts of God are increased. Finally, the perfection of old age comes. It consists in the full union through love, which Saint Paul called the perfect age of Christ and a perfect man in Christ (Eph. 4:13).[35]

This scheme is drawn from the mystical tradition, and Arndt, who freely utilized mystical sources in *True Christianity*, has often been described as a mystical teacher himself. Given a very general understanding of "mysticism,"[36] this may be appropriate. But on a stricter understanding (where "mysticism" involves hidden knowledge, the goal of losing self-consciousness in a complete union with the divine, and the pursuit of this goal in an ascetic community), Arndt cannot be described as a mystic. His understanding of the goal of union with Christ is ethical and affective (i.e., it was understood as a union of will and of love), not metaphysical. Far from Macarius's quest for "divinization" (*theiosis*), or Tauler's quest for the loss of the individual in the ocean of God's being, Arndt recognized that

> Perfection is not, as some think, a high, great, spiritual, heavenly joy and meditation, but it is a denial of one's own will, love, honor, a knowledge of one's nothingness, a continual completion of the will of God, a burning love for neighbor, a heart-held compassion, and, in a word, a love that desires, thinks, and seeks nothing other than God alone insofar as this is possible in the weakness of this life.[37]

In Arndt, then, the mystical tradition had been used and subtly changed, so that the form of religious life that Arndt advocated had more in common with the religion of the heart movements than with traditional mysticism.[38]

Arndt's influence may have "flowed in subterranean channels" from his time to that of Spener, but the seventeenth century was not lacking in expressions of affective devotion among Lutherans. *True Christianity* itself was widely read throughout this century, and it was in the period between Arndt and Spener that Lutheran hymnodists plundered the riches of medieval devotion to produce intensely personal hymns. The Silesian pastor Johann Heermann (1585–1647; Silesia is in present-day Poland) published in 1630 a collection of hymns entitled *Music of the Devoted Heart* (*Devoti Musica Cordis*), which included such highly personal lines as,

> Who was the guilty?
> Who brought this upon thee?
> Alas, my treason, Jesus,
>   hath undone thee!
> Twas I, Lord Jesus,
>   I it was denied thee;
>   I crucified thee.[39]

Just slightly later, Paul Gerhardt, one of Spener's predecessors in the Nikolaikirche of Berlin, offered the Church his deeply affective hymns, including,

> What thou, my Lord, hast suffered
>   was all for sinners' gain;
> mine, mine was the transgression,
>   but thine the deadly pain.
> Lo, here I fall, my Savior!
>   'Tis I deserve thy place;
> look on me with thy favor,
>   vouchsafe to me thy grace.[40]

Thus, if until Spener there was no recognizable Pietist movement in Lutheranism, there was nonetheless a deep well of affective devotion that was ready to be tapped by such a movement.

It was in the person and work of Philipp Jakob Spener[41] (1635–1705) that the Arndtian spirituality was combined with Reformed Pietism to produce a widespread Lutheran pietistic movement. Spener, born in 1635, was raised in a devout family and read *True Christianity* as a youth. He came to regard it as his favorite book. Arndt's influence on Spener was considerable, but it was not the only one. Spener

Philipp Jakob Spener

Engraving by Bartholomäus Kilian (1630–1696) after a painting by Johann Georg Wagner; in Wilhelm Hadorn, *Geschichte des Pietismus in den schweizerischen reformierten Kirchen* (Constance and Emmishofen: Verlag von Karl Hirsch, 1901), opposite p. 12.

had read widely in edificatory literature, including the Puritan Lewis Bayly's *Practice of Piety*.

It was during the course of his formal education that Spener directly encountered the tradition of Reformed Pietism. A native of Alsace, Spener had studied in Strasbourg between 1651 and 1653, then went on a tour of universities (a *Wanderjahr*), as was customary for young scholars at the time. While in Geneva in 1656, he fell ill, was required to stay in the city for nearly a year, and there made the acquaintance of Jean de Labadie. Soon after, Spener published a German translation of Labadie's *Manuel de Prière* ("Manual of Prayer"), and he would later read Labadie's *Reform of the Church through the Pastorate*. Early in his career, then, both the traditions of Arndt's distinctively Lutheran spirituality and Labadie's version of Reformed Pietism had come together.

Appointed senior pastor of the *Ministerium* in Frankfurt am Main from 1666, Spener began to preach the necessity of reform in the Church. In 1669 he suggested that believers should meet together for edification, rather than trivial conversation.[42] In the next year he organized a number of his followers into groups that met in his home on Sundays and Wednesdays to discuss the content of his sermons or some other edificatory literature. These groups came to be known as *collegia pietatis*, "gatherings for piety." (They are sometimes referred to as the "Frankfurt conventicles.") The groups had grown so large by 1682 (with numbers in the hundreds by then) that local authorities allowed Spener the use of one of the city churches for their meetings. At the same time, the conventicles spread to other cities, and Spener was becoming recognized as the leader of a widespread religious movement.

By this time, in fact, Spener had published the work which many regard as the clarion call for the Pietist movement. Originally written as a preface to Johann Arndt's *Postilla* on the Gospels, Spener's *Pia Desideria* (1675) was eventually published separately. In it, Spener laid out his program for a new Reformation of the Lutheran Churches.

Pia Desideria follows, in some critical respects, the pattern set by Labadie's *Reform of the Church through the Pastorate*. Like Labadie's book, it is principally directed towards the clergy, in the hope that they would spur on the reform movement. *Pia Desideria* has three main sections. In the first (corresponding to the first letter of Labadie's *Reform of the Church through the Pastorate*), Spener laid out his concerns about the present condition of the Church. Here, however, Spener showed that his concern was somewhat broader than Labadie's: his complaint was about the corruption of the whole Church, not just the clergy. Civil authorities and clergy were either indifferent to the cause of religion, or concerned themselves only with the maintenance of correct doctrine. The common people, likewise, were bereft of love, the distinguishing mark of a Christian, and many had fallen into superstitions or heresies.[43] In the second section of *Pia Desideria*, Spener laid out what he took to be the grounds for hope for a reform in the Church. Interestingly enough, this section is unparalleled in Labadie. Certain scriptural prophecies, he argued (such as the conversion of the Jews to Christianity and the fall of Rome), were as yet unfulfilled. Moreover, the life of the Church in the immediate post-apostolic period demonstrated that better conditions were possible even in the age after the apostles.[44] Finally, in the third section (answering to Labadie's second letter), Spener laid out his specific proposals for reform. Again, his proposals were broader than Labadie's, which had focused on the clergy. He proposed a more extensive use of scripture, in particular by the laity, who should exercise the spiritual priesthood by their study and teaching of the Bible in private settings. Teachers should stress that Christianity consists not only in orthodox doctrine, but also in the practice of love, and they should endeavor to set an example of piety for their students. Students should be instructed individually and in small groups about the nature of Christian piety. Sermons should be designed not to display learning, but to inculcate faith and to bring forth its fruits.[45]

The publication of *Pia Desideria* and the use of the *collegia pietatis* in Frankfurt provoked both support and suspicion. Spener received over three hundred letters, most of them supportive, in the next few years, and saw the widespread distribution of tract literature encouraging the reforms he had suggested. Many theologians, some of the Orthodox school, indicated their support.[46] But others felt threatened by the laity's claims to the "spiritual priesthood," and by the denunciations of the Church by many of Spener's followers. There was, indeed, a tendency in the *collegia pietatis* towards separatism, and this particularly threatened existing ecclesiastical structures. By the mid-1680s, Spener's followers were being called by the (then pejorative) term, "Pietists."[47]

In 1686 Spener was called to be the court chaplain to the Elector Johann Georg III of Saxony. His stay there (in Dresden) was quite short, due in part to the resentment of the Saxon clergy at the appointment of a foreigner, but more importantly due to Spener's falling-out with Johann Georg, who seldom attended chapel and whom Spener scolded for drunkenness. Nevertheless, it was during

Spener's five-year stay in Dresden that he came into contact with the young August Hermann Francke, then a lecturer in the University of Leipzig. Spener supported Francke's institution of a *collegium philobiblicum*, attached to the University. This *collegium* was in some respects like the *collegia pietatis*, but it was designed specifically for students and centered its exercises on Biblical study with practical exegesis.[48]

In 1691 Spener accepted the position of stated preacher in the Nikolaikirche in Berlin, with responsibility for inspecting the churches of the Consistory there. He remained in Berlin until his death in 1705, and his time there was taken principally with responding to the vociferous objections that were mounting against the Pietist movement, especially against excesses in the movement. To the end, and despite vigorous opposition, he remained optimistic about the prospects for reform. It is said that, a few days before his death, he requested that his coffin not be painted black:

> During my earthly life I have sufficiently lamented the condition of the church; now that I am about to enter the church triumphant, I wish to be buried in a white coffin as a sign that I am dying in the hope of a better church on earth.[49]

By the time of his death, Pietism was a flourishing movement in the Lutheran Churches throughout Germany.

Pietism flourished, at least in part, due to its acceptance in the increasingly powerful state of Brandenburg-Prussia. Under the Elector Friedrich Wilhelm (1640–1688), the state had been unified, and had begun to dominate German political and ecclesiastical affairs. The Prussian state, it is critical to note, was consistently wary of the inter-Protestant dogmatic struggles that had fueled Protestant Scholasticism: it was Friedrich Wilhelm's successor who built a "Union Church" in Berlin (the state capital) in 1708, with the Heidelberg Catechism and Luther's Catechism side-by-side.[50] Given this politically motivated concern for unity in the state, it is understandable why the Prussians would be receptive toward the Pietists, with their own concerns for the avoidance of dogmatic controversy.

The specific locus of the development of Pietism within Brandenburg-Prussia was the University of Halle, which, though organized somewhat earlier, was chartered by the Holy Roman Emperor Leopold I in 1694. Halle became the intellectual center for the Prussian state, and a major center for German culture throughout the eighteenth century. It has been called "the first modern university," because under Christian Thomasius a precedent was set for lecturing in the vernacular languages rather than Latin.

The organizing genius behind Pietism in the Prussian kingdoms was August Hermann Francke (1663–1727).[51] Francke's family background, like that of Spener, was that of a pious Lutheran family, and Francke, too, had read Arndt's *True Christianity* early in life. As a student at Leipzig, along with Paul Anton, Francke had founded the *collegium philobiblicum* in 1685. In 1687 he had provoked controversy in the University when he translated Miguel de Molinos's *Guida Spirituale* into Latin, and was accused of disseminating Molinos's Quietism.[52]

In the same year, Francke had a vivid conversion experience, which was to influence his vocation to reform the Church. After a long period of spiritual searching, Francke was set the task of preaching on John 20:31, ". . . these are written that you may believe that Jesus is the Christ, the Son of God, and that believing you may have life in his name." Francke recognized that he could not preach on the text, because he did not have the faith it described. On a Sunday evening soon after, Francke fell on his knees, and soon experienced the joy of conversion:

> Then the Lord heard me, the living God from his holy throne, as I was still on my knees. So great was his fatherly love that he would not take away such doubt and restlessness of heart little by little, with which I could have been quite content, but rather he suddenly heard me so that I would be all the more convinced and would bridle my strayed reason, to use nothing against his power and faithfulness; thus he suddenly heard me. Then, as one turns his hand [*in a twinkling*], so all my doubts were gone; I was sure in my heart of the grace of God in Jesus Christ; I knew God not only as God, but rather as one called my Father. All sadness and unrest in my heart was taken away in a moment. On the contrary, I was suddenly so overwhelmed as with a stream of joy that I praised out of high spirits the God who had shown me such great grace. I arose again of a completely different mind than when I had knelt down.[53]

Francke very soon allied himself with Spener's growing movement. He visited with Spener in 1689, who supported the work of the *collegium philobiblicum*. From 1689, Francke himself was attacked as a "Pietist," and the Leipzig faculty ordered him to cease his lectures on Paul's epistles in 1690 because of their suspicions of his pietistic teachings.

Two years later, Francke went to Halle, where he served as Professor of Oriental languages, and was also pastor of the Church in the Halle suburb of Glaucha. Francke built a kind of pietistic empire in Halle, and he was to dominate the city and the University for the next three decades.

Francke's organizational genius is seen in the variety of institutions, the so-called *franckesche Stiftungen*, or "Franckean Institutions," which he founded. Among these were an orphanage, a "normal seminary" for the training of teachers, a divinity school for the training of pastors, the "Seven Schools" for children, a Royal Paedagogium, for the education of the children of the aristocracy, a *collegium orientale* for the study of the scriptures in the original languages, an Institution to provide Board for Poor Students, a Book Store and Publishing Department, and a Chemical Laboratory and Apothecary. Together along a central street in the city, with impressive new Baroque façades, the *franckesche Stiftungen* stood as a powerful sign of Pietism's growing cultural dominance in the Prussian state.[54]

But Francke also influenced the movement as a preacher and a writer of edificatory literature. Francke stressed the process leading up to sincere repentance (the *Busskampf,* or "repentance-struggle"), the experience of the new birth, the path of continuing sanctification, and the prospect of Christian perfection.[55] His program was impressed upon the students of the University, the orphanage, and other schools, where Spener's dream of an education blending learning and piety was realized. Moreover, Francke followed Spener's pattern by organizing his parishioners and students into *collegia biblica,* answering to Spener's *collegia pietatis* and his earlier *collegium philobiblicum,* for mutual Biblical study and edification.

With Arndt and Reformed Pietism as its distant wellsprings, Spener as its herald, and Francke as its organizing genius, Lutheran Pietism became a dominant cultural force in the German states of the eighteenth century. In Brandenburg-Prussia, it was all but the state religion. In the area of Württemberg to the south, and especially at the University of Tübingen, Pietism also prevailed. There, the learned Biblical scholar Johann Albrecht Bengel produced his *Gnomon Novi Testamenti*, a commentary on the New Testament which offered not only a practical exegesis of every verse, but also a scholarly textual apparatus considered by many to mark the beginnings of modern New Testament scholarship.[56] During the eighteenth century, Pietism would spread to the Lutheran Churches of Austria and Scandinavia.

In Lutheran Pietism all of the characteristic traits of the religion of the heart movements came to full expression. True to its Lutheran setting, however, it bore some distinctive emphases. Unlike the Calvinist movements, including Puritanism and Reformed Pietism, Lutherans had taken a different attitude toward the question of election and reprobation,[57] and this would affect their understanding of

August Hermann Francke

Engraving after a copperplate by Bernhard Vogel (1683–1737); in Wilhelm Hadorn, *Geschichte des Pietismus in den schweizerischen reformierten Kirchen* (Constance and Emmishofen: Verlag von Karl Hirsch, 1901), opposite p. 40.

the way of salvation. Although Lutherans tended to hold to the language of election and reprobation, many argued that election to eternal life was based on God's foreknowledge (but not predetermination) of those. women and men who would choose to accept the offer of grace and believe in Christ. Lutheran Pietists were inevitably inclined towards this interpretation of election, and consequently could argue that Christ died for all of humankind, and that every person could repent, believe in Christ, and thus be saved. In Lutheran Pietism, then, the religious life was not dominated by the quest for the assurance of one's election that characterized the Puritans and the Reformed Pietists; it focused rather on the present possibility of repentance and faith for all.[58]

A second and very distinctive note of Lutheran Pietism is its ambiguity concerning the relationship between the sacrament of baptism and the new birth (or regeneration), and this reveals a great deal about the shift in forms of religious life that Pietism had brought about. Lutherans, following the ancient and medieval Church, had traditionally claimed that baptism is the outward means of regeneration. The Pietists were obliged to follow this teaching, and Arndt, Spener, and Francke all formally acknowledged the doctrine, but elsewhere they spoke of the new birth (Francke specifically calls it "conversion" [Bekehrung]) as the present challenge laid before their (already baptized) hearers.[59] Thus the Lutheran Pietists were forced into the somewhat awkward position of arguing, on the one hand, that baptism confers the divine grace of regeneration, but, on the other hand, that most adult hearers had already lost this grace and stood in need of a new regeneration.[60] Francke appeared to contradict Luther directly when he preached:

> Thus you ought not to say: "I am baptized, I go to church, I am a Christian." The hypocrites do the same. There is many a person baptized who yet went back on his oath and was faithless and fell out of his baptismal covenant.[61]

This awkwardness or ambiguity reveals the tendency of the movement: from an older form of religious life that had stressed the encounter with the divine through the appointed means of grace, the Pietists were struggling towards a new form of religious life in which the direct encounter with the divine, in "heartfelt" experience, was central. Their ambiguity on this issue reveals that although the tendency of the movement was toward the direct experience of the divine, nevertheless both forms of religious life were still operative.

Finally, the Lutheran Pietists took a more positive attitude than the Calvinistic pietistic movements had taken towards the possibility of conformity to Christ in this life. In this respect, they have almost all been identified as "mystics" at least in the broadest sense, but, as was the case with Arndt's view of union with Christ, so with Spener and Francke the goal of "Christian perfection" was understood as an ethical and affective goal, and considerable care was taken to state that "perfection," in the sense of complete conformity to Christ, was not possible in this life.[62] With these cautions, though, the Lutheran Pietists were able to offer a powerful vision of the transformation of life, a vision centering on the person of Christ in relation to the believer, and holding out the goal of a Christ-like life, even on this side of the grave.

The Moravians

It is ironic that one of the few denominations to result from Lutheran Pietism should be the Moravian Church. Ironic, because the Pietists, in general, and the Moravians in particular, began with a vehement opposition to the notion that denominations were important in themselves. Zinzendorf once preached,

> . . . who directed the people to do this? Who directed them to make a religion out of the family of Christ, in direct contradiction to the Holy Scriptures? It does not matter that men have confessions of faith; it does not matter that they are divided into religious denominations . . . it is a vulgar, mean disposition of the mind when people of one religious denomination take pleasure in opposing people of another.[63]

Perhaps the Moravians marked only the beginning of a tradition of "non-denominational" Evangelical movements that have seriously attempted to avoid sectarian controversies, only to find themselves a hundred years or so later comprising one more Protestant denomination. As tempting as this conclusion might be, however, it must be born in mind that the Moravian Church derived not only from Lutheran Pietism, but also from the independent tradition of the pre-Reformation *Unitas Fratrum*.

The Lutheran Pietist element of Moravianism was mediated to the movement in the person of Nicolaus Ludwig, the Graf (or Count) von Zinzendorf (1700–1760).[64] Zinzendorf was born into a noble Prussian family in 1700, and was baptized by none other than Philipp Jakob Spener. But if Spener and Francke had come to Pietism more or less on their own, Zinzendorf was born into it. Both sides of his family had been influenced by the movement, especially his maternal grandmother, the Baroness Gersdorf. He was given to frequent religious experiences as a child, and had spiritual conversations with members of his family. Following their lead, Zinzendorf developed a special devotion to the sufferings of Christ that was to mark his life and ministry.[65]

The family intended the young Count to take up a life of public service in the Prussian state. He was educated in Law at Halle, and then at Wittenberg, but in both places tended to pursue religious studies and involvements over his legal studies. At Halle, he gathered religious societies together, and at Wittenberg he organized an "Order of the Grain of Mustard Seed" which utilized pietistic conventicles. At Wittenberg he defended Francke and other Pietist leaders against charges of heterodoxy, and attempted to secure a reconciliation of the parties in the universities by a consultation between their faculties held on the bicentennial of the Reformation (1717). From 1719–1720 Zinzendorf went on a *Wanderjahr*, traveling through Europe, and making the acquaintance of many religious leaders, among them the Jansenist Cardinal Archbishop of Paris, Louis Antoine de Noailles (1651–1729), with whom Zinzendorf would correspond for many years.[66]

From 1722 through 1727, Zinzendorf was employed in public service in the Government of Saxony, but it was during this period that his religious vocation clearly emerged. Breaking a previous engagement in 1721, Zinzendorf married in the next year and purchased an estate near Berthelsdorf which he called "Herrnhut." He began gathering a circle of friends and advisers, including the Lutheran pastor of Berthelsdorf. On 12 May 1722, he allowed Austrian emigrants to stay at Herrnhut, among whom were some members of the Moravian *Unitas Fratrum*. During the next five years, he welcomed more of the Brethren to the estate, so that by 1727 Herrnhut had become a colony for the Central European emigrants.[67]

The history of the Moravian *Unitas Fratrum* ("Unity of Brethren") reached back to the late middle ages and the reforms suggested by Jan Hus in the early fifteenth century. One party that emerged from Hus's movement insisted that laity should receive both the chalice and the host in the eucharist, and were called "Calixtines" or "Utraquists." One party of Utraquists separated from the rest (and from Catholic communion) in the 1460s, and led a separate existence from that time as "Bohemian Brethren." (Bohemia is the western part of present-day Czechoslovakia.)

Nicolaus Ludwig, Graf von Zinzendorf

Engraving after a portrait (ca. 1740) by Johann Kupezky (1667–1740); in P. M. Legêne, *Zinzendorf* (Zeist: Zendingsgenootschap der evangelische Broedergemeente, 1938), frontispiece; published with the permission of Zeist Missionary Society of the Moravian Church in Holland.

By the end of the sixteenth century, most of the Bohemian Brethren had fled to Moravia (the easternmost part of present-day Czechoslovakia), but the group was persecuted there off and on for more than a century. Considerable numbers of them had already fled to the West, including Bishop Jan Amos Comenius, who was in Amsterdam in the mid-seventeenth century at the time of Jean de Labadie, Robert Barclay, and Antoinette Bourignon. It was a last, small remnant of the Brethren (now "Moravian" Brethren), including their bishop, Christian David, who found their way to Herrnhut in 1722 and thereafter. They brought with them a distinctive tradition, Protestantized, but yet retaining some elements of medieval Catholicism, such as a belief in the apostolic succession of their bishops, and the practice of hearing confessions.

Under Zinzendorf's leadership, the Herrnhut community developed an organizational structure and began to attract Christians from a variety of confessions. They instituted a press, established schools, and built a large Community House. The community was divided into "choirs" according to age, sex, and marital status. Ancient Christian patterns of worship were revived, and new services were developed: among these were the love feast, footwashing, and hymn singing. A stress was placed on daily scripture texts, and hourly prayers were offered.[68]

Zinzendorf soon extended the movement beyond the bounds of Herrnhut. While present at the coronation of the King of Denmark, Zinzendorf expressed an interest in a mission project that the Danish Church had undertaken (with the support of Halle University). In 1732, the Moravian community sponsored missions to the Danish colonies in St. Thomas (in the Virgin Islands) and Greenland. Within a few years, Moravian missions would be sent to Georgia and Pennsylvania in the British colonies of North America.[69]

In 1734, Zinzendorf made formal his intention to be an ordained minister. He was examined by the faculty of the University of Tübingen, and his beliefs were found to be in harmony with the Augsburg Confession. He was recognized as a Lutheran minister by the Tübingen faculty, then in 1737 he was ordained Bishop by the Moravian Bishop D. E. Jablonski, who at the time was serving as court preacher in Berlin.[70]

What finally forced Zinzendorf himself "into all the world" was a rising tide of opposition to his community, as a result of which he was exiled from Saxony (and thus from Herrnhut) from 1736 through 1747. During this period, Zinzendorf acquired new properties at Ronneburg and Marienborn, the latter of which became the site of the so-called "pilgrim congregation" where Zinzendorf and his highest associates maintained a strict regimen. Eventually he went to Pennsylvania (in 1741), where a community had been founded through the earlier work of August Gottlieb Spangenberg. The Moravian community in Pennsylvania, it may be observed in passing, had acquired a 5,000-acre tract of land they called "Nazareth," which had been abandoned by its previous owner, George Whitefield.[71]

The period between 1743 and 1750, punctuated by Zinzendorf's highly emotional return to Herrnhut in 1747, has come to be called "the sifting time." It was a period of unusual emotional fervor for the Moravian community, in which there was a heightened stress on the wounds and blood of Christ. Zinzendorf himself was caught up in this phase of the movement, and although by 1750 he had condemned its emotional excesses, they had discredited the community as a whole (especially the London society), and Zinzendorf's role as leader of the movement came to be overshadowed from then until the end of his life (in 1760) by Spangenberg and others.[72]

Zinzendorf reflected most of the salient emphases of Lutheran Pietism and other religion of the heart movements, and yet he presented his religious insights with a combination of traditional and innovative language that is, in some ways, puzzling to one accustomed to reading Puritan or pietistic literature. His concern about the religious life focused consistently on the necessity of a personal, experiential faith in the efficacy of Christ's work. Corresponding to the spiritual epistemologies of other pietistic writers, Zinzendorf distinguished between what he called "conceptual" knowledge and "experience." Only the latter, he argued, is constitutive of true Christian faith. Religion, he wrote, "is able to be grasped through experience alone without any concepts."[73] Here is an echo of Arndt's concern (and that of Spener and Francke, for that matter) that doctrinal learning and polemics should not take the place of inward religion. But in Zinzendorf's case it was pressed to the point where conceptual knowledge, including traditional dogmatics, was seen as a hindrance to inward faith.[74] Elsewhere, echoing a similar epistemological concern, Zinzendorf explained that faith is a spiritual "sight," a "sight" the object of which is Christ who, once seen, dominates the believer's life from that time on.[75]

This central concern for religious experience works itself out in the life of a believer, according to Zinzendorf, in a version of the way of salvation that progresses from "faith-in-distress" (answering to sincere repentance and "conversion" in other pietistic writers), in which one despairs of one's own spiritual condition, to "faith-in-love" (answering to justifying faith and the assurance of election, or of pardon) in which one leaves sadness behind "in love and thankfulness and attachment to him who died for his soul."[76] From this point Zinzendorf went on to explain that the Christian progresses from these earlier forms of faith (he calls both of them *fides implicita*, "implicit faith") to "explicit faith" (*fides explicita*), which itself is divided into the faith of one who is still learning about Christ, and the faith of one who shares Christ with the world.[77] Although this may answer to an older distinction between the "babes" in Christ and those who are "mature," the language itself is, to my knowledge, eccentric.[78] Again, Zinzendorf appears as an eccentric exponent of a religion of the heart, combining what were by then traditional concepts with his own rather distinctive vocabulary and conceptual scheme.

Equally distinctive of the Moravian version of the religion of the heart was its devotion to the wounds and sufferings of Christ—in this respect, it took up the medieval tradition that in their own way Jean Eudes and Marguerite Marie Alacoque had developed in their devotion to the sacred heart of Jesus. In a "Litany of the Life, Sufferings, and Death of Jesus Christ," Zinzendorf led his congregation in prayers that vividly portrayed the sufferings of Christ on their behalf:

Leader:	Christ, Lamb of God, you who take away the sins of the world
Congregation:	Give us your peace!
Leader:	By your willingness to die
Congregation:	Give us the mystery of your love!
Leader:	By your holy baptism of blood
Congregation:	Set us forth upon God's earth!
Leader:	By your tears and cry of dread
Congregation:	Console us in dread and pain! You shed so many tears for us, So many drops of blood flowed out from you, So many are the voices which pray for us and plead for us.
Leader:	By your head crowned with thorns
Congregation:	Teach us the nature of the kingdom of the Cross!
Leader:	By your outstretched hands on the Cross
Congregation:	Be open to us at all times!
Leader:	By your nail-pierced hands
Congregation:	Show us where our names stand written!
Leader:	By your wounded feet
Congregation:	Make our path certain!
Leader:	By your pale beautiful lips
Congregation:	Speak to us in consolation and peace!
Leader:	By the last look of your breaking eyes
Congregation:	Lead us into the Father's hands![79]

It was this devotion to the wounds of Christ that led to some of the excesses of the "sifting time," when Zinzendorf and the community would count themselves as "little blood worms in the sea of grace," or "little bees who suck on the wounds of Christ."[80] On the other hand, Zinzendorf's devotion could yield (in other times and circumstances) a more balanced spirituality, as in his hymn (here translated by John Wesley):

> O thou to whose all-searching sight
> The darkness shineth as the light,
> Search, prove my heart; it pants for thee;
> Oh, burst these bonds, and set it free!
>
> Wash out its stains, refine its dross,
> Nail my affections to the Cross;
> Hallow each thought; let all within
> Be clean, as thou, my Lord, art clean![81]

It was, moreover, precisely Zinzendorf's affective devotion, combined with his own eccentric genius, that led him (during the "sifting time") to address the Trinity as Father, Son, and Mother.[82]

It was because of his belief in the experiential nature of faith that Zinzendorf could downplay the theological controversies of the past: after all, they consisted for the most part in controversy over "concepts," whereas all true believers were united in the faith that comes by experience. This lay in the background of Zinzendorf's understanding of his own vocation to unite the divided Christian communities. He had not only been in correspondence with a wide range of Christian leaders—Catholic, Reformed, and Anglican as well as other Lutherans—but he developed a visionary, ecumenical conception of a united Protestant church, a "Congregation of God in the Spirit," composed of three principal *tropoi* ("training schools," implying that each was a distinct but equally valid way of coming to Christ): the Lutheran, Reformed, and Moravian. Zinzendorf's vision was that the Moravians should serve as a catalyst that would eventually unite the three into a common Church.[83]

Although this was not to be, the Moravian communities remained a vital expression of the religion of the heart, not only in the German states, but in England, North America, and throughout the world where their missionary endeavors had taken hold. Not only Zinzendorf's ecumenical vision, but the very fact that a Central European Christian community could find an alliance with Lutherans in the German states showed, indeed demonstrated, the ecumenical aspirations of the religion of the heart movements. And the Moravians, it should be noted, had an influence far beyond the bounds of their own communion. On board the *Simmonds* late in 1735, bound from Gravesend, England, to the Georgia colony in North America, where the Moravians planned a new settlement, August Gottlieb Spangenberg and a company of Moravians encountered an idealistic band of young Anglican clergy from Oxford, whose lives, as we shall see, were dramatically changed by the witness of the Moravians.

* * *

By the early decades of the eighteenth century, there was scarcely a religious community in Western Europe that had not been affected by the religion of the heart movements. By this time Jansenism was a vital force, persecuted but very much alive in France, and openly active in the United Provinces. Jeanne Marie Guyon had been silenced, but Quietism was very much alive, and devotion to the sacred heart of Jesus was being promulgated throughout Catholicism. It was a time of greater religious toleration in England; the old days of Puritanism and its offspring were well in the past, but its piety was expressed in the sermons of Richard Baxter and then in the moving hymns of Isaac Watts. Reformed Pietism was active in the Dutch and German Reformed Churches, and Lutheran Pietism, as we have seen, had become a dominant form of religious life in many of the German states. Although Labadism was declining by this time, the Quakers were at least holding their own, and the Moravians were expanding throughout the world. For some, the new century was to be an age of Enlightenment; for thousands more, it was to be the age of the religion of the heart.

Chapter Five

The Evangelical Revival

In 1743, defending the Methodist Revival in his *Earnest Appeal to Men of Reason and Religion,* John Wesley encouraged his readers not to be content with superficial piety, but to "inquire into the bottom of religion, the religion of the heart."[1] But it was not only John Wesley—it was Howell Harris, George Whitefield, Selina, Countess of Huntingdon, Anglican parish clergy, and a vast host of men and women—who preached, organized, and taught "the religion of the heart" as the basis or "bottom" of all religion in the Evangelical Revival[2] of eighteenth-century Britain. There were direct links between the earlier forms of the religion of the heart (especially Puritanism and Pietism) and the Evangelical Revival, and yet the eighteenth century revival proclaimed a religion of the heart in rather new social and cultural surroundings.

By the beginning of the eighteenth century the British Isles were well past the turmoil of the English Revolution, the Restoration, and the Glorious Revolution, and the mercantile economy that had fueled the Puritan Revolution was being transformed into an industrial economy. The invention of pumps to remove water from mines (thereby enabling deep mining), coupled with the development of the technique of smelting in the first decade of the century, were critical technological advances that gave rise to the Industrial Revolution.

What followed on these developments in the use of iron and steel was the eventual replacement of animal and human labor with machines, and the organization of labor into centralized units (textile mills and factories, to name two examples). The immediate effect on England was that masses of people began moving from the countryside to newly revitalized cities (such as Newcastle-upon-Tyne) and new industrial suburbs of existing cities (such as London and Bristol).[3] The importance of these developments for the growth of the Evangelical Revival cannot be underestimated, since it was generally in these new industrial cities and suburbs and often among the newly arrived immigrants to them that the earliest Evangelical societies developed.[4]

On the other hand, there were critical cultural and religious developments in the same age that should be understood in the background of the revival. Seventeenth-century reflection on the nature of human knowledge, in particular, had culminated in the philosophy of John Locke, whose influential works published in the 1690s argued that experience is the surest basis of knowledge, and developed an elaborate philosophical schema to account for the development of knowledge. Locke's epistemology provided a consistent basis for English thought (of wildly different persuasions) throughout the eighteenth century.[5]

Its implications for religion were drawn very quickly. If experience is the surest basis of knowledge, then traditional wisdom, including Biblical teaching, must be questioned. From the late 1690s a series of British thinkers explored the possibility that a benevolent creator God had endowed nature with all gifts necessary for human happiness. On their account, there was little, if any, need for special revelation or miracles; Jesus could be regarded as the human being who most adequately expressed the truth that was, in fact, "as old as creation." Others would shy away from this "Socinian" (as it was called then) or Deist conclusion, but would revive the ancient Arian claim that Jesus was the first of God's creatures, and only divine in a subordinate sense. By either option a crisis was posed for traditional faith, a crisis so severe that Christianity had become little more than a matter for joking among many sophisticated English people.[6]

If conventional beliefs about God and Christ were questioned, however, "morality," and especially "moral improvement" were the all but universally proclaimed values of the new century. There was a certain spirituality that had developed in England in the latter years of the seventeenth century, which focused on benevolence and moral rectitude, and is sometimes referred to as "Moralism." Anglican leaders of as widely varied theological opinions as the Latitudinarian John Tillotson or the staunchly orthodox George Bull, even clergy of the Dissenting churches, could maintain that, although our justification is by faith alone, God requires good works as a sign of true repentance before justifying faith will be granted. Bishop Jeremy Taylor's *Rules and Exercises of Holy Living* and *Rules and Exercises of Holy Dying,* written several decades before, became a popular text in this period. It was joined by republication of such medieval classics as Thomas à Kempis's *Imitation of Christ* and more recent exhortations of godly living, the most famous being William Law's *Serious Call to a Devout and Holy Life* (1728).[7] In Anglican Moralism, the moral-rigorist spirituality of the late middle ages, and something like its nominalist understanding of human nature and the need for grace, had been reborn. One of the most prominent signs of this moralistic spirituality was the foundation in the late seventeenth and early eighteenth centuries of a number of benevolent institutions for the improvement of social and cultural conditions, and for the advancement of piety. In 1698 Thomas Bray and four laymen founded the Society for Promoting Christian Knowledge (or SPCK), which helped to establish English language charity schools in England and Wales, and to distribute Bibles and other religious literature. Three years later Bray expanded the work that the SPCK had begun by founding the Society for the Propagation of the Gospel in Foreign Parts (SPG). The SPG had the double aim of providing Anglican chaplains for British persons living overseas, and of evangelizing non-Christian peoples who were subject to the British Crown. These were followed by the institution of charity schools and charity hospitals in England and Wales, and by the issuing of royal warrants soliciting charitable gifts for numerous causes.[8]

Another indication of the vigor of this moralistic spirituality was the development of a network of "religious societies" in England. The original inspiration for the societies came from Anthony Horneck, a German native familiar with the works of Johann Arndt who had emigrated to England just after the Restoration. In the latter years of the Restoration, Horneck's Anglican societies flourished in London and elsewhere, providing a means by which Christians could hold each other accountable for their personal moral behavior and for their pursuit of benevolent enterprises, such as providing food and clothing to the needy, and visiting imprisoned individuals. Horneck's work was carried on from the 1680s by Josiah Woodward, who published manuals detailing the institution and maintenance of such societies. By the early decades of the eighteenth century, the religious societies were flourishing among upwardly mobile, middle class Britons, and although they are sometimes compared to the *collegia pietatis* of contemporary Pietists, a better comparison might be with the "Precisian" conventicles of Voët, which focused on the precise following of the divine law.[9] In fact, despite their moralistic theology, the leaders of the SPCK and the religious societies were aware of the work of August Hermann Francke at Halle, and some of them had corresponded with him.[10]

The Evangelical Revival, then, emerged in an age when social structures were rapidly changing, when traditional religious beliefs had been challenged, and when moral improvement had become, for many people, the very essence of religion. None of these factors in itself accounts for the revival that began in the 1730s, but they contributed in their own way to the movement and provided the grounds in which the movement could grow.[11] Perhaps it is not surprising that the revival should begin in such a setting of social, cultural, and religious turmoil; what is somewhat surprising is that it began in a place that was in many ways farthest removed from these crises, namely, in Wales.[12]

The Welsh Revival

The revival in Wales began just slightly before the revival in England, at least if one can date the revival from the itinerant preaching associated with it.[13] It was largely the work of a group of young men who were in their mid-twenties when the revival began (most notably, Howell Harris and Daniel Rowland). But almost all of the younger leaders looked to an older clergyman for advice and inspiration, namely, Griffith Jones of Llandowror. Jones (1684–1761) was an Anglican priest ordained in 1708 by Bishop George Bull. He was appointed to the parish of Llandowror shortly thereafter, and it remained the base of his operations through his life. Jones's extant correspondence shows that he had hoped for a revival in the Church as early as 1714. In the 1730s, at the same time as English Schools were being instituted in Wales by the SPCK, Jones began to establish Welsh language schools for teaching children how to read and write, especially so that they could read the Welsh Bible.

By the time of his death in 1761, it is estimated that Jones had founded 3,225 schools, had circulated 30,000 copies of the Welsh Bible, and had taught some 150,000 persons to read. He had established a circuit of traveling teachers in Wales that paralleled, in some respects, the networks of religious societies in England. An important result of the work of these Schools was that important devotional works, including many Puritan works, were translated into Welsh. Among the latter were Joseph Alleine's *Alarm to the Unconverted*, and Bunyan's *Pilgrim's Progress*.

Although Jones's work at first could be understood as an extension of the same moralistic piety that had led to the founding of the SPCK and the SPG, it shows how work begun under the influence of such a moralistic outlook could be transformed into a very different, Evangelical outlook. Moreover, Jones had read *Pietas Hallensis*, Francke's account of the orphanage and other institutions at Halle.

Jones's name for his own publication, *Welch Piety*, imitates the name of Francke's influential book.[14] Jones himself had begun a revival of sorts in Pembrokeshire and Carmarthenshire in 1714, and the fact is that although his avowed aim in founding the Circulating Schools was to improve educational opportunities, Jones was a popular preacher on the "circuit" he had established, and others in the Circulating Schools would follow his lead. The Circulating Schools set the pattern of an informal network of societies linked to an informal network of itinerating preachers that was to characterize all sides of the Evangelical Revival. Despite Jones's opposition to lay preaching (that of Howell Harris, in particular), he remained a mentor to the younger evangelists.

If Griffith Jones's Circulating Schools provided the basic network for the Revival in Wales, however, the rhetorical inspiration for the movement was provided by the younger Welsh preachers, the most prominent of whom was Howell Harris of Trevecka.[15] Harris, born in the year of Jones's first revival (1714), was a schoolmaster in South Wales. At twenty-one years of age, on Palm Sunday, 1735, he experienced a religious awakening and a conviction of sin while attending the eucharist in his parish church (at Talgarth). On Pentecost Sunday of the same year, after months of searching and reading in Bayly's *Practice of Piety*, [16] his religious quest was resolved by an experience which he described in the following terms:

> At the table, Christ bleeding on the Cross was kept before my eyes constantly; and strength was given me to believe that I was receiving pardon on account of the blood. I lost my burden; I went home leaping for joy, and I said to my neighbor who was sad, Why are you sad? I know my sins have been forgiven, though I had not heard that such a thing was to be found except in this book. Oh blessed day! Would that I might remember it gratefully evermore![17]

Following this experience, Harris decided to seek ordination, and in November went to St. Margaret's Hall, Oxford, where he intended to take up studies. He remained in Oxford only six weeks, however, returning to Wales in late December, shocked at the laxity and immorality he had found in the university.

It was from December of 1735 that Harris, destined to remain a layman, took up his ministry of teaching and preaching among the people of Wales. At first, he seems not to have described his own work as "preaching," and in fact it consisted of little more than going from house to house, where he would read passages from *The Whole Duty of Man* and other devotional works, and then would continue

Howell Harris

Engraving of unknown provenance; in John Wesley, *Wesley His Own Biographer: Selections from the Journals* (London: C. H. Kelly, 1896), p. 130.

with exhortation. Harris had a fiery temperament, and seems to have utilized his preaching as a way to vent his strong emotions. Soon he was preaching outside of private homes, in the open air. His exhortations attracted crowds, who soon showed the characteristic signs of revivalism. His own account of his early preaching is strikingly reminiscent of Robert Blair's description of the thunderings of James Glendinning in Northern Ireland, over a hundred years before:

> At first I knew nothing at all, but God opened my mouth (full of ignorance), filling it with terrors and threatenings. I was given a commission to break and rend sinners in the most dreadful manner. I thundered greatly, denouncing the gentry, the carnal clergy, and everybody. My subjects, mostly, were death and judgment, without any mention of Christ.[18]

In 1737 he took a position overseeing some of Griffith Jones's schools, and despite Jones's opposition to his preaching (because he was not ordained), this position allowed him to travel about the country where he could carry on his work of evangelization. Harris was to continue as one of the most exuberant of the Welsh preachers, but his enthusiasm would eventually bring division to the movement.

Harris was joined in the work of evangelization by a somewhat calmer soul who was also a disciple of Griffith Jones, Daniel Rowland (1713–1790).[19] Rowland, unlike Harris, was ordained, and although he too preached itinerantly, his parish of Llangeitho was to become a gathering place for the Welsh Revival. If there was no direct link between the Irish and Scottish revivalism of the seventeenth century and the revival in Wales, there is a remarkable similarity in the manner in which these revivals were carried out. Here is Howell Harris's own description of a celebration of the Lord's Supper in Llangeitho in 1743:

> I was last Sunday at the Ordinance with Brother Rowlands where I saw, felt, and heard such things as I cant send on Paper any Idea of. . . . Such Crying out and Heart Breaking Groans, Silent Weeping and Holy Joy, and shouts of Rejoicing I never saw. Their Amens and Cryings Glory in the Highest &c would inflame your soul was you there. Tis very common when he preaches for Scores to fall down by the Power of the Word, pierced and wounded or overcom'd by the Love of God and Sights of the Beauty and Excellency of Jesus, and lie on the Ground.[20]

Whether there was any direct connection or not, the parallels between these phenomena and those of early revivalism among Presbyterians of Scottish descent are striking. Moreover, the Welsh Methodists soon took up the practice of Quarterly Communions, which sometimes involved several days of preaching in preparation for the celebration, and this too is reminiscent of the sacramental meetings of Scottish and Irish Presbyterians in the seventeenth century.[21]

By the 1740s, Harris and Rowland had been joined by a number of other evangelists—lay and clergy—who were busy preaching and organizing societies. William Williams of Pantycelyn (1717–1791), by way of translations and original compositions, gave Welsh Evangelicalism a distinctive hymnody. In 1743, after contacts had been established with leaders of the revival in England, a "conferring together," or "Conference," as they called it, was held in 1743, and would meet annually thereafter. Though the Welsh preachers remained Anglican (nominally Anglican through the eighteenth century), the Annual Conference offered an alternative structure by which the movement could be organized.

Howell Harris's emotionalism led to a serious division in the movement in 1750. Throughout the previous decade Harris had been attracted to Moravian teachings. It was the "sifting time" in the British Moravian community,[22] and Harris's preaching stressed more and more the devotion to the wounds and sufferings of Christ that the Moravians had advocated. Harris even proclaimed in this period that God the Father had suffered and died in the person of Jesus Christ. This teaching was quickly recognized by other Evangelical leaders as "Patripassianism" (or "Sabellianism" or "Modalism"), the ancient (and long condemned) teaching that denied any difference between the members of the Trinity. Harris was ostracized from the company of the evangelists, and his "party" seceded from the movement, with many following Harris back to Trevecka, where he established a farm for his religious community (the "Family," as he called it), modeled after the Moravian settlement at Herrnhut.

In the twelve years between 1750 and 1762, Harris refused to itinerate, and Rowland consequently emerged as the leader of the revival. In 1762, with signs of a new outburst of the revival already present, Rowland and Harris were reconciled, and Harris again took up the work of itinerant preaching, though he never again would recover the status of leadership that was his in the first decades of the revival. His friendship with the Countess of Huntingdon, who supported Calvinistic Methodist preachers in England and Wales (see the next section), led her to establish at Trevecka in the late 1760s a training college for preachers, to foster the work of revival.

The Welsh revivalists, like their counterparts in England, were almost uniformly referred to as "Methodists," and when in 1811 the independent status of the Welsh Evangelical societies was made formal, they were called the "Welsh Calvinistic Methodist Church." The name itself suggests that the Welsh Revival was but part of a larger religious movement that swept through the British Isles and the British provinces of North America in the eighteenth century. Though distinctively Welsh in language and culture, the theology and practices of the Welsh Methodists were essentially the same as those of the English Evangelicals, at least, of the Calvinistic English Evangelicals of "The Countess of Huntingdon's Connexion," to whom we now turn.

The Countess of Huntingdon's Connexion

The Evangelical Revival in England was in many ways the result of a collaboration between a common man and a noble woman. The common man was George Whitefield, born in the same year as Howell Harris (1714), the son of a Gloucester tavern keeper.[23] The noble woman was Lady Selina Shirley Hastings, the Countess of Huntingdon, born five years before Whitefield in 1709, and married in 1728 to Lord Thomas Hastings, the Earl of Huntingdon.[24] The alliance of Lady Huntingdon and Whitefield dominated what might be called the "Calvinistic Wing" of the revival in England, but it took organized form as "The Countess of Huntingdon's Connexion."

Both Whitefield and Lady Huntingdon underwent conversion experiences in the 1730s. Whitefield's conversion in 1735 (the same year as Howell Harris's) came as a result of his participation in a religious society in Oxford. Having decided to seek ordination as a priest, and having matriculated at Pembroke College in 1732, Whitefield had attached himself to a society modeled after those of Josiah Woodward. Through his reading of spiritual literature with the group, he had become keenly aware of his own sinfulness, and the terms he used to describe his "awakening" to this realization were similar to those of so many religious seekers of his age: he felt his sins as a "burden," as fetters or chains that bound him, as being "barren and dry." He gave himself to unusual austerities of food and dress, and spent many nights "groaning" for redemption, the vision of hell ever before him.[25]

Seven weeks after Easter in 1735, completely unconnected with, but apparently within hours of Howell Harris's experience in Talgarth, Whitefield found release in a vivid religious experience:

One day, perceiving an uncommon Drought and a disagreeable Claminess in my Mouth, and using things to allay my Thirst, but in vain, it was suggested to me, that when *Jesus Christ* cried out, "I thirst," His sufferings were near at an End. Upon which I cast myself down on the Bed, crying out, I thirst! I thirst!—Soon after this, I found and felt in myself that I was delivered from the Burden that had so heavily oppressed me! The Spirit of Mourning was taken away from me, and I knew what it was truly to rejoice in God my Saviour, and, for some Time, could not avoid singing Psalms wherever I was . . .[26]

He then carried on the typical work of the Religious Societies, visiting the sick and prisoners, but began proclaiming the possibility of a present justification by faith alone. Whitefield was also ordained deacon soon after his conversion experience. Within a few months, his benevolent enterprises would take on more and more the character of evangelistic enterprises.[27]

The conversion of Lady Huntingdon four years later came as a result of a similar experience on the part of her sister-in-law, Lady Margaret Hastings. Lady Margaret had heard a preacher, Benjamin Ingham,[28] proclaiming repentance and faith; she had believed the message, and told Lady Selina, "Since I have known and believed in the Lord Jesus Christ for salvation, I have been as happy as an angel."[29] The words came back to Selina some months later as she lay ill. A nineteenth century biographer tells the story of her conversion in romantic terms:

There she lay, with every alleviation which the best skill and the tenderest nursing could impart, but there was a malady of the soul which these could not reach. Was there no balm in Gilead, and no Physician there? Then it was that the words of Lady Margaret came laden with wonderful meaning. "I too will wholly cast myself on Jesus Christ for life and salvation," was her last refuge, and from her bed she lifted up her heart to God for pardon and mercy through the blood of his Son. With streaming eyes she cast herself on her Saviour: "Lord, I believe; help thou mine unbelief." Immediately the scales fell from her eyes; doubt and distress vanished; joy and peace filled her bosom. With appropriating faith, she exclaimed, "My Lord, and my God!" From that moment her disease took a favorable turn; she was restored to health, and what was better, to "newness of life."[30]

Despite the later romanticization of this account which contrasts with the eighteenth-century "plainness" of Whitefield's conversion narrative, it makes clear that the spiritual pilgrimage of this noblewoman ran roughly parallel to the experiences of common persons such as Harris or Whitefield. From this point, Selina began to utilize her considerable financial resources and her social position to foster the work of the revival.

It would not be until 1748 that the Countess and the evangelist met each other face to face. In the meantime, Whitefield was busy developing his evangelistic enterprise both in Britain and in the North American colonies. Three years after his conversion, in 1738, Whitefield traveled to the newly-established colony of Georgia with the intention of founding there an orphanage, explicitly modeled after that of August Hermann Francke in Halle.[31] He returned to England after four months, intent on raising funds for his orphanage. After his return, he visited Wales, making the acquaintance of Howell Harris, and witnessing Harris's itinerant preaching. Despite rumors about Whitefield's own "irregular" preaching already circulating (this referred only to his vigorous preaching of repentance and faith in Anglican churches), the Bishop of London ordained him a priest in January of 1739.

It was scarcely a month later, on 17 February, that Whitefield began to preach in the open air, following the pattern that Harris had shown him. The location was Kingswood, a coal-mining settlement outside Bristol, where Whitefield had met with existing religious societies. He described the event, evoking an obvious parallel to Jesus's Sermon on the Mount, in these words:

> After Dinner, therefore, I went upon a Mount, and spake to as many People as came unto me. They were upwards of two hundred. Blessed be God, *I have now broke the Ice; I believe I was never more acceptable to my Master than when I was standing to teach those Hearers in the open fields.*[32]

Returning to London, Whitefield found parish churches consistently closed to him, and he wrote to Howell Harris his intention of repeating the "mad Trick" of field preaching.[33] He proceeded to preach at Moorfields, just outside the City, and at Kennington Common. Whitefield attracted not only large crowds, but also a great deal of publicity, and Lady Huntingdon was at least aware of Whitefield's activities from 1739.

In the summer of 1739, Whitefield returned to North America, leaving his Bristol societies in the hands of another evangelist (John Wesley) who had himself recently returned from Georgia. Whitefield arrived in Philadelphia, and carried on his church and field preaching as he moved southward through the colonies. Along the way, he made the acquaintance of Gilbert Tennent, who was already involved in the work of evangelistic preaching in the middle colonies following the patterns of Scots-Irish Presbyterian revivalism. Whitefield remained in America through 1741, principally concerned with building

George Whitefield's First Open-Air Preaching

Engraving by J. W. Barker; in John Gillies, *Memoirs of Rev. George Whitefield* (New Haven: Whitmore and Buckingham and H. Mansfield, 1834), opposite p. 37; used with permission of the Special Collections Department, Duke University Library.

his orphanage in Savannah (he laid the first brick for it in March 1740), although he made a preaching tour of New England before his departure, meeting Jonathan Edwards at Northampton.

Whitefield returned to Britain in 1741. He opened a large preaching house in Moorfields, "the Tabernacle," a few months later, then embarked on a preaching tour of Scotland and Wales, where he was accompanied by Howell Harris. At the first Conference of "Methodist" preachers in Wales, in January of 1743, he was made their moderator, and a few months later was named moderator of the Conference for life. He was not able to serve often, however, for after the tragic death of an infant son early in 1744, Whitefield and his wife again departed for North America, spending four years there, attracting huge crowds and building on his reputation as an evangelistic preacher. Finally, in 1748, they returned to England.

While Whitefield had been building his evangelistic empire, Lady Huntingdon had been developing her own network among the Evangelicals. After her conversion in 1739, she had become a participant in the "Fetter Lane Society," a joint Moravian-Anglican Religious Society that met within a few miles of her home in Chelsea. After her husband's death in 1746, she gave herself to full-time support for the revival. She attempted to attract other aristocratic women to the Evangelical experience, both by inviting them to hear the preachers, and by correspondence. Her letters sometimes drew the ire of her high-born correspondents, as the following excerpt from a letter from the Duchess of Buckingham shows:

> I thank your ladyship for the information concerning the Methodist Preachers. Their doctrines are most repulsive and strongly tinctured with impertinence and disrespect towards their superiors, in perpetually endeavouring to level all ranks and do away with all distinctions. It is monstrous to be told that you have a heart as sinful as the common wretches that crawl the earth.[34]

Here it is apparent that among the upper classes, the Evangelicals were feared because of the "leveling" tendencies in their understanding of original sin.

But the Countess found two ways in which she could support the work of the Evangelicals among the upper classes. First, she began to appoint numerous preachers, including Howell Harris, to the post of personal chaplain, and then personally allowed them the freedom to preach itinerantly. Second, she built elegant chapels in the spas frequented by the nobility, Bath and Tunbridge Wells in particular. Moreover, she opened her Chelsea residence for the Evangelical

The Countess of Huntingdon

Engraving of unknown provenance; in [Aaron Seymour], *The Life and Times of Selina, Countess of Huntingdon* (London: William Edward Painter, 1839), frontispiece.

preachers and invited friends to hear them. In these ways, the Countess was able not only to attract a few wealthy patronesses to the movement, but, what is perhaps more important, she lent the movement an air of respectability.

When George Whitefield arrived from his third trip to North America in 1748, the Countess dispatched Howell Harris to bring him to her Chelsea residence. He preached for a week there, and joined ranks of other preachers by being made her personal chaplain. It was fortunate timing for Whitefield, who had arrived to find his Moorfields Tabernacle congregation nearly bankrupt, the furniture having been sold in his absence to pay off debts. With the Countess's spiritual and fiscal backing, Whitefield was able to set the congregation on a new footing before launching off on a preaching mission to the north of England and (in 1751) to Ireland.

From 1748 there remained a staunch alliance between Harris, Whitefield, and the Countess, the various preachers appointed by Selina now collectively referred to as "The Countess of Huntingdon's Connexion." They met in Conference annually, with Whitefield as their (at least titular) moderator. Whitefield spent the remaining twenty-two years of his life on preaching missions alternating between Great Britain and North America. He died on his seventh trip to North America in 1770, leaving the Countess of Huntingdon as the proprietrix of his Georgia properties.

Whitefield's preaching had a dramatic flair that heightened his stress on the religious affections. On one occasion he described the sinner as a poor, blind beggar who, having lost his dog, groped blindly on the brink of a bottomless abyss. As Whitefield held the congregation in suspense, the otherwise reserved Lord Chesterfield (who had been invited as the guest of the Countess) suddenly cried out, "By Heaven, he's gone!"[35] Reported by some to have had the ability to put a congregation in tears by pronouncing the word "Mesopotamia," Whitefield's preaching attracted the same kind of attention, and evoked the same emotional responses, as Howell Harris's oratory had done.

Selina outlived George Whitefield by more than twenty years (she died in 1791). In her later years her movement became more and more sectarian. In 1768 she founded Trevecka House, Talgarth, at Harris's home village, as a kind of Methodist seminary for the preachers in her "Connexion," and eventually her chapels were registered as independent Protestant Churches.

Harris (at least from 1736), Whitefield, and the other preachers of the Countess of Huntingdon's Connexion preached a Gospel at harmony with their understanding of an Anglican Calvinism they believed to have been expressed in the Articles of Religion and Homilies. When challenged on the doctrine of election by other Evangelicals, they defended the Calvinistic theological heritage.

The evangelists of the Countess of Huntingdon's Connexion (English and Welsh) had adapted the old Puritan theology in their new social and cultural setting. It is true that they made a broad, popular appeal, so much so that some have argued that although their "theology" or "doctrine" was Calvinistic, their "faith," the practical import of their message, was essentially Arminian.[36] The Evangelicals of the Countess's circle would surely have repelled this suggestion: Harris, Whitefield, Augustus Toplady and others repeatedly affirmed and defended the doctrine of election, and they would break communion with the Wesleys over the issues of election and "antinomianism." The Evangelical preachers did indeed appeal to new classes of hearers, from the Kingswood colliers to the blue-blooded associates of the Countess, and in this respect the Methodists of the Evangelical Revival (Calvinist and Arminian) may have embraced a broader range of social spectra than Puritans in the previous century had done.

Consistent with the older Puritan theology, the Evangelicals of the Countess of Huntingdon's circle stressed the experiences of repentance (or awakening) and assurance as critical responses to the troubling questions of their age. They seemed to answer not only the general epistemological question, "How do I know?" but also the specific "case of conscience" that had haunted the Calvinists, including the Puritans and Reformed Pietists: "How do I know that I am among the elect?" Among other "signs of grace revealed," the Evangelicals valued the experiences of conviction of sin and the assurance of pardon as certain confirmation of one's election. One could argue (but scarcely prove) that they tended to stress "assurance" more than conviction, with the reverse being true of the Puritans, but both moments of religious awakening were encouraged.

Finally, the Evangelicals of the Countess of Huntingdon's Connexion brought the moral stresses of the late seventeenth century into their theological understanding as the proper *fruit* (though not the *prerequisite*) of justifying faith. Sanctification naturally followed justification, so that the two were inseparable. Augustus Toplady's well-known hymn expresses the connection between the two in this manner:

> be of sin the double cure:
> save from wrath, and make me pure.[37]

Again, the older Puritan stress on sanctification was proclaimed, but in this case in more or less conscious opposition to the Moralism of the day. The revival may indeed have begun as a moralistic quest for holiness as a necessary requirement for pardon, but with Harris, Whitefield, and others it was transformed into a movement that stressed an Evangelical quest for pardon ushering in a life of graced holiness.

The Wesleys

Intertwined also in the lives and efforts of Harris, Whitefield, and the Countess of Huntingdon, were the careers of John (1703–1791) and Charles (1707–1788) Wesley.[38] The grandsons of Non-Conforming preachers whose own children, Samuel Wesley and Susanna Annesley, had turned "High Church" (that is, had turned not only to conformity to the national Church, but also to a conservative form of Anglicanism), John and Charles Wesley were raised in a Lincolnshire rectory characterized by poverty, on the one hand, and high standards for education and moral life, on the other. Both were educated at "public" schools in London, then at Christ Church, Oxford. In 1726 John Wesley was elected a Fellow of Lincoln College, with the responsibility of "Greek moderator," and a stipend that would fund him (even away from the college) so long as he remained single.

John Wesley had decided to be a priest in 1725, and from that time undertook a program of devotional reading and religious exercises, including the keeping of a personal diary that grew more elaborate as the years went on. By the early 1730s, after a brief period in which John had served as curate to his father, both John and Charles Wesley were involved in an Oxford religious society structured after the model of those of Horneck and Woodward. The group held each other accountable for daily devotional life, regular attendance at the eucharist, works of charity (visiting prisoners and helping the needy find clothing and food), and devotional reading. Eventually they came to stress regular observance of the "stationary" fasts (on Wednesday and Friday every week, from sunup until about 3:00 P.M.).[39]

The readings as well as the activities of the Oxford group reflected the rigoristic stress of Anglican Moralism, and included works by Horneck and Woodward themselves, Taylor's *Holy Living* and *Holy Dying*, the anonymous work entitled *The Whole Duty of Man* (which Harris had used in his earliest preaching), and à Kempis's *Imitation of Christ*. Perhaps through the influence of William Law (whom John

John Wesley Preaching to a Segregated Congregation at Nottingham

Engraving of unknown provenance; in John Wesley, *Wesley His Own Biographer: Selections from the Journals* (London: C. H. Kelly, 1896), p. 276.

Wesley had met), the group became interested in Christian mysticism. When this, along with their fasting, became publicly known, one London newspaper reported that a group of Oxford students had taken up ascetic austerities after the pattern of the ancient Alexandrian mystic, Origen.[40]

By 1733, John Wesley had become acquainted with a group of Manchester Non-Jurors who maintained their own episcopal succession. (The "Non-Jurors" were Anglicans who refused to take oaths [*jures*] of allegiance to William and Mary.) This group, which included John Byrom, Thomas Deacon, and Wesley's friend John Clayton, was convinced of a mission to restore the Church to its primitive purity, which they believed to be represented in the so-called *Apostolic Canons*, the *Apostolic Constitutions*, and other early Christian literature. They were also committed to certain practices or "usages" found in the first Prayer Book of Edward VI (1549), including the use of a prior blessing of the eucharistic elements, an epiclesis in the eucharistic prayer (that is, a prayer for the descent of the Holy Spirit upon the elements), and prayers on behalf of the dead. These practices, too, they held to be part of the unbroken tradition of ancient Christianity. One of John Wesley's earliest writings, an "Essay upon the Stationary Fasts," was published by Thomas Deacon, and it shows Wesley's attachment to the ideal of reviving ancient Christian practices.[41]

By the year of Harris's and Whitefield's conversions, then, John and Charles Wesley had been attracted to a variety of contemporary forms of religious life, including Anglican sacramentalism and mysticism, although moral rigorism seems to have predominated. This is evident not only in their participation in the Oxford Religious Society and in the devotional literature they read, but most obviously in their decision, following their father's death in 1735, to go to the newly founded colony of Georgia in North America. Charles went as personal secretary to General Oglethorpe, the colony's founder. John went as chaplain and missionary of the SPG, loaded with SPCK books and pamphlets.[42]

John Wesley's concern for the restoration of primitive Christianity continued through his early months in Georgia. He divided the Sunday services between a service of Scripture and preaching, and the communion proper. He evidently implemented the "usages" to which the Manchester sect was attached, he insisted on baptizing by immersion, even for infants, and stated that baptisms of women should be performed by deaconesses, as they had been in the primitive Church. His reading included a heavy fare of works relating to ancient Christianity, such as William Beveridge's enormous volumes on the canons of the ancient Church.[43]

It was in Georgia, however, that John and Charles Wesley directly encountered the European strands of the religion of the heart movements, in the form of German Pietism. On board the *Simmonds* with the brothers bound for Georgia were August Gottlieb Spangenberg and a company of Moravian pilgrims traveling to their Georgia commune. On board ship, and throughout his stay in Georgia, Wesley held religious conversations with the Moravians, and sometimes they inquired as to his spiritual condition. Moreover, Wesley found in Georgia a group of refugees from Salzburg in Austria whose pastor, Johann Martin Bolzius, had been appointed from Halle University, and who represented the main stream of Lutheran Pietism, the tradition of Spener and Francke. Both John and Charles Wesley traveled to the Salzburger settlement, and engaged in religious dialog. The Wesleys were impressed with the piety of the German Christians, and when John Wesley discovered the Moravians' claim to have maintained an unbroken episcopal succession from the ancient Church, many of his prejudices against them were relieved.[44]

John Wesley's days in Georgia ended late in December of 1737. Angered at the betrothal and eventual marriage of his friend Sophia Hopkey to another suitor, Wesley refused to admit her to the eucharist, citing quite old Anglican canons. Her uncle and guardian, an alderman of Savannah, then posed a dozen or so counts against Wesley in the provincial court, most having to do with his irregular ecclesiastical practices. After waiting several weeks for the trial to come up, John Wesley simply departed, went to South Carolina, and in early January 1738 sailed from Charleston to England. On board ship, he wrote down a lengthy self-inspection, of which he later included a portion in his published *Journal*. The document reveals his frustration with Moralism and with the program of the Manchester Non-Jurors, and indicates that he was undergoing a serious spiritual crisis.[45]

Back in England, in the midst of explaining his actions to the Georgia trustees, Wesley made contact with London Moravians, including a minister named Peter Böhler, who became his confidante. Charles soon joined him, and both brothers became attached to the Fetter Lane Society. Böhler and the Moravians continued to press them on the question of whether they had experienced the assurance of pardon that the Moravians and other Pietists had stressed.

It was on Pentecost Sunday, 21 May 1738, that Charles Wesley found this assurance. Within hours, he wrote a hymn describing the experience:

O how shall I the goodness tell,
    Father, which thou to me hast showed?
That I, a child of wrath and hell,
    I should be called a child of God!
Should know, should feel my sins forgiven,
Blest with this antepast of heaven![46]

Three days later, on Wednesday evening, John had a similar experience, which he described in the following terms. After telling of his long quest for a sense of pardon, Wesley's *Journal* account continues:

13. I continued thus to seek it (though with strange indifference, dullness, and coldness, and unusually frequent relapses into sin) till Wednesday, May 24. I think it was about five this morning that I opened my Testament on those words: Τά μέγιστα ἡμιν καὶ τίμια ἐπαγγέλματα δεδώρηται, ἵνα γένεσθε θείας κοινωνοὶ φύσεως— "There are given unto us exceeding great and precious promises, even that ye should be partakers of the divine nature." Just as I went out I opened it again on those words, "Thou art not far from the kingdom of God." In the afternoon, I was asked to go to St. Paul's. The anthem was, "Out of the deep have I called unto thee, O Lord. Lord, hear my voice. O Let thine ears consider well the voice of my complaint. If thou, Lord, wilt be extreme to mark what is done amiss, O Lord, who may abide it? But there is mercy with thee; therefore thou shalt be feared. [. . .] O Israel, trust in the Lord: For with the Lord there is mercy, and with him is plenteous redemption. And he shall redeem Israel from all his sins."

14. In the evening I went very unwillingly to a society in Aldersgate Street, where one was reading Luther's Preface to the Epistle to the Romans. About a quarter before nine, while he was describing the change which God works in the heart through faith in Christ, I felt my heart strangely warmed. I felt I did trust in Christ, Christ alone for salvation, and an assurance was given me that he had taken away *my* sins, even *mine*, and saved *me* from the law of sin and death.[47]

When he returned home that evening, where his brother Charles lay ill, John entered and said, "I believe."[48]

A few weeks later, John traveled to Germany, where he visited the Moravian settlement at Herrnhut. He interviewed several persons there, but was rejected from communion as *homo perturbatus*, "a very disturbed person": the Moravians were still not convinced of his faith. On his way back to England in August, he visited Halle, where again he encountered the main stream of the Lutheran pietistic tradition.[49] This is important to note, since Wesley's later rejection of

Moravianism is sometimes represented as a rejection of the pietistic tradition as a whole.

Back in Oxford in November, he began studying the Articles of Religion and *Homilies* of the Church of England. There, in the constitutional documents of the Elizabethan Reformation, he seems to have found a theology that countered the Moralism of his age, and with which his new-found Evangelicalism seemed at harmony. He published at that time a tract on the doctrine of justification according to the teachings of the Church of England, which remained a standard Methodist pamphlet through the decades to come.[50] In this way, just as Reformed and Lutheran Pietists had reinterpreted their own doctrines concerning salvation, placing the stress on the personal apprehension of faith, so Wesley reinterpreted the teachings of the Anglican tradition in the light of his new-found experience of the assurance of pardon.

John and Charles Wesley had been preaching a more or less Evangelical doctrine of justification, even before they themselves experienced the assurance of pardon. Peter Böhler had encouraged John Wesley to "preach faith *till* you have it . . ."[51] Their doctrine was perceived as innovative, and several London churches had already been closed to them. John Wesley's sermon on "Salvation by Faith," preached at St. Mary's, Oxford, on Sunday 11 June 1738, was probably composed before the Aldersgate Street experience.[52] Moreover, in the Fetter-Lane Society in London and in a religious society in Bristol which John Wesley had visited, the brothers had come into contact with George Whitefield. It was under Whitefield's influence that on 2 April 1739 John Wesley preached in the open air at Kingswood, just as Whitefield had done there for the first time less than a month before. Like Whitefield's account, Wesley's draws an obvious parallel with Jesus' preaching:

> At four in the afternoon I submitted to be more vile, and proclaimed in the highways the glad tidings of salvation, speaking from a little eminence in a ground adjoining to the city, to about three thousand people. The scripture on which I spoke was this (is it possible any one should be ignorant that it is fulfilled in every true minister of Christ?), "The Spirit of the Lord is upon Me, because he hath anointed Me to preach the gospel to the poor . . ."[53]

It was in fact John Wesley to whom Whitefield entrusted his Bristol societies when Whitefield left for North America in the summer of 1739, to return to the Georgia work that the Wesleys had only recently left. Whitefield was never to recover the Bristol society from the Wesleys' control.

Within a decade of John Wesley's first field preaching, the Evangelical movement that he and Charles led had developed a large organizational structure. An open letter to a sympathetic priest, the Reverend Vincent Perronnet, written in 1748, describes their elaborate system of societies, subdivided into classes, with special "select bands" and "penitent bands" to meet the needs of members who were progressing in holiness or notoriously backsliding (respectively). The letter went on to describe the quarterly love feasts observed by the societies (following the Moravian precedent), their annual Covenant Renewal (following at least partially the patterns of Scots-Irish Presbyterianism), their fasting and watch-nights (or vigils), and their charitable institutions.[54] Not mentioned in the letter but already in place by 1748 was an organized circuit of ordained and lay preachers who met together annually in a Conference, structured after that of Howell Harris.[55]

Throughout their works, John and Charles stressed the centrality of religious experience and the way of salvation punctuated by such experiences. John Wesley had developed an epistemology of religious experience (sometimes utilizing Lockean terms) by which he understood that "faith" in a general (not specifically Christian) sense denotes the religious apprehension shared by all human beings as a result of divine, "preventing" (preparatory) grace. Self-knowledge, knowledge of moral principles (including conscience), and a rudimentary knowledge of God were all given by the religious "sense" of faith, which then ushered in consciousness of sin (repentance) and eventually a knowledge of one's pardon (assurance).[56] Having this spiritual epistemology, Wesley could then proceed by a more or less scientific method to observe and describe the affective progress of the religious life.

John Wesley's personal diaries and his published *Journal* resemble in some ways the scientific diaries and journals of the age, and show a fascination with the accurate recording of his own and others' religious experiences. Many of his published sermons read more like generalized treatises on specific aspects of the Christian life (such as "Heaviness through Manifold Temptations," "Wandering Thoughts," or "The Repentance of Believers") than the oral sermons he delivered.[57] The sermons represent the distillate of Wesley's reflections on the "way of salvation," drawn from his study of Scripture, Christian tradition, and the experiences of those whom he had observed. In addition to them, Charles Wesley's hymns provided a popular means of teaching the "way of salvation" to the Methodist people. The *Collection of Hymns* published by the Wesleys in 1780 is

William Hogarth, "Credulity, Superstition, and Fanaticism"

An engraving believed to caricature John Wesley, published by Hogarth in 1762; in Sean Shesgreen, ed., *Engravings by Hogarth* (New York: Dover Publications, Inc., 1973), no. 95 (n.p.).

organized along the lines of the way of salvation, with specific hymns for each stage of the Christian life (for example, the hymn "Love Divine, All Loves Excelling" describes entire sanctification).[58]

The Wesleys' understanding of the way of salvation shows clear signs of their Anglican commitment, and is more like that of Lutheran Pietists than of the Puritans or Reformed Pietists. The Wesleys rejected the doctrine of election, maintaining that Christ had died for all human beings and that all could come to pardon. They staunchly defended sacraments and other divinely appointed "means of grace" in the pilgrim way, and consequently fell into the same ambiguity that the Lutherans had done in maintaining both baptismal regeneration for infants and the necessity of an experience of regeneration for those who had fallen.[59] With caveats much like those of Arndt, Spener, and Francke, they taught the possibility of "Christian perfection," the possibility that God can bring human beings to perfect love for the divine.[60]

The Wesleys' concern for the communication of religious affections is seen not only in their formal sermons and treatises, and in the *Collection of Hymns* they published, but also in the way in which John Wesley tried to train preachers for their work. His "Directions concerning Pronunciation and Gesture" illustrates this concern with the communication of affective devotion, and affords us a window through which we may imagine what it might have been like to attend upon an eighteenth-century Evangelical sermon. In the first place, it should be noted that Wesley encouraged a certain reserve on the part of preachers:

> To avoid all kinds of unnatural tones, the only rule is this,—Endeavour to speak in public just as you do in common conversation. Attend to your subject, and deliver it in the same manner as if you were talking to a friend.[61]

The preachers were not to scream, and their gestures and expressions should not detract from the subject of the sermon. But given this reserve, the preachers were to illustrate their subjects by expressions of affection, gestures, pitch and speed of the voice, and facial expressions. "Conversation" is the key word: the preachers were not to speak as if they were discoursing about some disinterested subject, but they were to speak as friends to friends about matters of ultimate concern to the human soul:

> 7. You should always be casting your eyes upon some or other of your auditors, and moving them from one side to the other, with an air of

affection and regard; looking them decently in the face, one after another, as we do in familiar conversation. Your aspect should always be pleasant, and your looks direct, neither severe nor askew; unless you design to express contempt or scorn, which may require that particular aspect.

8. If you speak of heaven or things above, lift up your eyes; if of things beneath, cast them down; and so if you speak of things of disgrace; but raise them in calling God to witness, or speaking of things wherein you glory.[62]

These techniques could be taught, learned, and practiced: Wesley encouraged the preachers to stand in front of a mirror (or even a friend), and rehearse their sermons with a careful eye to their gestures, pronunciation, and expressions.[63] The medium of communication, then, their very style of preaching, was itself part of the message of affective piety that the Evangelical preachers sought to express.[64]

John Wesley's reflection of the religion of the heart traditions was by no means coincidental. He had been influenced directly by Pietism (both by the Salzburgers and the Moravians he had met in Georgia) and somewhat less directly by the pietistic impetus of English Puritanism (perhaps especially by Richard Baxter).[65] Wesley read widely, and published editions (sometimes abridgments) of books for his preachers and others in the Methodist societies. Although he sometimes severely edited books for his constituents, all the stands of the religion of the heart movements were represented. His *Christian Library*[66] and other editions included Saint-Cyran (published separately) and Blaise Pascal (vol. 23), representing the Jansenists, and Antoinette Bourignon (published separately), Miguel de Molinos (vol. 38), and François Fénelon (vol. 38), representing Quietism. He also published the *Life* of Gascon Jean-Baptiste de Renty, a close associate and supporter of Jean Eudes.[67] The *Christian Library* included a variety of Puritan spiritual writers, among them Thomas Goodwin (vols. 11–12), Joseph Alleine (vols. 24–25, 30–31), John Bunyan (vol. 32), and Richard Baxter (vol. 37). He gave an honored position to Arndt's *True Christianity* in the first volume of the *Christian Library*, immediately following the Apostolic Fathers and the *Spiritual Homilies* attributed to Macarius of Egypt. John Wesley, then, was not only influenced by the varied strands of the religion of the heart movements; he more or less consciously understood himself as transmitting their spiritual teaching to the Methodist people for whom he felt responsible.

"The Parting of Friends"[68]

The Fetter Lane Society had been a remarkable gathering of men and women who in very different ways would lead the Evangelical Revival. In 1739 it included Anglicans, Dissenters, and Moravians, and had seen George Whitefield, the Countess of Huntingdon, and John and Charles Wesley among its adherents at various times. Within five years, however, this original nucleus of the Evangelical Revival would splinter into a number of kindred but separate movements, and all attempts to reunite them would eventually fail.[69]

The first division came in 1740, and amounted to a rift between Anglicans and Moravians. Some of the English Moravians (prior to the "sifting time"), led by P. H. Molther, insisted that, because all acts performed without justifying faith have the nature of sin, an unregenerate person should be "still" or "quiet," that is, engage in no religious acts, until that person should receive the gift of faith and the assurance of pardon. To John and Charles Wesley and other Anglicans, this teaching of "stillness" seemed a denial of the efficacy of the sacraments and other "appointed means of grace." John Wesley maintained, against Molther and the English Moravians of this period, that God has appointed certain "ordinary means" by which grace is given to human beings (among these he included prayer, the reading and study of scripture, and the eucharist). The implication, for the Anglicans, was that the unregenerate person should "seek the Lord" in the ways which God had ordained, namely, through the regular means of grace. The implication of the "stillness" teaching, by contrast, was that the unregenerate should be strictly "fenced" from the sacrament and other religious acts.

In June of 1740, the Moravian-dominated Fetter Lane Society voted to prohibit John Wesley from preaching because of their disagreement over this issue. A few days later, after accusing the Moravians of mysticism, Wesley led his followers out and they formed their own society at an abandoned canon foundry in Moorfields, near the site of Whitefield's original Tabernacle. The Foundery Society, as it came to be called, served from that time through the 1770s as the London base for the Wesleyan branch of the revival.[70]

The controversy over "stillness" had separated Anglicans and Moravians: a further controversy would separate Anglican Evangelicals from each other. This second controversy emerged in 1742, originally between John Wesley and Howell Harris, and focused on the question of the "extent of the atonement." The controversy grew, as

Whitefield and other Calvinistically inclined Evangelicals stood with Harris, and the Wesleys refused to give ground.

In understanding this controversy, it is important to note what all sides held in common. Wesley, Harris, and Whitefield all agreed that there is no possibility of human free will (free will, at least, to believe in Christ) apart from a special act of grace. Their characteristic way of stating this was to assert that there is no "natural" human free will, the term "natural" in this context having decidedly pejorative connotations.[71] The question that remained, then, was the question of the "extent of the Atonement": did Christ die for the specific number of the elect who had been predestined to grace, or did Christ die for every human being?

Harris, Whitefield, and others, largely those associated with the Countess of Huntingdon, insisted on the traditional Calvinistic teaching that those not elect to salvation are necessarily damned (not by God's intention, but because of the fall of humankind in Adam). This teaching alone, they maintained, could hold salvation to be entirely the work of God. John and Charles Wesley, by contrast, maintained that the "extent of the atonement" embraces all human beings. God, they taught, by a special "preventing" or preparatory grace, has given all persons the possibility of believing in Christ. Charles Wesley's controversial hymn put it in this manner:

> Come, sinners, to the gospel feast;
> Let every soul be Jesu's guest;
> Ye need not one be left behind,
> For God hath bidden all mankind.[72]

John and Charles Wesley were generally willing to accept the term "Arminian" as describing their view of the extent of the atonement, though neither had read any of Arminius's writings.

The controversy divided the movement, the Arminians hurling the epithet "antinomian" at the Calvinists, the Calvinists returning the epithet "Pelagian" at the Arminians. Despite the theological controversy and the ill will that accompanied it, by 1749 there was a possibility that the two sides would unite. Wesley had met with Howell Harris at the latter's request in 1747, and by 1749 George Whitefield's alliance with the Countess of Huntingdon was firmly in place. In that year John Wesley entered into serious negotiations with Whitefield and the Countess in the hopes of forming a sort of general alliance of Evangelical clergy. Although the scheme did not work as an organizational plan, Wesley, Whitefield, and Harris all agreed to circulate the *Minutes* of each others' Conferences, and the disputes largely died down for two decades. In the early 1760s, negotiations were again carried on between Wesley, the Countess, and George Whitefield. There was again a general agreement to respect each others' ministries, and through 1769 there was growing cooperation between them.[73]

It was, most unfortunately, in the year of George Whitefield's death (1770) that the Calvinist-Arminian controversy broke out again in earnest. In this year, the published *Minutes* of the Wesleyan Conference included an assertion that good works are, in a sense, "necessary" to justifying faith.[74] To the Calvinistic Evangelicals, this seemed to be a return to the Moralism against which the Evangelicals had reacted in the first place. Wesley responded that he only meant "necessary" in a "remote" sense, that is, if one had time and occasion between the time of her awakening and the time of her justification, she should necessarily "bring forth fruits worthy of repentance." But the controversy grew rapidly, with Augustus Toplady defending the Calvinist cause, and John William Fletcher's *Checks against Antinomianism* defending the Wesleyan *Minutes*.

In the midst of the controversy, Whitefield died in North America. John Wesley was placed in an embarrassing position when it was discovered that Whitefield's will, written a few years before, mandated that Wesley should preach Whitefield's funeral sermon. Although some suggested that because of their recent disputes Wesley should relinquish the responsibility to another preacher (and many funeral sermons for Whitefield were preached), Wesley went ahead, and stressed the common ties that had bound the earliest leaders of the revival.[75]

But by this time the damage was done, and in the next two decades all sides proceeded along their own paths towards separation from each other, and most proceeded towards separation from the Church of England. Many of the preachers associated with Whitefield, loosely confederated as the "Tabernacle Connexion" or "Whitefield Methodists," became associated with Independent or Congregationalist churches. In 1779 the Consistory Court of London disallowed the Countess of Huntingdon's practice of appointing personal chaplains, and in that year she registered her chapels according to the Act of Toleration. Although the Methodist chapels in Wales did not form a separate "Welsh Calvinistic Methodist Church" until 1811, they traditionally date their existence as a church to 1743 (when Harris first organized the Conference), and most of the congregations were effectively separate from the Church of England by the middle of the eighteenth century.

The Wesleyan societies also progressed gradually towards separation, with Wesley himself denying to his death that he had separated, and yet approving moves that would make his societies a *de facto* denomination by the end of the 1780s. In 1778 he had opened a new chapel on City Road, London, which was designed for sacramental worship. In 1784, he registered his chapels according to the Act of Toleration, protesting all the while that he dissented in no way from the doctrines or practices of the national Church. In the same year he prepared a Prayer Book designed along the lines of the Book of Common Prayer, complete with an ordinal. In September he ordained two lay preachers to serve as "elders" among the Methodists in North America, and consecrated Dr. Thomas Coke, already ordained an Anglican priest, to serve as "General Superintendent" among the North American Methodists, with the authority to ordain. By the end of the 1780s, John Wesley had ordained Methodist elders for Scotland, Wales, and England, and Methodist chapels were celebrating the eucharist at the same time as neighboring Anglican parish churches. Four years after John Wesley's death, in 1795, the Wesleyan Conference in Great Britain formally adopted a denominational structure.[76]

*   *   *

Despite these separations, there were some Evangelical clergy who remained within the national Church. Sometimes with only remote connections with the Wesleys or the Countess of Huntingdon's Connexion, such clergymen as Samuel Walker of Truro, William Grimshaw, and John Newton would provide the seed of an Evangelical movement within the Church of England that would come to dominate that Church in the early decades of the nineteenth century.[77] At the same time, there were many groups who had separated long before the Countess of Huntingdon's Connexion or the Wesleyan Conference became separate, and who towards the time of the French Revolution would break forth into a multitude of new sects.[78]

In fact, if the Evangelical Revival appears complex on the surface, with tedious interrelations of Anglicans, Dissenters, and Moravians, Calvinists and Arminians, and preachers "in connexion" with Harris or Whitefield or Wesley, the fact is that below the surface the movement was an even more complex maze of preachers, societies, chapels, classes, and charitable institutions. In addition to the Welsh, Calvinistic, and Wesleyan strands of the revival mentioned above, there were many independent preachers and societies with no formal connections with these groups. There was, moreover, considerable flux in the movement from the first: individuals and whole societies might pass back and forth between connections with the Wesleys, the Countess of Huntingdon, Whitefield, Harris, or any other preacher, and they might simply function as independent individuals or groups.

By the time of the American and French Revolutions, the Evangelical movement was undergoing significant changes. Howell Harris and Charles Wesley had already died. In 1791 John Wesley, the Countess of Huntingdon, and William Williams of Pantycelyn all died, leaving Britain without the first generation of Evangelicals. But by this time, the revival was slowly beginning to take on the institutional forms (denominations and Church parties) that were to sustain its life through the century ahead.

Chapter Six

Distant Echoes:
Eastern Christian Piety and Hasidic Judaism in the Seventeenth and Eighteenth Centuries

John Wesley's inclusion of the *Spiritual Homilies* attributed to "Macarius of Egypt" in the first volume of the *Christian Library* indicates something of the romantic view of the Christian East held in Wesley's age. Arndt, Spener, and other Western European religious leaders had studied the Macarian homilies as well, and in their own ways were intrigued with the Christian East (especially in antiquity).[1] A similar romantic tendency may be seen in earlier English Non-Jurors' attempts to forge an alliance with Constantinople, and then in later Methodists' fascination with a (supposedly) Orthodox bishop whom John Wesley had met, and who (for a small fee) ordained some of the Methodist preachers.[2] Beyond these romantic fancies, however, there were some actual liaisons between East and West in the seventeenth and eighteenth centuries, and both the Jews and the Christians of Central and Eastern Europe would experience religious movements similar to the religion of the heart movements of Western Europe, although they most often grew from the distinctive spiritual roots of Eastern Christianity and of Central European Judaism.

By the middle of the eighteenth century various strands of the religion of the heart movements were coalescing in Western Europe, where expanding commerce had enabled cultural patterns to be transmitted readily from one nation to another. Although Eastern Europe did not have extensive transportation and communication links as the West did, there was a growing and significant cultural interchange throughout the Continent. It was, after all, the age in which a Calvinist would be elected Patriarch of Constantinople (Cyril Lukaris, patriarch 1620–1638), reflecting the influence of Dutch and English theologians. It was the age in which a Russian Tsar would attempt to Europeanize the Russian state and Russian culture (Peter the Great, Tsar 1682–1725). It is not surprising, then, that some influences of the Western European "religion of the heart" movements should have been felt in Eastern Europe in the seventeenth and eighteenth centuries.

Beyond these direct influences, however, religious movements arose in Eastern Europe in the same period which parallel the Western movements, but which arose out of their own cultural traditions. In Russia, a congeries of sectarian movements arose, many of which stressed personal illumination and apocalyptic speculation. In Greece, older traditions of meditative prayer were renewed in the *Philokalia* tradition, which became a form of popular devotion throughout Eastern Orthodoxy. In southern and eastern Poland, the Hasidic movement transformed traditional Jewish mysticism into a movement of popular, affective devotion and personal illuminism. These movements suggest that beyond the direct cultural links that may have existed, there were social and cultural circumstances in Central and Eastern Europe similar to those of Western Europe, and similar religious movements developed there on their own grounds.

Influence of the Western Movements in the Christian East

Both Greek and Russian Orthodoxy were influenced by Western Christianity in the sixteenth through eighteenth centuries. The connection between the West and Greek Orthodoxy was made as a result of commercial contacts, initially by the Venetians, who had traded with Greece and Constantinople from the late middle ages. The Venetians had been the last bastion of support for the Byzantine Empire before it fell in 1453, and in fact they came into control of the Peloponnesus for a twenty-year period early in the eighteenth century (1699–1719). The fact that Orthodox leaders of the eighteenth century were familiar with Jesuit and Oratorian writings is a direct result of the Venetian connection.[3]

During the sixteenth and seventeenth centuries, English and Dutch merchants began trading with Greece and Turkey. As a result of their activities, Protestant theologians and civil leaders came into contact with Constantinople. There were ongoing attempts by various Protestant churches to establish an alliance with Constantinople against Rome, sometimes promising support against the Turks. It was under these circumstances that Cyril Lukaris, Patriarch of Constantinople from 1620 through 1638, wrote a confession of Faith for the Greek Orthodox communion that was essentially Calvinistic.[4] Although Cyril's program was not accepted, it stands as an indication that Protestant theologies were known and studied in the Christian East throughout the sixteenth and seventeenth centuries.

Russian Orthodoxy was also influenced by the Western Christianity in these centuries. Catholic influence on Russia came through

Roman missionaries working in Eastern Europe, and eventually through the "Uniat" churches, that is, churches that maintained Eastern rituals, but were in communion with Rome. A large Uniat communion had existed in the Ukraine from the late fifteenth century, when the Metropolitan of Kiev accepted the formulations of the Council of Florence (1448). This Church remained in communion with Rome through the early eighteenth century, when it was suppressed under the Tsarina Catherine. In opposition to the Uniat influence, an Orthodox Theological Academy had been established at Kiev in the 1640s, but in their dialog with the Uniat Catholics, the Orthodox theologians of Kiev had learned a great deal about Western theology and Church practices. Peter the Great would call on the Kiev theologians for his reform of the Russian Orthodox Church in the 1720s.

In the early eighteenth century there was a direct liaison between the Russian Orthodox and French Jansenists. Peter the Great's interest in Western European culture had led him to visit Paris in 1717, where he proposed the initiation of a dialog concerning the unification of Eastern and Western Churches. After the invitation had been extended, however, he refused to debate with the papal *nuncio* who had been dispatched to meet him, electing instead to carry on his discussion with the Jansenists of France (represented by Cardinal Noailles), carrying back to Russia specific proposals for reunion drawn up by the Jansenist- (and Gallican-) leaning theologians of the Sorbonne. It was probably the Jansenists' view of papal authority that attracted the Tsar, more than their theology or spirituality, but on the other hand Peter's expulsion of the Jesuits from Russia (in 1719) could not but have pleased the Jansenists.[5] The Russian bishops to whom the proposals were forwarded could not agree on a plan to implement them. Undaunted, however, the Sorbonne theologians sent their own emissary, Jacques Jubé, to Russia in 1727 (during the reign of Peter II). Jubé remained there for three years, conducting meetings with Church leaders and teaching in Orthodox churches. He was expelled from the country in 1730, however, with the accession of the Tsarina Anna Ivanovich, who virulently opposed Catholicism in any form.[6] In these instances, it was Jansenism's rejection of papal autocracy that was appealing to the Russians. Nevertheless, Jansenism's spirituality had lent the movement a certain ecumenical spirit: it was, then, the same Cardinal Noailles who had met and corresponded with Zinzendorf, who was also instrumental in the negotiations with the Russian Orthodox.

Protestant Churches also came into contact with the Eastern Orthodox communion in the seventeenth century. The patriarchate of

Cyril Lukaris in Constantinople has already been noted. Perhaps even more significantly, German Pietists began to forge links with Eastern Christians at the beginning of the eighteenth century. As a result of the general outreach of Pietism, the Spener-Francke tradition had extended as far eastward as the Lutheran congregations of Teschen, on the borders of Silesia, central Poland, Moravia, and Hungary, during the first three decades of the eighteenth century. The Pietism of Herrnhut, likewise, had been extended through its missionary activities to Latvia and Estonia in the Baltic by the middle of that century, and had also been established among German peoples living along the Volga in Russia.[7] But institutional links with the Eastern Churches came as a result of Halle Pietism's broader plans for influence in the Christian world, beyond the limits of the Lutheran or Moravian communions, and especially as a result of the Oriental Institute which Francke had established at Halle.

The agent of Halle Pietism in Russia was Heinrich Wilhelm Ludolf, a German-born diplomat familiar with several Eastern European languages who at one time served a joint special appointment as an agent both of the English Court of Queen Anne and of the Danish government. Ludolf, a friend of Philipp Jakob Spener, had devised with August Hermann Francke a plan for supplying a pastor for the Lutheran congregation in Moscow. Francke seized the occasion as an opportunity for expanding the Oriental Institute at Halle, both by bringing Russian scholars to Halle and by bringing Pietistic Lutheran ministers to Moscow. After Russia's defeat of Sweden in 1721, moreover, Swedish immigrants to Moscow increased the number of Lutheran congregations there, and again Halle supplied the pastors. Meanwhile, the study of Russian, Church Slavonic, and other Slavic languages was underway in Halle, and numerous pietistic works were translated into Russian. Perhaps most significantly, these included Arndt's *True Christianity*—with its own reverence for "Macarius of Egypt." The pietistic books would have a significant influence on Russian religious culture: the Orthodox saint Tikhon of Zadonsk (1724–1783), for example, held Arndt to be among his favorite authors, and Tikhon's own work on *True Christianity* echoes Arndt's both in its title and its concern for the out-working of the Christian life.[8]

Francke's plans extended beyond Moscow, however. He envisioned a large-scale Christian mission to the East, and recognized the importance of Constantinople in this scheme. Ludolf proposed the establishment of two theological institutions in Italy (at Venice and Livorno) where Greek theologians could come into contact with the Lutherans of Halle. Further, he hoped that from Venice, and then from Constantinople, Halle missionaries could move east and set up a station at Astrakhan (north of the Caspian Sea, where there already existed a school run by Italian Capuchins), and from there eventually spread their influence to China. Although this elaborate plan did not work out, Francke did establish a Greek seminary at Halle, which was well-funded and came to be preferred by Greek Church officials to a similarly planned program at Oxford sponsored by Anglicans.[9]

By the time that the Evangelical Revival was underway in England, then, Eastern Christians had seen Western Christian literature translated into their languages, Jansenist teachers in their midst, Pietist pastors in the Lutheran congregations of their lands, Moravian missionaries in Great Russia, and emissaries from Halle University who had established formal institutions for intercultural theological education. The influence of Western religion of the heart movements was being felt throughout the Christian East. And yet, at the same time, the Christians and Jews of Central and Eastern Europe witnessed the rise of religion of the heart movements that grew, not so much from the influence of the Western movements, but from cultural patterns and contemporary conditions in their own countries.

Orthodox Piety and Russian Sectarianism

In the larger picture, Western contacts with the Christian East were but one, perhaps minor, factor in the complex story of the Eastern Christian Churches in the seventeenth and eighteenth centuries. The ancient Greek Church was reeling from the fall of Constantinople to the Turks, and was living under a corrupt system of patriarchal rule. Although the Russian Church was growing in power and influence, it underwent a serious schism late in the seventeenth century, and the centralization of the state under Peter the Great brought with it an attempt to stifle individualistic or eccentric spiritualities. Both of these factors would influence expressions of popular piety in Eastern Christian lands. At the end of the seventeenth century a number of religious sects emerged at the time of the "Great Schism" within the Russian Orthodox communion. Originally a revolt against Constantinopolitan liturgical practices imposed in Russia, many of these groups drifted more and more towards spiritualism (i.e., rejection of sacraments in favor of a purely spiritual understanding of the means of grace) and illuminism (i.e., claims to immediate divine revelation) as they grew further and further from traditional Eastern Christian liturgy and discipline. Both the Greek and Russian Churches, though, saw a renewal of older orthodox traditions of devotional life in the eighteenth century, a renewal which first affected monks, but which spread rapidly among pious laity. To understand these movements on their own terms, it is important to bear in mind their background in the decline of the ancient Patriarchate of Constantinople, and the simultaneous ascent of the Patriarchate of Moscow.

Constantinople had fallen in 1453 to the Ottoman Turks. The last Byzantine Emperor died in the struggle, and all of Asia Minor and Greece fell under Turkish control as a result. The Ecumenical Patriarch, head of the Greek Orthodox communion, became a servant of the Turkish sultans, and was given the title of "ethnarch" *(millet bashti)* of the Greek people as well as his religious position. He was forced to pay a heavy tax to the Turks, and this led subsequent Patriarchs to sell episcopal sees and to impose levies on the Greek people under them. Many were kidnapped or murdered, and for long periods there were rival Patriarchs contending for the headship of the Church.[10]

On the other hand, the same period witnessed the rise to global power of the Russian Empire, whose Church was in communion with Constantinople. Just after the fall of Constantinople, Ivan the Great (Tsar, 1462–1505) had consolidated the power of Moscow and began the process of "the gathering of the Russian lands." A period of anarchy set in in the early decades of the seventeenth century when Polish and Cossack peoples invaded the Russian lands. These events, known as the "Time of Troubles" in Russian history, led eventually to a coalition of Russian and Ukrainian power late in the seventeenth century. Building on the strength of this coalition, Peter the Great (Tsar, 1682–1725) embarked on a program of centralization and Westernization, including reforms in the state and the Church.

Just before Peter became Emperor, sectarian movements began to appear in the Russian Church, some of which offer striking parallels to more radical Western movements such as the Labadists or Quakers. Particularly important in the background of Russian religious movements was the *Raskol*, or "Schism" in the Russian Orthodox Church in the late seventeenth century.[11] The *Raskol* was in its origins a reaction against an attempt to Byzantinize the Russian church. Under the *millet* system, the Patriarch of Constantinople had been scarcely able to govern the wide ranges of Eastern Europe that had traditionally looked to him as the symbol of Eastern Christian unity. It was for this reason that in 1589 the Metropolitan of Moscow was elevated to the status of Patriarch. Ties to Constantinople remained firm, however, so much so that in 1652 a newly elected Patriarch of Moscow, Nikon, attempted to revise the Slavic liturgy, to bring it into conformity with Greek practice. Though Nikon at first had the favor of the Tsar, his reforms had raised such a controversy by 1658 that he was deposed. The controversy continued however, and in 1667 those who refused to accept the reforms were excommunicated. Nikon's reforms may seem trivial—he wanted priests to use three fingers in blessing the congregation instead of the customary two, for instance, and he wanted three alleluias sung in the liturgy instead of the customary two—but they provoked an enormous, emotional response. Thousands of Russians burned themselves to death (some in mass suicides) rather than being forced to conform to the new practices.[12] Although their fervor was at least partly nationalistic, it speaks also to the prominence in the Christian East of a form of religious life stressing the encounter with the Divine through sacraments (or, to use the more characteristically Eastern Christian term, "mysteries").

From 1667 the separated Russians referred to themselves as "Old Believers" (sometimes "Old Ritualists"), but they were called *Raskolniki*, "schismatics," by the Orthodox. The Old Believers, as their name suggests, claimed that the Russian Church was itself heretical, and that they represented the true continuation of Orthodoxy in Russia. Although they originated as staunch supporters of the old Russian forms of liturgy, their beliefs were further fueled by apocalyptic speculations concerning the imminent downfall of the Church. Peter the Great, with his plans to Westernize the Russian Church, provided a convenient Antichrist, and his reforms provoked more people (especially peasants) to side with the *Raskol*. Peter, moreover, attempted to curb religious enthusiasm by persecuting the sectarian groups and by limiting extreme forms of traditional monastic life (especially anchoritism).[13]

His efforts hardly succeeded. The *Raskolniki* soon divided into two large subgroups. One faction, the *Popovtsy*, believed that a priesthood was necessary to the continuation of the Church, and, because they had no bishops, relied on Orthodox priests who defected to their movement, and (later) on bishops who came over and ordained priests for them. The *Popovtsy* were not actually liturgical fundamentalists: in their own understanding, it was Nikon's party who had quibbled over liturgical details that were not of supreme importance, and which should have been left to ethnic churches to determine. In their form of religious life, except for the critical differences in liturgical practices, the *Popovtsy* generally resembled the Orthodox.[14]

More radical groups, though, identified together as *Bezpopovtsy* ("priestless"), were determined to carry on the life of their communities without priests (ironically, not because they *objected*, at first, to the idea of priesthood, but actually because they believed even more strongly than the *Popovtsy* that priests must be legitimately ordained—and they had no legitimately ordained priests). The *Bezpopovtsy* came to argue that the mysteries were of two types: those absolutely necessary to salvation (including baptism, the eucharist, and penance), and those only remotely necessary to salvation (including anointing or chrismation, holy orders, and marriage). Although there were precedents for the administration of baptism and penance by laypersons in cases of necessity, there was no precedent for the administration of the eucharist; consequently, the *Bezpopovtsy* were forced either to use eucharistic elements already consecrated by (Orthodox) priests, or to believe that a "sincere desire" for communion would suffice in place of the eucharistic liturgy.[15] The latter case shows how the *Bezpopovtsy* could be drawn to a spiritual interpretation of the eucharist:

> If I live a good life, then I am saved even without communicating in the holy mysteries. Live you a life of good works, they say to the orthodox, and God will not forsake you; only set your hope on communion with him. Communion is reached in a life that imitates Christ's, according to his saying, if a man loveth me and keepeth my word, my Father will love him and come unto him and make his dwelling with him.[16]

Holding to this spiritualized interpretation of the eucharist, however, the *Bezpopovtsy* were divided on the question of marriage: some argued that marriages could be blessed without a priest simply by the consent of the parties, the blessing of their families, and their intention to live in perpetual union; others argued that without priests no marriages could be legitimated, and so insisted on the celibacy of all believers.[17] Again, in the case of the *Bezpopovtsy* who allowed marriage (the majority of the movement), it was spiritualized in the sense that it was held to be constituted by the consent of the parties, not by a ritual. So it was that the *Raskol*, which began as a movement opposing liturgical reforms, could itself end up in a variety of sects, many of which stressed the spiritual meaning of the mysteries. In this way the movement within the *Raskol* towards the *Bezpopovtsy* displayed a parallel tendency to the Western religion of the heart movements.

The *Raskol* led to a proliferation of new sectarian movements and provided an occasion when previously existing movements came to light. There is a certain parallel with the English Revolution, where it has been argued that the sectarian movements that emerged at that time were continuations of underground movements that simply came to light under the circumstances of the Commonwealth.[18] Not all of the new Russian movements of the late seventeenth and early eighteenth centuries, in fact, were directly inspired by the reaction against Nikon's reforms: a number of new movements were distinguished by spiritualities of religious experience from the very beginning. Advocates of such movements were often classed together as "Spiritual Christians." In some cases they were accused, by Orthodox and *Raskolniki*, of reflecting Western Christian influences, and in one case (that of the *Doukhobors*) they acknowledged that they had been founded by Western itinerants.[19] Some of the "Spiritual Christian" groups emerged in the southern areas of modern Russia and in what is now the Ukraine, and this fact has led some interpreters to distinguish them rather sharply from the *Raskolniki* of "Great" (or central) Russia. The *Bezpopovtsy*, however, included many spiritualizing groups within themselves (*Stranniki, Netovski*, "Self-Baptizers," "Prayerless"),[20] and so it is impossible to draw a sharp distinction between them and the southern spiritualist groups that emerged at approximately the same time.

One group of "Spiritual Christians" emerged in the 1690s and were called by their opponents *Khlysti*, or "flagellants." They denied the ascetical excesses implied by this term, preferring to call themselves "People of God," or advocates of the "Christ-Faith" *(Khristovshchina).*[21] The People of God were renowned for their ascetic feats, including prolonged fasts. They renounced all sexual relationships, although they customarily took "spiritual friends" of the opposite sex (as earlier monks had done). Their communities they called "ships" (using the Latin *naves*), each of which had a leader that might be designated as a "Christ" or a "Mother of God."

The People of God were a spiritualist sect in the fullest sense: they held that true Christians are immediately inspired by the Spirit, and they practiced a form of ecstatic dance called *radenie*, a dance in which they would receive visions and illuminations. They would recite the Jesus Prayer, or would sing rapturous choruses celebrating the Spirit's presence among them:

> It floated down, it floated down,
> The Holy Spirit, the Holy Spirit!
> 'Twill blow where it will, where it listeth,
> The Holy Spirit, the Holy Spirit.

O I burn, O I burn,
The Spirit burns, God burns!
Light is in me, Light is in me,
The Holy Ghost, the Holy Ghost![22]

The People of God claimed, moreover, that during their *radenie* they had the abilities to speak in, and to interpret, unknown tongues, as suggested in Acts 2. Sometimes they would fall down, exhausted, and sleep until morning. This led to accusations of sexual immoralities among them; but the accusations seem to have no documentable grounding. They replaced the eucharist with love feasts, and baptism with a "spiritual baptism" or "bath of regeneration," which they held to occur during *radenie*.[23]

The People of God did not avoid communion with the Orthodox (at least at first), but did hold themselves to be the true Church, and the fact that they referred to their leaders as "Christs" and "Mothers of God" indicates their heterodox christology. Some interpreters point out that this did not prevent their communities from worshiping Jesus Christ as uniquely divine, or from venerating the Theotokos ("Mother of God").[24] It could be argued that theirs was the same case as that of Montanism (in the second century), whose prophets and prophetesses spoke *in the person* of the Holy Spirit, and whose utterances were then (falsely) taken to mean that they themselves claimed to *be* the Spirit. Eastern Christians, moreover, were accustomed to speaking of the goal of Christian life as *theiosis*, "divinization" (or even "deification").[25] On the other hand, the leaders of the People of God did self-consciously accept the titles "Christs" and "Mothers of God," and they believed their founder, Danila, to have become the "Lord of Hosts" at the time he was called to found the sect. In this respect, the People of God illustrate a common extreme to which spiritualist movements can be pressed, namely, the extreme of blurring the distinction between the Divine and the human in their stress on direct, human apprehension of the Divine.

Another group of "Spiritual Christians" appeared in the Kharkov region, between Astrakhan and the Ukraine, around 1740. According to the traditions of the *Doukhobors*, as they came to be called, the instigator of this movement in Kharkov was an anonymous, retired Prussian military officer, said to have been a Quaker. Although it is probable that the general background out of which the *Doukhobors* arose was the People of God movement, it is just possible, given the Western contacts noted above in the Ukraine and Astrakhan, that an itinerant Quaker (or perhaps a member of some other Western sect such as the Labadists) made his way to Kharkov.[26] Whatever the case may be, the fact is that the teachings of the *Doukhobors* bear a remarkable resemblance to those of the Society of Friends.

The *Doukhobors* are described in traditional literature as being contemptuous of all authority. Although this characterization was used to justify their persecution, it is grounded in the *Doukhobors'* teaching that the "Living Word," the prophetic revelation to living persons, stands above all other authority, including that of the written scriptures. Like the People of God, the *Doukhobors* maintained that they alone represented the true Christian faith, holding all other Churches to be "dead." They acknowledged one God, and held that Christ was divine, but only in the sense that all human beings can be divine by Christ dwelling within them. A contemporary description of the doctrine of a late-eighteenth-century *Doukhobor* teacher, Sabellius Kapustin, expresses this central teaching:

> He attached peculiar importance to the doctrine of the transmigration of souls, which was already known among them; he also taught that Christ is born again in every believer; that God is in everyone; for when the Word became flesh, it became this for all time, like everything divine, that is, man in the world; but each human soul, at least as long as the created world exists, remains a distinct individual.[27]

Leaders of the *Doukhobors*, then, could refer to themselves as "Sons of God," recalling the self-descriptions of the People of God mentioned above.[28]

The *Doukhobors*, under a series of leaders, developed a distinctive communal and agrarian lifestyle. They were almost constantly persecuted, and in the nineteenth century they wandered from Kharkov to the Crimea, then to Georgia, then to Siberia, eventually finding a home in western Canada. At the same time, there existed throughout Russia during the eighteenth century a variety of sectarian movements, who were joined early in the nineteenth century by "Stundists," apparently German Pietists of the Spener-Francke tradition who had migrated to Russia and there took up a program of reform within the existing churches, much as Pietists had done in Germany.[29]

The People of God and *Doukhobors* represent extremes of the Russian sects. There is a kind of continuum running from the Orthodox to them, which might be represented in this manner:

Orthodox	*Popovtsy*	*Bezpopovtsy*	Radical Sects
			(People of God,
			Doukhobors)

In this continuum, the Orthodox represent a form of religious life stressing an encounter with the divine through sacraments (or "mysteries") available to all, with the possibility of unmediated experience of the divine available to the ascetic elite, and the sectarian movements represent the form of religious life stressing the encounter with the divine through an unmediated personal experience available to all. One might draw a parallel with a similar continuum in Western religion of the heart movements, here represented as the transitions in the career of Jean de Labadie:

Catholic	Jansenist	Reformed	Pietists	Radical Sects
(Jesuits)				(Labadists)

Again, the continuum is from Catholics, representing the medieval stresses on the encounter with God through the sacraments or through ascetic mysticism, to the radical sects such as the Labadists (or Quakers), which most clearly rejected the sacramental system and insisted on personal illumination as the center of religious life.

But despite the similarities, these two continua point to some critical differences between the Western and Eastern movements. In the first place, it should be noted that the Western movements were preoccupied in this period with the Reformation's questions about human nature and salvation: the quarrels between Jesuits and Jansenists on the issue of "Molinism," and the quarrels between traditional Calvinists and "Arminians" indicate the degree to which the question of the priority of grace had dominated Western thought. By contrast, issues of the relationship between human initiative and divine grace in salvation seem to have affected the Eastern movements very little: note in the quotation from the *Bezpopovtsy* source above the casual throwing-together of moralistic suggestions that good works lead to salvation, and the call to respond to God's love shown in Christ. This in itself gives a distinctive character to the Eastern movements, where illuminism and spiritualism arose more out of the long tradition of mystical piety without the typically Western preoccupation with the assurance of salvation.

A second critical difference indicated in these continua is in the forms of religious communities available for these groups. The Eastern movements could be characterized as more radically sectarian in their sociological forms than the Western movements; at least, none of the Eastern movements understood themselves as a reform movement existing within a larger Church, as the Jansenists saw themselves within the Roman Catholic Church, or as the Pietist and

Evangelical movements saw themselves as existing within Reformed, Lutheran, or Anglican communions. Here the difference may lie in social conditions. The Western movements (Jansenist, Pietist, Evangelical) included various strata of the emerging northern European bourgeoisie; in Russia, by contrast, there was only a small middle class prior to the nineteenth century, and the religious movements inevitably attracted the peasantry. There appears to have been no precedent in Russia for the Western notion of a voluntary society of laity existing within a larger Church communion. Consequently, once the *Raskol* occurred, even the *Popovtsy* were left as a congeries of small, unconnected settlements and movements.

If the Russian sectarian movements appear more like Labadists or Quakers, though, at the fringes of traditional religious communities, the point should not be lost that there were also movements within the Orthodox Churches in the seventeenth and especially the eighteenth centuries in which their traditional mysticism developed into a popular piety. We should liken these latter movements, perhaps, to the Quietists, or perhaps even to more traditional advocates of divine love, within Catholicism. But although there were some Catholic (and even Protestant) influences on the Orthodox piety of the seventeenth and eighteenth centuries, popular Orthodox piety grew in some respects from a reaction *against* Western influences— perhaps much in the way that the *Raskol* originated as a reaction against foreign (in their case Constantinopolitan) liturgical practices.

The Greek Orthodox communion reacted decisively against Catholic and Protestant theology in the last three decades of the seventeenth century. The Patriarch Dositheus (Patriarch 1669–1707) convened a Council of Orthodox theologians in Jerusalem in 1672, and authored many of its decrees and its Confessions of Faith. Although the Confession of Dositheus itself reflects some Catholic influences (such as its affirmation of transubstantiation), and follows the form of Western confessions, its intent was to clarify Orthodox teachings in light of the questions that had been raised since the Reformation. In his own writings, Dositheus attacked both Reformed and Uniat Churches, and defended the Orthodox ownership of the Holy Places in Palestine.[30]

In the middle of the eighteenth century, this move to affirm the integrity of Orthodoxy expressed itself in a monastic reform movement, the advocates of which were called *Kollyvates*. (The term derives from *kolyva*, a sweet cake traditionally blessed during funeral services.)[31] Two of the *Kollyvates*, Nicodemus of the Holy Mount (also called Nicodemus "the Hagiorite") and Macarius of Corinth, revived the Orthodox traditions of hesychasm, that is, prayer in "stillness" or "quiet" (ήσυχία). They did this by compiling loci from traditional Orthodox spiritual writers, from Anthony of Egypt up until their own time, who had written on hesychastic prayer. Their completed work, entitled *Philokalia* or "Love of the Beautiful," was published in Venice in 1782.

Although Nicodemus of the Holy Mount had read Latin Christian works, and had even produced Greek versions of works by Jesuit and Oratorian authors, the *Philokalia* stands in the tradition of Eastern Christian spiritual literature. It includes sayings and stories about Eastern ascetics, and in some cases stories that relate other stories or sayings. At any given point in reading the work, the reader may encounter, for example, an eighteenth-century account of a treatise by a fourteenth-century monk of Mt. Athos, itself repeating a story about the fourth-century monk, Anthony of Egypt.[32] Above all, the selections in the *Philokalia* stress the necessity of concentration and of prayer in stillness or silence (ήσυχία), often translated as "prayer of the heart" or "prayer of mind and heart."[33] Selections from Gregory of Sinai and others advocate the use of the "Jesus Prayer," i.e.,

> Lord Jesus Christ,
> Son of God,
> have mercy upon me.[34]

By the recitation of this prayer, either in full, or broken into smaller units for meditation, the Hesychast could attain to "Wisdom," that is, perfection of the mind-heart unity.

The *Philokalia* was originally conceived by Nicodemus and Macarius as a means of renewing the life of Eastern monasticism, and the lifestyle it advocates could be fully pursued only by men and women in a monastic setting. In itself, then, it reflects what we have called an ascetic mystical form of religious life. But the book and its practices became widely popular in Orthodox circles and incited a widespread revival of meditative practices among laity as well as women and men in religious orders. The *Philokalia* was translated into Russian by a Ukrainian monk of the Kiev Academy, Paisii Velichkovskii, and published in 1793. By the time the *Philokalia* had been rendered in Russian, a number of Russian teachers (called *startsy*, "elders," or perhaps "spiritual directors") had advocated a way of personal and affective devotion. Among these was Tikhon of Zadonsk, mentioned earlier as an avid reader of Johann Arndt, who utilized *True Christianity* as the basis for his own pietistic works.[35]

The *startsy* led a revival of religious life which inspired the founding of thousands of new monasteries beginning in the late eighteenth century. These included houses led by women *startsy* who played a critical role in the social upheavals of nineteenth-century Russia.[36] Although the *startsy* were mainly monks, they included some lay men and women, an indication that the piety of the *Philokalia* had spread beyond the confines of the monasteries. By the middle of the nineteenth century the recitation of the Jesus prayer and the reading of the *Philokalia* had become common among Russians of all regions and of every walk of life.[37] In this manner, older forms of Orthodox religious life focusing on the presence of God in the mysteries and the way of ascetic discipline were joined by a newly emerging form of religious life stressing the popular assimilation of the mystical quest.

It might indeed be argued that the form of religious life centering on a personal experience of the divine was relatively less influential in the Christian East than in the Christian West in this period. The development of the *Philokalia*, though later popularized, was in its origins an expression of a typically mystical form of religious life. The Russian sectarian movements were not able to influence the Russian Orthodox communion at large precisely because they were sects, cut off from communion with the Orthodox. Nevertheless, in the popularization of the *Philokalia* tradition and in the presence of the Russian sects themselves, some Eastern Christians had moved away from sacramental and mystical forms of religious life and towards popular and affective forms of religious life. In this respect, they represent a distant echo of the religion of the heart strains that were heard more strongly in the Christian West. But it was not only in the Christian communities of Eastern Europe that these echoes were to be heard.

Hasidic Judaism in the Eighteenth Century

The Christian communities of Central and Western Europe had seen the development, throughout the late middle ages, of a growing Jewish community in their midst. Sometimes barely tolerated, and frequently persecuted, European Jews (*Ashkenazim*, from *Ashkenaz*, the Hebrew for "Germany") developed distinctive cultural and religious traditions, in some cases reflecting the influence of Christian theology and practices. With the rise of *Hasidism* among the Jews of southern and eastern Poland in the eighteenth century, a distinctively Jewish "religion of the heart" movement emerged. Although there is some evidence of the borrowing of cultural motifs from Christian movements (especially from more radical Russian sects, such as the People of God)[38] Hasidism's roots were firmly planted in the soil of

Talmudic and Kabbalistic teachings, and the movement was essentially Jewish in its sense of ultimate religious realities and values. It was, then, a distant echo of the cultural impetus of the religion of the heart movements within the Central European Jewish tradition.

It is believed that Jewish communities had existed in Poland, in particular, since the twelfth century, and that most of the Polish Jews immigrated there from Germany. There was a particularly strong influx into Poland in the fifteenth century, when persecutions in Germany forced many Jewish families to flee to the east. Like other Ashkenazi Jews, the Polish community utilized Yiddish in ordinary life, Hebrew in religious devotion and study, and the languages of the Christian majority (in this case, Polish, but in some areas Russian) in commerce.[39]

Just as Western pietistic movements emerged from the aftermath of the Thirty Years War and the English Revolution, the Hasidic movement emerged in the aftermath of "the Deluge," a nineteen-year period of warfare and displacement throughout Poland. The problems began in 1648 when bands of Cossacks from the Ukraine invaded Poland from the south. Six years later, Russians took advantage of the Poles' weakened position and launched an invasion from the east. A year after that, the Swedish army, rejuvenated after its struggles in the Thirty Years War, invaded Poland from the west. Throughout this period, Poland managed to hold most of its lands, and by the Truce of Andruszowo (1667) the struggles were ended. Meanwhile, the Jewish community in Poland had suffered not only from the general atrocities of the war, but also from specific persecutions in which they were made a popular scapegoat for the economic and social problems of the age.[40]

It was during the last years of the "Deluge" that a messianic movement affected the Jewish communities of the whole world, and especially the Jews of Podolia and Volhynia, in southeastern Poland.[41] The major events of this movement occurred far away on the eastern shores of the Mediterranean, where around 1648 a Sephardic (non-European) Jewish leader named Sabbatai Tsevi began to prophecy the coming of the Messiah, and eventually made it clear that he was himself the Messiah. Tsevi's movement gathered strength very rapidly throughout the Sephardic Jewish communities of the Mediterranean basin, and his work attracted attention in Ashkenazi circles. It was the cult of Sabbatai Tsevi that Jean de Labadie had commended in Amsterdam in the 1660s. In the early 1660s, Tsevi began to sign his letters, "I am your God Sabbatai [Ts]evi."[42] In 1666, however, Tsevi was captured by Turkish officials, and when offered the options of death or conversion to Islam, he chose the latter, becoming a Muslim in 1667. This shocked the communities that had gathered around him, and although many deserted him, others attempted to devise an explanation for the Messiah's advent among the Muslims.

In the Polish Jewish communities as elsewhere, Sabbatai Tsevi was regarded as a traitor, and persons suspected of following him were persecuted by Jewish authorities. They were forced underground, but records from the late seventeenth century and even the early eighteenth century indicate continuing suspicions of Sabbataianism among the Jewish communities of southeastern Poland. Thus, although messianism had largely been discredited by the defection of Tsevi, there existed in Podolia and Volhynia at the beginning of the eighteenth century an underground messianic movement which would prove fertile ground for the rise of Hasidism.[43]

At the beginning of the eighteenth century, then, the Jews of Volhynia and Podolia were slowly recovering from the warfare and persecutions of the "Deluge." There were lingering suspicions of Sabbataianism among them, although immediate hopes for the advent of the Messiah had been discredited. Moreover, the Jews of these regions were living in contact with Russian refugees, *Raskolniki*, in fact, and possibly People of God, who had fled to Poland after their excommunication.[44] All of these factors lay in the immediate background of the work of the Baal Shem Tov and the rise of Hasidism.

The founder of Hasidism was a Jewish miracle worker from Podolia (now in the western Ukraine, but then in southeastern Poland) named Israel ben Eliezer, who was born in 1700.[45] He came to be called the *Baal Shem Tov*, "Master of the Good Name" (or possibly, "Good Master of the Name"). Sometimes an acrostic is formed of the initials for these words, and he is called the "Besht." The term *baal shem* had been used in Polish Judaism to describe a wandering teacher who performed cures and other miracles.[46] Described as an *am haarets*, a peasant (literally "a person of the land"; it also denotes an uneducated person), the Besht married the daughter of a prominent rabbi, held a number of odd positions (school assistant, janitor in a synagogue, lime digger, and tavern keeper), and was said to have studied Scripture, Talmud, and Kabbala in secret.[47]

It was after the Besht's thirty-sixth birthday that he took up a career as an itinerant wonder worker (that is what *baal shem* denoted), and for the next decade or so built a reputation among the common people for his cures, which he worked utilizing odd combinations of remedies and herbs, coupled with meditative prayer. His enthusiasm and fervor were spectacular:

> Rabbi Abraham was reciting Shaharith before the ark, and the Besht was praying in his usual place. It was his custom to pray before the ark beginning with the Hallel. During the voiced eighteen benedictions, the Besht trembled greatly as he always did while praying. Everyone who looked at the Besht while he was praying noticed this trembling. When Rabbi Abraham finished the repetition of the prayer, the Besht was still standing at his place and he did not go to the ark. Rabbi Wolf Kotses, the Hasid, looked at his face. He saw that it was burning like a torch. The Besht's eyes were bulging and fixed straight ahead like those of someone dying, God forbid.
>
> Rabbi Ze'ev motioned to Rabbi Abraham and each gave his hand to the Besht and led him to the ark. He went with them and stood before the ark. He trembled for a long time and they had to postpone the reading of the Torah until he stopped trembling.[48]

The Besht was also renowned for his alms giving to the poor, and for his clairvoyant gifts.[49]

In the 1740s, the Besht gave up his career as an itinerant wonder worker, settled in the town of Medzibozh in Podolia, and began to attract a circle of better-educated persons around himself. He remained there for the rest of his life (he died in 1760), except for some journeys to visit other leaders of his movement. He seems to have given up the spectacular miracle working that characterized his earlier life, but continued to have ecstatic visions, which his followers recorded. He advocated his views in private homes and in the *bet hamidrash*, the local house for Talmudic study.

The Baal Shem Tov maintained the traditional Jewish stress on following God's Law (Torah) as expressed in the Hebrew Scriptures and as interpreted by the Talmud. His doctrine also utilized traditions of Jewish mysticism, especially Kabbalistic teaching, a set of mystical interpretations of the Torah involving speculation on the descent of the powers of God, the use of the Hebrew letters as secret symbols, and the path of disciplined meditation. In each case, however, the Besht popularized the older Jewish traditions.[50]

The Besht popularized the legalistic tradition by moving the focus of religious life from the careful study of, and commentary on, the Talmud, to the practice of the religious life, and especially to the fervor and devotion of the religious adherent. There is considerable disagreement as to his own abilities as a scholar of the Talmud: his

his opponents represented him as an ignorant charlatan, and accused the Hasidim of contempt for traditional scholars.[51] In any case, it is clear that for the Besht, the *study* of Torah and Talmud was not the focus of religious life:

> The soul once told the Baal Shem that sublime things had been revealed to him not because he had studied much the Talmud and its commentaries, but on account of his praying. Because he always prayed with great fervor, he was found worthy of high estate.[52]

It may be recalled that traditions about the Besht represent him as learning the Talmud and Kabbala in secret. Stories about the Baal Shem Tov consistently represent him as confounding the wisdom of local rabbis. Given this attitude toward Torah and Talmud, it is possible to understand how the Besht excited not only a popular following, but also considerable opposition from more conventional rabbinic circles: his opponents *(Mitnaggedim)* saw him as overturning the traditional basis of Jewish life in his stress on the priority of faith and devotion over the long tradition of written and oral interpretation of the Torah.[53]

The Besht also popularized Jewish mysticism. Rejecting the asceticism of traditional mystics (and of his own early life), he summarized his teaching in these terms:

> I am come into the world to show a new way. Let man strive for three things: love for God, love for Israel, and love for the Torah. And self-mortification is unnecessary.[54]

To Hasidism the Besht bequeathed his belief that even the smallest, commonest acts of life could be hallowed by devotion.

Consistent with his rejection of extreme asceticism, the Besht stressed joy, even ecstasy *(hitlahavut)*, as being at the center of Jewish religious life. He himself reported visions, especially on Holy Days, and he encouraged his followers to sing songs and engage in dances (here perhaps reflecting the influence of the People of God or other radical Christian sects) in which they could attain to ecstasy. His followers reported seeing light and fire exuding from him while he was in ecstatic states.

The term used consistently by the Baal Shem Tov and other Hasidic leaders to describe the ideal of the human relationship to God was *devekut*, "adhesion" or "cleaving." Again, his teaching on *devekut* shows how he had popularized the Talmudic and Kabbalistic traditions:

Devaykuth is the element of mystery in the Torah. The mystery is not
Cabala, as some seem to think. For all the books of Cabala stand open
to the reader, and he who does not understand them might just as well
call the Written and Oral Law a mystery. No, the mystery lies in
devaykuth.[55]

For the Besht, then, the essence of religious life lay not in orthodox
opinions or practices (though he did not oppose them), nor in ascetic
rigor coupled with mystical meditation; the essence of religious life,
for him, lay in *devekut*, the affective devotion of the human soul towards the God of Israel. Later Hasidic teachers would inculcate the
ideal of constant *devekut*, adhesion to God in every aspect on life.[56]
Devekut was for the Hasidim the fulfillment of the Great Commandment given to Israel and recited in the *Shema:* "You shall love the
Lord your God with all your heart . . ."

After the death of the Baal Shem Tov in 1760, the leadership of
the movement passed from him to Dov Baer of Mezeritch (1760–
1772), also called the *Maggid*, or "Preacher." Baer was a recognized
Jewish leader, and it was he who gave the Hasidic movement its earliest institutional forms. He moved the center of the movement, in
the first place, to Mezeritch in Volhynia, closer to central Poland.
During the period of his leadership, Hasidism spread throughout central, southern, and eastern Poland, and a number of teachers and rabbis were attracted to the movement. He also had to combat staunch
opposition to the movement (the *Mitnaggedim*, "Opponents") which
developed in tandem with its popularity. Shortly before his death, he
was pronounced excommunicate by one synagogue.

After the death of the Maggid in 1772, no single leader emerged
to guide the whole Hasidic movement, but a number of individuals,
zaddikim ("righteous ones"), assumed the guidance of particular
groups of Hasidim. The *zaddikim* patterned themselves after the
Besht and the Maggid, and were understood as divine-human inter-
mediaries, endowed with unusual *devekut*, who were capable of ascent
to the divine (and to the Messiah in Heaven), redeeming sinners by
the sinners' adhesion to the *zaddik* and altering the material world by
performing miracles and healings. The traditional rabbinical office
was utilized in the Hasidic communities, but their rabbis were devotees of the *zaddik* of the community. Thus, if the earliest Hasidim
had challenged the elite hierarchies of rabbis and Kabbalistic adepts,
the *zaddikim* formed a new, spiritual elite for their movement, and
throughout the nineteenth century the Hasidic *zaddikim* would struggle with conventional rabbis for leadership of Central and Eastern
European Jewry.[57] It has been estimated that the Hasidim numbered

a few thousand when the Besht died, hundreds of thousands after the death of the Maggid, and millions by the end of the nineteenth century.[58]

*   *   *

Although John Wesley was fascinated by early Eastern Christianity (represented by "Macarius"), one can argue that Hasidism provides a closer parallel to the Evangelical Revival than any of the Russian movements considered above. The Besht was born in 1700, John Wesley in 1703. In 1736, at the age of 36, the Besht began his ministry of itinerant teaching and healing. In 1739, at the age of 36, John Wesley began his ministry of itinerant preaching. The fact that both took up their itinerant ministries at this age is probably no coincidence: the mid-thirties are apt to be the point when a young woman's or young man's youthful optimism gives way to a more mature self-understanding, and it is an apt time for experiences of religious vocation. Still, the parallels are striking. The Besht carefully trained his disciples to avoid the "alien thoughts" that could distract a believer during prayer; Wesley's sermon on "Wandering Thoughts" (1762) carefully analyzes stray thoughts to determine which are occasioned by sin and which are not. At times, descriptions of the Besht seem to replicate those of the Evangelical preachers (though perhaps more of Howell Harris than of John Wesley):

> Before the commencement of the service, he preached to the multitude, urging them once more to repent; he wept, laid his head upon the pulpit, groaned and uttered loud wails.[59]

As George Whitefield put his hearers in tears by his pronunciation of "Mesopotamia" (so reported, at least), so the Besht struck awe into the people with the fervor of his recitation of the Hallel.

The point has already been made, at several different junctures, that parallels in forms of religious life do not imply essential likeness: just as the Jansenists differed widely from the English Puritans, but paralleled their moves towards affective devotion, so the relationship between the Evangelical preachers of England and Wales and the early Hasidim of Poland is strictly a parallel. They differed in language, cultural traditions, influences, and most critically, they differed in their conceptions of ultimate or religious values; to put it somewhat differently, they differed in the objects of their worship. Even if there were some influences of Christian sectarianism on early Hasidic leaders, they are not obvious, and they were probably indirect.

The parallels, then, and not direct influences, are most striking, and they lie in the simultaneous movement on the part of each of these movements towards a form of religious life that stressed an experience of the divine available to all; not just to the ascetic elite, but to the Kingswood colliers, or the *amei haarets* of Poland, to England recovering from its Revolution and the religious millenarianism it brought, and to Polish Jewry recovering from the "Deluge" and the false messianism of Sabbatai Tsevi. What John Walsh has written of early Evangelicalism could be equally applied to the religion of the heart movements throughout Europe. Their history

. . . shows how men faced by similar intellectual or spiritual crises can, in isolation from each other, pass through a strikingly similar odyssey towards similar conclusions.[60]

Chapter Seven

Conclusion

A Moravian synod meeting in 1740, at the time when English Moravians had come into conflict with Anglican Evangelicals, identified itself with a broad religious movement throughout Europe, specifically naming

> . . . those zealous servants of God, who, in Germany, by some were called Pietists, in England, Methodists, in France, Jansenists, in Italy and Spain, Quietists, in the Roman Church in general often known by the character of preacher of repentance and ascetics, but in the Protestant Church generally thought Mystics. . . .[1]

The Moravians' extraordinary ecumenical spirit placed them in a unique position in their age to see the similarities between these movements, and although the synod went on to distinguish the Moravian witness from (or within) the other groups mentioned, they understood "Pietist," "Methodist," "Jansenist," "Quietist," and others as but different names for the same religious movement that had spread through the continent. This claim may be laid beside Wesley's *Christian Library* as evidence that even in the eighteenth century the "religion of the heart" movements were understood as kindred religious forces in quite different cultural contexts.

By the last decade of the eighteenth century, however, the religion of the heart movements were in a state of flux: some were dying out, and others were assuming more lasting institutional forms that would carry them into the nineteenth century. The French Revolution had rendered Jansenism passé, although a small Jansenist Church continued in Holland. All the major leaders of Quietism were long since dead, and no new figures had arisen to take up the claims of Molinos, Guyon, and Fénelon. Devotion to the sacred heart of Jesus continued to be popular, a Mass celebrating it having been officially sanctioned by the Vatican in 1765, and it would grow in prominence through the nineteenth century.

By the time of the French Revolution, all the early leaders of Pietism (and of the Moravians) had died, but by that time Pietism had become a dominant form of religious life in most of the German Protestant Churches, Lutheran and Reformed, and a dominant intellectual force in the German universities. With its secure bases in Prussia and Württemberg, Pietism had given rise to some colorful offspring by the end of the eighteenth century: the pietistic mysticism of Gerhard Tersteegen and other "radical" Pietists, the pietistic rationalism of Christian Wolff, and the intensely emotional (and antirational) secular plays produced by the *Sturm und Drang* literary movement, which Goethe represented.

By the 1790s, British Evangelicalism was more than a half-century old. The first generation of Evangelical leaders had died within two years of the French Revolution. Some Evangelical clergy remained attached to Anglican rectories and vicarages, but many, perhaps most Evangelicals, belonged to movements that were by this time either cleanly separate from the Established Church or rapidly moving towards formal separation. An Evangelical culture was emerging in Britain among a new generation of leaders, a new generation who had not passed through the crucible of Moralism on their way to the Evangelical experience, but who could take that experience as a given.

Although the character of the Russian sects changed little at the end of the eighteenth century, Hasidism was at a crucial turning point, with the Besht and the Maggid both dead, and a new generation of *zaddikim* emerging. Questions of succession in Hasidic communities show that the movement was very much in flux: in most cases, the community's *zaddik* was replaced by a disciple of the old *zaddik* who exhibited exceptional spiritual gifts; in some circles, though, the belief was developing that a *zaddik* is a *zaddik* from birth, and this legitimated the passing of leadership hereditarily to a son of the older *zaddik*.

The religion of the heart movements, then, faced at the end of the eighteenth century the classic problem of how a movement that originated in a concern for personal religious affections and illumination could be reconciled to the social structures necessary to transmit its spiritual impetus to new generations of women and men in new cultural settings. They faced the problem of the "institutionalization" or "routinization of charisma."[2] In the last decade of the eighteenth century and the earliest three or four decades of the nineteenth century, a variety of patterns emerged. It should not go without mention that at the time of the French Revolution a number of new sectarian movements arose, some of which bequeathed to the nineteenth century an array of millenarian, utopian, communistic, and other sects. In other cases, such as those of Pietism, Evangelicalism, and Hasidism, the movements took on new institutional forms. Beyond these, nineteenth-century European culture often reflected the motifs of the religion of the heart movements, sometimes even in secularized belief systems, and so we might perceive the religion of the heart "in dilution" in early nineteenth-century culture. We may now consider each of these options in turn.

Radical Sectarianism

The religion of the heart movements moved along parallel paths away from sacramental, ascetic, and moralistic religious life toward a form of religious life stressing personal encounter with the divine. From the very beginning, this general motion led to the secession of sectarian groups, and at the end of the eighteenth century the process of sectarian division flourished. Not only did the French Revolution inspire revolt against authority, but the very fact of the institutionalization of the religion of the heart movements provoked sectarian reactions within their own ranks.

The radical sectarianism that emerged in the 1790s involved both apocalyptic speculation and claims of personal revelations, and as such the movements were precedented by an earlier period of speculation and prophecying in the eighteenth century. It was in 1706 that a group of French Protestants, called "Camisards," were driven, after an unsuccessful attempt at revolt, from their native country. Some made their way to Halle, where the young Graf von Zinzendorf encountered them, but a significant number made their way to England.

The Camisards, who came to be known in England as "French Prophets," had become convinced in the 1680s by the writings of Pierre Jurieu and others that the prophecies of the Revelation were near to fulfillment; in particular, they believed that the Papacy was soon to be overthrown and Protestantism established in France. Many had given themselves to ecstatic frenzies, and claimed immediate divine inspiration. Their movement had led to political revolt in 1702; it was crushed by 1705, and hence their exodus in the following year. Once in England, however, the prophets continued their speculations on the coming of the Year of Jubilees and the establishment of the Messiah's kingdom, and they continued the tradition of ecstatic prophecying, which attracted considerable public interest. Late in

1707 they predicted that an Englishman, one Dr. Emes, then on his deathbed, would rise from the dead five months later. Huge crowds gathered, but Dr. Emes remained in his tomb in Bunhill Fields cemetery.

Despite their disappointment, the prophets had attracted a number of English followers. One of them, John Lacy, had come into contact with the prophets in 1706. He produced translations of the Camisards' works, and began developing his own circle of prophets. Lacy was committed to Bridewell prison in 1737 on the charge of opening an unregistered "oratory" in London, and was never heard from after his imprisonment, but his community continued, and many of the prophets continued to travel about the countryside, eagerly received by Quakers and others.

In 1747, a group of Quakers in Manchester, who had come into contact with the French prophets, became a separate sect under the leadership of James Wardley. They believed in the immediacy of the second advent of Christ, and stressed ecstatic visions and inspirations. Because of their bodily movements, they were described as "Shaking Quakers." Eleven years later, a Manchester woman named Ann Lee took over the leadership of the group. Ann Lee was capable of remarkable, even spectacular, physical manifestations in her ecstasies: she was reported to have sweated blood during her convulsions. Imprisoned in the 1770s because of her claims to special revelation, Ann emerged with a new teaching.

After 1770 Ann Lee claimed that as Jesus was the "male principle" in Christ, she was the "female principle," the embodiment of the second advent of Christ in the flesh. She taught her disciples to oppose marriage as the "root of depravity," and was again imprisoned for her teachings. In 1774 she left England for North America, where her disciples established "The United Society of Believers in Christ's Second Appearing," known colloquially as the Shakers.

The story of the French Prophets, their English converts, and the lineage through James Wardley to Ann Lee and the Shakers serves to alert us to what some have described as the "underworld" of British religion in the eighteenth century. The story of this underworld is not well known, partly because it is precisely what other Evangelicals would have liked to conceal or at least forget. John Wesley frequently encountered French Prophets and other ecstatic groups, such as the "Jumpers" in Wales, and warned his followers against them: they "bring the real work into contempt," as Wesley put it.[3] But after the American and French Revolutions, these spiritualities flourished again.

The last decade of the eighteenth century saw a resurgence of millennial speculations, directly related to the revolutions. Two books published in the decade have the titles, *Popular Commotions Considered as Signs of the Approaching End of the World*, and *The Present State of Europe Compared with Ancient Prophecies*.[4] These works laid out an understanding of the contemporary events against the background of the prophecies of Daniel and the Revelation, and both foresaw an immediate, second advent of Christ. The same decade saw a resurgence of personal claims to immediate divine inspiration, nowhere more apparent than in the poetic works of William Blake, who claimed frequent visions and illuminations, and conversations with angels and demons. Blake, too, could see the hand of God and the fulfillment of biblical prophecies in contemporary events. He wrote,

> . . . terrors appeared in the Heavens above
> And in Hell beneath, & a mighty & awful change
>   threatened the Earth.
> The American War began. All its dark horrors
>   passed before my face
> Across the Atlantic to France. Then the French Revolution
>   commenc'd in thick clouds,
> And My Angels have told me that seeing such visions
>   I could not subsist on Earth.[5]

Among various millennial movements that emerged in this period, one of the best documented is that of Joanna Southcott. Born in a Devonshire village in 1750, Joanna Southcott joined a Methodist society at age forty-one, in the year of John Wesley's death. A year later, she had a vision in which it was revealed to her that she was "the woman" spoken of in the twelfth chapter of the Revelation. She was rejected by the Wesleyan society, and sought the advice of a Calvinistic Methodist preacher, but soon turned against him. From the middle of the 1790s she was convinced that she should remain within the Church of England: "As high as the Heavens are from the Earth," she wrote, "so high are my Writings from the thoughts, knowledge, and understandings of the Methodists."[6]

She insisted throughout her career, in fact, that her doctrines were in keeping with the teachings of the national Church. Her teachings were distinguished, however, by her millennial views, and her followers expressed their faith in the following terms:

> We believe that there will be a New Heaven, as declared by the Spirit, and a New Earth, wherein dwelleth righteousness. We believe that Man will be created anew in Hart and Life. We believe that there is a Time to come for the millennial World, a Rest for the People of GOD;

that he will come to destroy the works of the Devil, and send his Holy
Spirit up—on the Sons of Men.[7]

Southcott insisted, moreover, on the availability of the Gospel to all,
rejecting with particular vehemence the doctrine of election as setting up a "spiritual aristocracy."[8]

Joanna Southcott began traveling through the country, sharing
her prophecies, and attracting followers. Many of her prophecies were
sealed, not to be opened until later; others were published. Within
her lifetime, she published sixty-five books of prophecy, which were
widely distributed. At one point her book distributor was said to have
on hand £785 of her books.[9]

In 1803, while in Yorkshire, she began the practice of "sealing"
her followers. For a fee (between twelve and twenty-one shillings)
she gave the disciple a slip of paper with an inscription indicating
that they had been sealed unto Christ's second coming. The slip was
then folded and marked with a seal which Joanna had found, and
which bore the initials "I. C." After 1809, when one of her "sealed"
disciples committed a murder, she ceased the practice.

Joanna's disciples included not only persons from the working
classes, but eventually a number of wealthy patrons who had been
convinced by her teaching. William Blake wrote a poem "On the
Virginity of the Virgin Mary & Johanna Southcott," though he was
not himself convinced of the validity of her prophecies.

Among her followers, moreover, Southcott attracted a number of
men and women who became actively employed in preaching themselves. Within her lifetime, "Southcottian" chapels were established.
Many of the preachers were drawn from the ranks of the Wesleyan
Methodists, and they appear to have been organized into circuits following the Methodist pattern. Although some were drawn from the
Church of England, and Joanna originally insisted on baptizing according to the Anglican ritual, she later undertook to celebrate the
eucharist herself, and allowed lay preachers to do so.[10]

In 1814, faced with lagging interest in the movement, Joanna
Southcott unexpectedly announced that the Spirit had revealed to
her that she was to have a son (she was sixty-five years old at the
time). The child was to be named Shiloh, and would usher in the
millennial age. Though Southcott herself did not make the connection, many of her followers were convinced that Shiloh would in fact
be Christ in his second advent. Some followers left the movement,
shocked, but the announcement attracted enormous attention, and
devout disciples began sending a barrage of baby gifts, among them a
crib valued at £200.

Toward the end of 1814 excitement grew. Joanna Southcott was ill, frequently bedridden, and her stomach was growing. She never lost faith in Shiloh's advent, but on Christmas day, she died. An autopsy revealed that the growth of her abdomen was due to an accumulation of fat from her disease. Even still, her followers set a constant watch on her grave, many convinced that she would rise with the child Shiloh in her arms. They sang:

> The glorious Flag of Liberty,
> Which heads all Zion's host;
> Jesus suffered death on Calvery,
> To redeem the world that's lost;
> And Shiloh, he shall reign the King,
> Of everlasting peace;
> When Christ shall reign a thousand years
> All sorrow it shall cease.
>
> God's spirit now does strive again,
> His standard is unfurl'd,
> Joanna's children again shall bid
> Defiance to the world![11]

Joanna Southcott's movement provides an example of a consistent process within the religion of the heart movements, and especially within its more radical expressions: the farther a community is removed from a sacramental focus, the easier it is for subgroups to claim their own inspiration and to separate. We have already noted the plethora of sects that emerged during the English Revolution and during the period following the *Raskol* in Russia. At the same time as Joanna Southcott was leading out her disciples, the Hasidism were dividing into smaller units, each with its own *zaddik* claiming divine inspiration.

Through the nineteenth century, and well into this one, the descendants of the religion of the heart movements continued this process. The "Primitive" (or "Camp Meeting") Methodists separated from the Wesleyans in England in the second decade of the nineteenth century, when the larger Wesleyan Conference decried the practice of Camp Meetings (imported from North America) as improper and tending to mischief. In a similar move, William and Catherine Booth seceded from the Methodist New Connexion in 1865 and eventually formed the Salvation Army. Across the Atlantic at about the same time "Camp Meeting" or "Holiness" Methodists were growing further from their denominational parents, and by the beginning of this century would give rise to Holiness and Pentecostal denominations throughout the world.[12]

There is a certain truth to be conceded, then, in R. A. Knox's diatribe against *Enthusiasm:* "here, I would say, is what happens inevitably, if once the principle of Catholic unity is lost!"[13] The truth is that sacramentalism tends to breed unity, where illuminism tends to breed schism. But, granting this truth, historical understanding cannot simply dismiss the sectarian movements as the products of a general ill will, or of an intentional rejection of "the principle of Catholic unity." There were other, critical factors involved.

It should not go without remark that Ann Lee's disciples, and Joanna Southcott's disciples, and the Primitive Methodists, and the Salvation Army, and the Holiness and Pentecostal sects of late nineteenth-century America (and on and on) spoke for classes of people—if not the abject poor, then the lower middle classes— who scarcely had spokespersons elsewhere. It is sometimes pointed out as an irony that movements (such as the Methodists) who began with an identification with "the poor" (seldom carefully defined) should end up so irremediably middle-class that the poor have to secede from them (as in the Salvationists' secession in 1865). While it may be true that Methodists and others underwent a process of social climbing (*embourgeoisement* or "bourgeoisization") during the nineteenth century, this should not obscure the fact that from the very first the religion of the heart movements embraced a fairly wide spectrum of social classes: Blaise Pascal as well as the Jansenist *convulsionnaires,* the Countess of Huntingdon as well as the Kingswood colliers.

If, then, the religion of the heart bore within itself a tendency toward schism, it also offered a kind of power not contingent upon a traditional religious hierarchy (Catholic, Anglican, or Methodist, for that matter). This power was inherent in the self-understanding of the religion of the heart movements: once the center of religious life moved from specific moments in the space-time continuum (sacraments or "mysteries") administered by an established priesthood, and shifted towards the personal experience of redemption or the charismatic exhibition of spiritual gifts, a way was open (not necessitated, just open) for women and laity and common folk—for those traditionally excluded from religious power—to set up a kind of religious anti-structure. When the conflict over religious power was sharp, this anti-structure would take a sectarian form.

The Institutionalization of the Religion of the Heart

Radical sectarianism represents one pole of the religion of the heart movements at the transition from the eighteenth to the nineteenth century. The other pole is the institutionalization of the religion of the heart movements that was in process throughout Britain and the European Continent. Institutionalization took a variety of forms: we have already seen how the Quakers, Labadists, Moravians, and various Evangelical groups had become formally separate religious denominations throughout the seventeenth and eighteenth centuries. The process of denominational formation continued through this period. In other cases, however, institutionalization would take the form of an organized party within an existing denomination (such as the Anglican Evangelicals), or of a hereditary succession within family groups (such as the Hasidim).

The possibility of religious movements formally constituting themselves as religious denominations was raised by the allowance of religious toleration in varying degrees following the English Revolution and the Thirty Years War; it was, thus, a relatively new idea in the eighteenth century. Jansenists could persist as a schismatic church only in the United Provinces, where a greater degree of religious toleration prevailed than in France. In Britain, the Act of Toleration of 1689 had specified the steps necessary for the constitution of a tolerated 'Dissenting' denomination: in particular, a deed had to be registered naming a specific place of worship, and stating that the group was not Catholic. At the beginning of toleration in Britain, the Dissenting denominations included Presbyterians, Congregationalists, Baptists, and Quakers. By the end of the eighteenth century, though, they included the "Whitefield Methodists," the Countess of Huntingdon's chapels, the Wesleyan Methodists, and a host of smaller Evangelical denominations (in the strict sense, a denomination could be a single, registered chapel). These were joined in 1811 with the official registration of the Calvinistic Methodist Church of Wales.

The point at which a particular group ceased to be a movement within the Church of England and started to be a separate denomination, however, was not obvious, despite the overt action required in registering a chapel. By the time of John Wesley's death in 1791, the Methodist people "in connexion" with him had their own ordained ministers, their own places of worship which had been registered according to the Act of Toleration, and were conducting religious services, sometimes the Lord's Supper, at the same time as neighboring Anglican parishes. In spite of all of this, Wesley protested until the end that he had never "dissented" from the Church of England in doctrine or practice.[14] It was not until 1795, four years after Wesley's death—and eleven years after he formally registered his chapels—that the Wesleyan Conference acknowledged itself to be a separate denomination.

It can be argued that the United Provinces and Britain were exceptional in allowing denominations to be formed: the only parallel cases would be European sectarian movements like the Labadists or Russian sects, or the highly unusual case of the Moravians (unusual because of its link with the pre-Reformation *Unitas Fratrum*). Toleration, then, had afforded British and Dutch society in the eighteenth century the exceptional privilege of being able, under controlled circumstances, to form independent denominations, and this allowed the religion of the heart movements there to form a structure that would enable them to carry on their lives into the nineteenth and twentieth centuries.

In Britain, another mode of institutionalization emerged, in addition to the Evangelical denominations, and that was the development of continuing institutions among the Evangelical party of clergy and laity within the national Church. This party (or "cause," as they might prefer to be called), in contrast to the sectarian movements, displayed clear signs of social and cultural conservatism and shows how the religion of the heart might become an entrenched part of the cultural *status quo*. The same events, especially the French Revolution, that stimulated radical political thought and radical religious expressions in late eighteenth-century England also stimulated a conservative response. In 1790 Edmund Burke published his *Reflections on the Revolution in France*, denouncing the revolutionaries and warning his nation against their excesses. Parliamentary leaders became concerned about the threats to England. In 1795 they passed stronger Sedition and Treason Acts than had been in place before, and in 1799 they passed a Combination Act, forbidding the "combination" of working people in clubs and societies. The Combination Act would be used to suppress the nascent movement towards Trades Unions, and also lay in the background of the suppression of Primitive Methodist Camp Meetings.

The same decade saw the rise to prominence of a new group of Evangelicals, committed to the Established Church and to the stability of the political state. But this new coalition of Anglican Evangelicals represented, in many respects, a continuation of the tradition of those Evangelical clergy who had elected to remain in parishes within the national Church, rather than joining the Wesleyans, the Countess of Huntingdon's Connexion, or any of the other independent denominations that had arisen in the last half century.[15]

John Newton (1725–1807) provides an example of a transitional figure from the old to the new Evangelicalism. Newton was converted in 1748 while serving in the British navy. He made the acquaintance of George Whitefield, and took up an Anglican-Calvinistic theology similar to that of Whitefield's circle. He studied ancient languages, and was ordained and appointed to the curacy of Olney in Buckinghamshire in 1764. While at Olney, he developed his talent for hymn composition, and with the poet William Cowper produced *The Olney Hymns* (1779). Newton wrote a number of the hymns himself, including one which was to become a hallmark of the Evangelical tradition:

> Amazing grace! How sweet the sound
> That saved a wretch like me!
> I once was lost, but now am found;
> was blind, but now I see.[16]

And Cowper's contributions also influenced the movement:

> There is a fountain filled with blood
> drawn from Immanuel's veins;
> and sinners plunged beneath that flood
> lose all their guilty stains.[17]

In the 1790s a new generation of Anglican Evangelicals rallied around the parish of Clapham, south of London, and so were dubbed, by a later historian, "the Clapham Sect." John Venn, installed as the rector of Clapham in 1792, was the son of Henry Venn, who himself had been an associate of both George Whitefield and John Wesley. John Venn held the incumbency of Clapham for nearly twenty years (until 1813), and attracted a number of prominent clergy and laity there. The members of the "Clapham Sect," like John Venn himself, tended to be well-educated, middle-class, second-generation Evangelicals. They also included representatives of the upper classes, such as Lord Teignmouth, and eventually influential Members of Parliament identified with the group.

Perhaps the best-known member of the Clapham circle was William Wilberforce, who provides a kind of case study in the interests of these Evangelicals. Wilberforce (1759–1833) had become a Member of Parliament in 1780, and four or five years later, as a result of his study in the New Testament, had a conversion experience and identified himself with the Evangelical cause. Although he considered ordination, John Newton discouraged him from this move, arguing that his position as a Member of Parliament could be used to great advantage by the Evangelical cause. Wilberforce befriended John Wesley, who encouraged his efforts, already underway by 1791, to abolish the slave trade, and eventually the institution of slavery.

Wilberforce settled in Clapham in 1797, and in the same year published *A Practical View of the Prevailing Religious System of Professed*

William Wilberforce

Engraving by J. Jenkins after a portrait (1833) by George Richmond (1809–1896); used with permission of the Special Collections Department, Duke University Library.

Christians, in the Higher and Middle Classes in this Country, Contrasted with Real Christianity. The book focuses on the need for a stricter morality. It is interspersed with quotations from Adam Smith, and argues, among other things, that a revival of moral rigor would be to the best advantage of the political state. Such a revival would, Wilberforce insisted, encourage persons to pursue the duties appropriate to their "station" in society, and so would result in political stability:

> If any country were indeed filled with men, each thus diligently discharging the duties of his own station without breaking in upon the rights of others, but on the contrary endeavouring, so far as he might be able, to forward their views, and promote their happiness; all would be active and harmonious in the goodly frame of human society. There would be no jarrings, no discord. The whole machine of civil life would work without obstruction or disorder, and the course of its movements would be like the harmony of the spheres.[18]

Wilberforce's Christianity was no retreat to Anglican Moralism: he counseled earnest seekers to respond to the grace they found, so that the Christian life should be a joyful response to God's work. But by his time the Evangelical experience was no longer a surprising discovery on the part of a few individuals struggling against the burden of Moralism; his was an evangelical experience generalized to the point that it could serve as a basis for a cultural tradition. The ethos of Victorian England was present, *in nugo* in Wilberforce's proposals.[19]

The religious program sponsored by the Clapham group led to specific benevolent undertakings. The group developed Sunday Schools for poorer children in Anglican parishes. They were critically involved in the struggle to abolish slavery. Wilberforce agitated throughout his adult life for the abolition of the slave trade, and of the institution of slavery itself. Other members of the Clapham Sect, such as Zachary Macaulay, supported the founding of Sierra Leone in West Africa as a haven for freed African slaves.

The group was also involved in the thrust for missionary activity in this period. With Newton and others, they aided in the foundation of the Church Missionary Society ("CMS," 1798), formed in direct response to the London Missionary Society, which was almost entirely composed of Dissenting groups. In 1803 they cooperated with some of the dissenting groups in the founding of the London and Foreign Bible Society ("LFBS"), which had as its goal the translation and distribution of the Bible in foreign countries in support of the missionary enterprise.

The Clapham group also engaged in the publication of popular tracts and other literature. Their tracts encouraged their religious and benevolent program, and could be utilized as reading material in their Sunday Schools. Somewhat more sophisticated literature came from the writer Hannah More, an acquaintance of Samuel Johnson who had been converted under the influence of Evangelicals and had taken John Newton as her spiritual adviser. More joined the Clapham community after moving to the London area in 1802. Her literary productions included plays and novels, as well as religious tracts.

By the beginning of the nineteenth century, the Clapham Sect had influenced English society and the English Church in each of these enterprises. But the flourishing of Anglican Evangelicalism in the early decades of that century resulted from another innovation from a member of the Clapham circle. Charles Simeon (1759–1836) was a clergyman of the Church of England who had met both Henry and John Venn, and was in sympathy with their views. He had been a co-founder of both the CMS and the LFBS with the Clapham group. Simeon began using his wealth, and encouraged other Anglican Evangelicals to use whatever resources they had, to purchase the "livings" of Anglican parishes (that is, to purchase the right to control what vicars were appointed to certain parishes). In this manner, Simeon and his associates were able to utilize a medieval Catholic institution to see to it that Evangelical clergy were appointed to the parishes they controlled. His work resulted in the formation of the Simeon Trustees, which took responsibility for the screening of incumbents for the parishes controlled in this manner.

In Britain, then, the religion of the heart was institutionalized in the form of denominations registered according to the Act of Toleration, and as the Evangelical cause that remained within the Church of England and which had to rely upon informal links (such as the circle of friends at Clapham) or on structures beyond those of the Established Church, such as the Simeon Trustees, which could influence the appointment of vicars to Anglican parishes. In addition to both of these, there remained the institutional (or perhaps "anti-institutional") structures of the sectarian groups that had multiplied after the French Revolution.

The institutionalization of Pietism had to follow a different course. On the one hand, there was not the same degree of toleration for dissenting denominations in the German states that the Act of 1689 had allowed in Britain; on the other hand, Pietism had forged a more powerful presence among the upper middle classes, the clergy, and the universities than had been the case with British Evangelicalism.

As a consequence, Pietism did not produce independent denominations as Evangelicalism had done (except in the case of the Moravians), and its powerful influence throughout the German states at the beginning of the eighteenth century made it more susceptible to influence by other cultural movements (such as rationalism) than Evangelicalism had been.

The influence of Pietism on the Protestant theological faculties of Europe is striking, especially when compared with the Evangelical Revival in England. Although Wesley remained a fellow of Lincoln College, Oxford, through 1751 (when his marriage forced him to resign his fellowship), he did not teach there after 1735, and Evangelicalism had few advocates in the British universities through the earliest decades of the nineteenth century. Pietism, by contrast, had been a university movement since its earliest decades, with the work of Francke at Halle University, and the presence of Bengel and others at Tübingen. Older Protestant universities such as Marburg, Jena, and Königsberg also saw the advent of Pietist faculty and conventicles during the eighteenth century.

Pietism's place in the universities opened the way for rationalism—the distinctively European version of the Enlightenment—to meld with it from the middle of the eighteenth century. The German Reformed Pietist Friedrich Adolph Lampe (1683–1729), who ended his career teaching at the University of Utrecht, had already produced an influential systematic theology that utilized the analytical methods of Cocceius. Marking a clear synthesis between Pietism and Enlightenment thought was Christian Wolff (1679–1754), a Halle teacher influenced both by Halle's Pietism and also by the philosophy of G. W. Leibniz. Wolff was expelled from Halle in 1723 for his rationalism and spent the next seventeen years in Marburg, but was invited to return to Halle in 1740. From this time, a rationalistic Pietism (sometimes described as "Neo-Pietism") was a prominent theological option in the Dutch and German universities, and lay in the background of the nineteenth-century development of Protestant Liberalism.

Pietism's ecumenical outlook influenced the Prussian state's eventual union of Reformed (Calvinistic) and "Evangelical" (in this case, the term means "Lutheran") Churches early in the nineteenth century. It was, after all, the Hanseatic coast of Prussia where Reformed Pietism had flourished late in the seventeenth century, and it was the state of Brandenburg-Prussia which had supported the development of Halle University and Pietism in the days of August Hermann Francke. The Prussian King Friedrich Wilhelm III, urged by a number of progressive theologians, proposed a Union of the Churches in 1817 to commemorate the three-hundredth anniversary of the Protestant Reformation. This proposal provoked a vociferous rebuttal from more conservative (anti-rationalist and anti-Pietist) Lutheran theologians, and the 1817 plan failed. In June of 1830, though, Friedrich Wilhelm forced the Union by royal decree. It was a high moment for Pietist ecumenism; but it was also a moment when new and very different religious forces surfaced.

In the German-speaking Protestant states, then, Pietism was institutionalized in at least two ways. The first was the continuing existence of pietistic conventicles (*collegia pietatis*) that functioned in parishes well into the nineteenth century. In Württemberg, in fact, the conventicles became a regularly organized feature of the state (we should perhaps say, regional) church. The second form that institutionalization took was in the Prussian state's advocacy of Pietism: in this case, we might, say, pietistic Lutheranism actually *became* the state religion, and the Union of Reformed and Evangelical Churches in Prussia symbolizes the ascendancy of Pietism there. It was, in a sense, a pyrrhic victory, since it opened the way for Pietism, as a theological school, to be overshadowed by other schools in the next decades; but at least at the very beginning, it was understood as a victory for the Pietist cause.

None of the precedents for institutionalization we have seen so far—the formation of independent denominations, an organized "party" within the national Church, or an ascendancy as the predominant school within the national Church—could work for Hasidism. The Hasidim at the beginning of the nineteenth century might well be described as a congeries of sects (and there remained some eccentric Hasidic sects into the nineteenth century), but a parallel with Eastern or Western Christian sects breaks down, since the Hasidim had brought within their circles most of the elements of traditional Judaism, including traditional liturgical observances and Talmudic learning. Through the early decades of the nineteenth century, however, patterns of leadership among the Hasidic groups of Central Europe began to shift, from the charismatic pattern predominant in an earlier period of passing leadership to a disciple of the old *zaddik*, to the pattern of passing leadership to a son (typically the oldest son) of the old *zaddik*. This process was not uniform: charismatic leadership persisted in some circles, with revolts against the older *zaddik*, and in some cases the designated hereditary *zaddik* was rejected in favor of a brother or uncle thought to be more gifted. By the 1830s, however, hereditary leadership had become the norm in the Hasidic communities.[20]

The hereditary principle enabled the Hasidic communities— which had by this time spread to central Poland, Hungary, Belorussia, Lithuania, and the Ukraine—to settle into dynastic family groups, typically associated with a particular town where a *zaddik* (or *Rebbe*) presided. Even within the bounds of these family groups there was considerable diversity. The Hasidic dynasty of Lubavich (in Belorussia) developed a distinctive intellectual tradition, blending Kabbalistic learning with Hasidism. By contrast, the somewhat later dynasty of Bratslav (in the Ukraine) was founded by a Rebbe who wished to return to the more charismatic styles of the Besht and earlier Hasidism.[21] This diversity should alert us to the fact that after the time of the Besht and the Maggid, there was no center of unity for the Hasidic movement: dynasties such as the Lubavichers or the Bratslav Hasidim were self-contained, with devotion to their Rebbe and their own community the bonds that united them together. The Hasidim existed (and continued to exist) as separate communities united only by the common historical tradition of their origins with the Besht and the Maggid.

By the early decades of the nineteenth century, then, the religion of the heart movements of Europe had become part of the whole fabric of Western religious life, an established and institutionalized part of Western culture. Papal approval of a mass celebrating devotion to the sacred heart of Jesus (later to be elevated to a feast observed throughout Catholicism) had given a lasting form to Baroque Catholicism's affective devotion. Pietism, already tinged with Enlightenment rationalism, remained a formidable theological option in the German states, where conventicles transmitted the movement's religious genius to new generations of laity. Evangelicalism lived in the Wesleyan and Calvinistic Methodist denominations of England and Wales, and in the benevolent work of the Anglican Evangelical party. It had extended its influence to the older Dissenting Protestant Churches of England (Presbyterians, Congregationalists, and Baptists) who had been little influenced by the revival in its early years, but who by the beginning of the nineteenth century had been revitalized by the Evangelical tradition of itinerant preaching.[22] The Hasidic family circles of Central Europe (and soon of Palestine and America), were settled into a pattern of hereditary leadership in family dynasties. And just below the relatively calm surface of these institutional forms ran the turbulent and ever-changing flow of Evangelical, Pietistic, Eastern Christian, and Jewish sectarian movements.

The Religion of the Heart in Dilution

By the time the religion of the heart movements had found stable institutional forms early in the nineteenth century, significant changes were underway in European Christian and Jewish cultures. In the German states, the influence of the Enlightenment had already been felt by Neo-Pietists such as Christian Wolff, and this influence would soon lead to Liberalism. One of the most active advocates of the Prussian Church Union of 1817, in fact, was Friedrich Schleiermacher, widely regarded as the founder of Protestant Liberalism. At the same time, many German Christians found the Romantic stress on emotive experience, and its anti-rationalist bias, attractive. Further, the Church Unions of 1817 and of 1830 had forced the secession of the "Old Lutherans," conservative Lutherans who opposed the Union, Pietism, and the Enlightenment.

Changes were also underway in Britain's religious life. William Wilberforce died in 1833, just months before Parliament finally abolished slavery, and Charles Simeon died in 1836. But just over a decade after their deaths (in 1848) an Evangelical was elected Archbishop of Canterbury. It was the high watermark for Anglican Evangelicalism; but already the signs of change were apparent. A Unitarian Church had been registered according to the Act of Toleration in 1773, and Unitarianism attracted converts among the educated classes through the early decades of the nineteenth century. In the same year as Wilberforce died, moreover, John Henry Newman published the first of the "Tracts for the Times," in defense of apostolic succession, and by the time the Evangelical John Bird Sumner became Archbishop of Canterbury, the Oxford Movement, a kind of English parallel to the Old Lutheranism, was well underway.[23]

Typically, then, the religion of the heart movements early in the nineteenth century faced opposition or resistance from two different sides: on the one hand was the pervasive influence of the Enlightenment (represented in English Unitarianism, in German Liberal Protestantism, and in the *Haskalah*, the European Jewish Enlightenment), and on the other hand were a range of conservative reactions against the Enlightenment, which often blamed the religion of the heart movements for doctrinal laxity, and might even accuse them of having opened the way for the Enlightenment (these conservative reactions included the Oxford Movement, the Old Lutherans, and the continuing presence of the *Mitnaggedim*, Hasidism's rabbinical orthodox opponents). Despite the tension, however, the religion of the heart movements began to interact with broader cultural trends in the nineteenth century. One might say that certain stresses of the religion of the heart movement pervaded Western culture, and so were diluted into the mixture of European cultural traditions.

Friedrich Schleiermacher, whose systematic study of *The Christian Faith* paved the way for the Prussian Church Union, reflected the influence of the religion of the heart on early Protestant Liberalism. Schleiermacher's parents were converts to Moravianism, and he was trained originally at a Moravian seminary, then at Halle University after he converted to the German Reformed Church. In Halle he encountered the tradition of Neo-Pietism that Christian Wolff had initiated. In his attempt to give a universal basis for religious claims, Schleiermacher insisted that there is a "feeling of absolute dependence" experienced by all human beings, which is the ground of all religion and morality.[24] Building on this basis in the religious affections experienced by all human beings, Schleiermacher developed his entire theological system. True to his Pietist roots, then, Schleiermacher began with religious experience; but his was a universalized religious experience, not the particular experiences of repentance and assurance prized in the older Pietist tradition. Despite a vociferous reaction against Pietism on the part of later Liberals (such as Albrecht Ritschl), Protestant Liberalism continued to follow Schleiermacher in stressing religious experience as the empirical grounds for its religious claims.

Schleiermacher stood at a threshold: he has been called the executor of Pietism's last will and testament as well as the founder of Protestant Liberalism; he has also been identified by some as a religious exponent of Romanticism. Reacting against the classical formality and rationality of the eighteenth century, Romanticism celebrated human emotion and imagination. Pietism had already influenced the German literature of the *Sturm und Drang* ("Storm and Stress") school, a late eighteenth-century precursor of Romanticism. In the Romantic literature of the nineteenth century, the religion of the heart's concern with the experience of the supernatural appears, again in a diluted or universalized fashion, from Friedrich von Schiller's "Ode to Joy" (the text used by Beethoven in the finale of the Ninth Symphony) to Wordsworth's almost pantheistic sense of the omnipresence of God. Romanticism also expressed the darker side of religious experience: one can perceive, even in the antirational torment of Kierkegaard, a lingering impression of Pietism's "repentance-struggle" (*Busskampf*).

Similar influences appeared in Eastern European literature. If *Busskampf* can be sensed in Kierkegaard's writings, how much more so in the work of Feodor Dostoevsky, in whose novels religious emotion plays a guiding role, and whose vehement rejection of the institutional Church is reminiscent of the Russian sectarian movements. The eccentric religious genius of the Russian sectarian movements found an explicit literary expression in the work of Leo Tolstoy (1828–1910), who in 1876/1877 began to conceive of the ideal of Christian love as complete self-giving. Very much like the *Bezpopovtsy*, cut off from the mysteries of the Church (Tolstoy himself was excommunicated in 1901), the heroes of Tolstoy's later works exhibited the purely spiritual values of compassion and self-sacrifice. Not surprisingly, Tolstoy ardently defended the cause of the oppressed *Doukhobors*, making them the subject of his last novel, *Resurrection* (1899).

It was only in the middle of the twentieth century that Hasidism came to be appreciated both for its literary and religious contributions—perhaps because of the relative isolation of the Hasidic families, or because of the continuing prejudices of the *Maskilim* (Jewish advocates of the Enlightenment). The Viennese theologian Martin Buber (1878–1965), who was persecuted by the Third Reich and forced to immigrate to Palestine in the 1930s, discovered in early Hasidism a precedent for contemporary religious life, especially in its stress on the sanctification of common life and the accessibility of God to all persons. Hasidic stories (some collected by Buber in his *Tales of the Hasidim*) continue to provide a basis for contemporary Jewish literature, including the stories of Isaac Bashevis Singer.

With Buber and Singer, it is relatively easy to trace the influence of the religion of the heart, since its influence was explicit in their case, and only slightly less so with Tolstoy, who at least in his later years sympathized with the Russian sects. In other cases, though, the traces of the religion of the heart become so diffuse, so diluted that it is not really possible to tell where they leave off and where other influences begin. Who was that well-dressed but unbelieving man following Joanna Southcott and distributing tracts among her followers? It was Robert Owen, a founder of modern socialism who found the millennialist fervor and popular ideas of Southcott's followers a fertile field for his ideas. But were the first trade unions really clones of the *collegia pietatis* or Methodist classes, with "shop stewards" where the Methodists had "class stewards"? And was the Bolshevik Revolution, among the masses, as indebted to Russian Christian sectarianism as it was to the Marxism of its educated leaders? The historian has no instruments to gauge these claims; one can only wonder.

Conclusion

While we are wondering about the farther and more diffuse reaches of the religion of the heart's influence, though, the point should not be missed that its influence in other areas of modern, indeed of global, culture is unmistakable and unavoidable. Members of Hasidic families, and for that matter Methodist or Baptist, Holiness or Pentecostal families, and the latter-day descendants of Quakers and Russian sects, feel its influence in the round of their weekly lives. Jews and Christians outside of these traditions feel its religious power in quieter tones: faithful Catholics observing the solemnity of the sacred heart will be called to affective devotion; Protestants singing the hymns of Joachim Neander or Charles Wesley will sense its warmth. Women and men with no traditional religious commitments will hear its echoes in literature, art, and music, perhaps even in political speeches.

North Americans will sense a particular connectedness with the religion of the heart movements. The Great Awakening of the eighteenth century, powerful force as it was in melding the cultural conscience of North America, was in its origins a distant expression of the Evangelical Revival. In the early American republic, the religion of the heart's stress on individual responsibility before God and its inherent leveling tendencies found fertile ground, and blossomed into a plethora of democratically inclined religious movements, including the Disciples of Christ, the Holiness movement, the first distinctively Afro-American Churches, and even American sects such as the Mormons.[25] We turn, in conclusion, to the religion of the heart movements in their own contexts.

On a clear winter night, through a small telescope, one may see the Pleiades—thousands of small but brilliant stars clustered together, with faint wisps of nebula connecting them. This is how I think of "the religion of the heart" in seventeenth- and eighteenth-century Europe: it was a brilliant cluster of women and men, a cluster of churches, sects, and societies, a cluster of religious movements against a varied background of Christian and Jewish cultures, connected by the nebulous ties of wandering religious teachers, shared books, translated hymns, and popular religious traditions. Its edges—the areas where it seems to blend into ascetic mysticism, older sacramentalism, or moralism—are rather fuzzy, but its center lay in the form of religious life characterized by affective devotion and the possibility of a direct, personal encounter with God.

Simply beholding this cluster at a distance, it hardly seems appropriate to speak of its consistent or general traits: one fears that the brilliance and eccentricities of its members will be lost, or painted over, by generalizations. One is tempted to let these brilliant and eccentric individuals lie still in their unique place in space and time, neither to explain, nor to draw morals from them. But since it is also possible to trace the nebular links or cosmic strings that lace these members together, we may with caution describe some concomitant traits that more or less consistently characterize the religion of the heart movements.

We should note, however, one crucially important matter that was *not* characteristic or constitutive of the Christian and Jewish movements, and that is a consensus about ultimate or religious values. For the Christian religion of the heart movements (with the possible exception of the "People of God" and *Doukhobors*), Jesus Christ was worshiped as God, and in this the movements were consistent with the Orthodox, Catholic, and Protestant understanding of the deity of Christ as a constitutive, Christian claim. Hasidism, for its part, was perfectly clear that the God its adherents worshiped was the one God of Abraham, Isaac, and Jacob, as traditional Judaism had maintained. Despite the accusations of Protestant scholasticism and the *Mitnaggedim*, fundamental religious values were not at stake in the religion of the heart movements. Hasidism, then, was not "fundamentally the same" as the Christian pietistic movements: it was fundamentally different. What *was* distinctly similar in the religion of the heart movements was their parallel manners of *approaching* the religious ultimate, what I have called their forms of religious life.

In the first place, then, among the consistent concomitant traits of these religious movements, we should note what Joseph P. Schultz has called the "religious excitation" that characterized them.[26] Religious excitement does not necessarily follow from affective devotion, but did accompany the religion of the heart movements in many of their expressions. It often provoked their opponents, whose reactions indicate the novelty of these movements in their own time. Whether it was Jansenist *convulsionnaires*, the "Stewarton sickness" of Scottish revivals, the *Schwarmerei* of Lutheran Protestantism, the "enthusiasm" of British Evangelicals, or the epithet "Quaker" hurled at Russian sectarians, the outward manifestations of religious excitation provoked a vociferous reaction from religious establishments. Although moderate advocates of these movements (such as Wesley or

174 The Religion of the Heart

Spener) wished to stifle or at least conceal the more offensive signs of religious excitation, their very defensiveness on the issue should indicate what, in their time, was understood to be culturally offensive: the lurking danger of "enthusiasm" threatening the well-known structures of ecclesiastical, social, and cultural order.

In the second place, it is important to discern two distinct religious options that consistently threatened the religion of the heart movements internally: on the one hand, there was the threat that their members would be drawn into millenarian sects; on the other hand, there was the equally persistent threat that their emphasis on the experience of God would lead members into mystical aberrations, such as Quietism or metaphysical speculation. The Quakers (and other sectarian movements that arose during the English Revolution), the Labadists, the Russian sectarian movements, and then the Southcottians and certain later Evangelical sects show the persistence of the former threat. Perhaps the recent failure of Sabbatai Tsevi prevented Hasidism from spawning millenarian sects. For religious teachers like Johann Albrecht Bengel and John Wesley, who themselves speculated about the date of the second advent of Christ (but dated it comfortably beyond their own deaths), this tendency was avoided only with great difficulty. On the other hand, the Quietists, the Labadists (because of their mystical speculations), the Moravians who advocated the "Stillness" teaching, and the so-called "Radical Pietists" who taught mystical doctrines, all indicate the persistence of the threat of ascetic mystical aberrations. Again, teachers like Wesley and Francke, who advocated the possibility of "Christian perfection" in this life, had to work very hard to distinguish their doctrine (and to discourage their disciples) from the teaching of a metaphysical union with God.

A third rather consistent concomitant of the religion of the heart movements is the fact that (in Knox's words), "the history of enthusiasm is largely a history of female emancipation. . . ."[27] Angélique Arnauld among the Jansenists, Antoinette Bourignon and Jeanne Marie Guyon among the Quietists, Lady Huntingdon, Mary Bosanquet, and a host of others among the English Evangelicals, Ann Lee and Joanna Southcott as leaders of radical sects—the list goes on and on. With the exception of the Jansenist *convulsionnaires* and Joanna Southcott, none claimed the priesthood or ordained ministry; but Angélique Arnauld and Antoinette Bourignon (at least in her days as a Carmelite) transmitted to the seventeenth century the role model of women leaders of religious orders, and Mary Bosanquet and other Evangelical women eventually claimed (with the belated blessing of John Wesley) the "extraordinary" ministry of preaching.

On the one hand, the emergence of women in prominent roles of religious leadership congrues with the rise of the middle classes, if for no other reason than that women's roles in the upper classes and among the peasants were determined by long-standing cultural precedent, whereas the mores of the bourgeoisie were still in flux. On the other hand, the form of religious life centering on affective devotion and personal religious experience was also conducive to the development of women's leadership, precisely because of its distance from the power structures of the sacramental system.[28]

A final concomitant trait to be observed throughout the religion of the heart movements is the manner in which each of them had to compete with the simultaneous development of the Enlightenment. Blaise Pascal lived in both the worlds of Jansenism and nascent experimental science; English Puritans such as William Ames utilized the new philosophy of Ramus, and later Puritans would be influential in the development of British observational science; rationalism and Pietism made their peace early on in the eighteenth century. On the other hand, Whitefield, Wesley, and other Evangelical leaders perceived the threat posed by Deism, and Jewish Enlightenment leaders (*Maskilim*) were one of the two main sources of opposition to the Hasidim.

It is sometimes said that the pietistic movements—Evangelicalism in particular—were not as opposed to the Enlightenment as one might guess from the later polemic between science and religion. One historian of the Evangelical Revival has suggested that the early Evangelicals understood themselves to be "allied with the Enlightenment."[29] This claim, however, relies on a crucial ambiguity in the term "Enlightenment." In a very broad sense, "the Enlightenment" denotes a certain understanding of human nature, stressing rationality, freedom, and scientific inquiry. With this broad definition, one can argue that the Evangelicals, early Pietists, Jansenists and others shared much in common with the Enlightenment. On the other hand, Peter Gay and others take Enlightenment in a somewhat more restricted sense: ostensively, they point to Hume and Voltaire as the paradigms of the Enlightenment, and they make the claim that the Enlightenment implies an explicit rejection of the most distinctive of Christian and Jewish teachings.[30] In this more restricted sense, the Enlightenment and the religion of the heart movements were competing, throughout the seventeenth and eighteenth centuries, for predominance in European culture.

Even so, it is possible to understand the Enlightenment (in either sense) and the religion of the heart movements as nearly simultaneous cultural phenomena. Bacon and Descartes offered the first versions of empiricism and rationalism at the same time as Puritanism and Jansenism were emerging in their respective cultural settings. Locke's philosophy was employed not only by the Deists, but by Jonathan Edwards and John Wesley as well, in their attempts to forge an empirical account of religious experience. Hume and Voltaire flourished in the same period as the Evangelical Revival, Pietism, and Hasidism were in their ascendancy. Perhaps both movements responded, in different ways, to the crisis of understanding and authority that the Reformation and the century of religious warfare following it had raised.

The concomitant traits of the religion of the heart movements described above—the phenomena of religious excitation, the threats posed to them by sectarianism and mysticism, the leadership roles exercised by women in the movements, and their offering of a cultural parallel to the Enlightenment—these do not *define* the religion of the heart movements, they only show some respects in which the similarity in their form of religious life was linked to similarities in other areas. Is it possible, then, to explain why Christian groups of so many different persuasions should turn to the cultivation of affective piety in the seventeenth and eighteenth centuries? Several candidate explanations are often given: pietistic movements may be explained as a reaction against Protestant Scholasticism, as an "internalization" of Christianity following the warfare of Christian states in the seventeenth century, or as an alternative way of knowledge parallel to the empirical epistemologies of the Enlightenment. Each of these has its grain of truth; but each, I am convinced, is but a part of the larger picture of transitions in Western culture which gave rise to the religion of the heart movements.

I would be inclined to explain the rise of the pietistic movements on a larger scale, at least in Western Europe, in the following fashion. The Protestant Reformation had brought about an unprecedented, visible disunity in the fabric of Western European culture. In the century following the Reformation, this disunity became even more visible in overt conflicts between Catholics and Protestants and in inter-Protestant struggles. Scholastic theology in Lutheran and Reformed states, the cult of Christian antiquity among Anglicans and Gallicans, and the appeal to the unbroken tradition of the church for Catholics, each of these functioned to legitimate the ever-widening cultural rifts that by the end of the sixteenth century were breaking out into open warfare. Each of these, however—Protestant Scholasticism, or appeals to Christian antiquity or the continuous tradition of Catholicism—relied on "traditional" authorities, i.e., on the "objective," publicly accessible authorities of the Bible and the traditions of the Christian churches.

By the beginning of the seventeenth century these conflicts were perceived as dysfunctional by many Western Europeans, and by the end of the Thirty Years War and the English Revolution, there was an emerging consensus that the inter-Christian strife had been contrary to the essential spirit of Christian faith. Not surprisingly, some well-educated Europeans rejected traditional authorities altogether and sought a *novum organum*, a surer or better way of knowing. The Enlightenment would arise from their quest for knowledge.

The religion of the heart movements arose simultaneously, I am convinced, among Europeans of widely different confessional traditions who, disgusted with what corporate Christian states had done to each other since the Reformation, and disillusioned with "objective" appeals to scripture and tradition, turned inwardly to a more individualistic and (in a certain sense) "subjective" appropriation of the Christian faith. The quotation from the Moravian synod (at the beginning of this Chapter), and the extent of John Wesley's borrowing from Puritan, pietistic, and Catholic devotional literature in his *Christian Library*, demonstrate that these movements were perceived in the eighteenth century as breathing a certain kindred air despite the vast confessional and cultural differences between them.

* * *

The power that held this unique cluster of men and women, of ideas and movements, together was a fresh way of approach to the religious ultimate, an insistence that "the heart," the human will and the affections, was the crucial link between divinity and humanity, that the way to God was the way of heartfelt devotion. It was a way to God symbolized in the flaming heart held aloft by the ancient bishop of Hippo in Jansen's *Augustinus*, the flaming heart of love that called out to Marguerite Marie Alacoque, the heart of Christ in heaven calling out to sinners on earth proclaimed by Thomas Goodwin, the bleeding, wounded heart of Christ celebrated in Moravian hymns; it was the human heart "strangely warmed" in Wesley's Aldersgate experience, or the heart of a Hasid filled with love for God, for Torah, and for Israel.

The experience of divine love was not, indeed, a universal human experience; after all, it came as a surprise to so many Europeans in the seventeenth and eighteenth centuries. And yet it was an experience paralleled at select moments in human history, not only in the charismatic gifts of first- and second-century Christianity, but also in Shinran Shonen's insistence on the experience of Amida's grace, or the Hindu *bhagavan*'s devotion (*bhakti*) to Krishna or Vishnu. Even beyond the limits of cultural-linguistic systems, "language games," and religious texts, and despite the overt differences in ultimate values (or worship), the religion of the heart's consistent call to affective devotion had been echoed long, long ago and far, far away in the great revelation of the *Bhagavad Gita:*

> Even if a very evil doer
>   Reveres Me with single devotion,
> He must be regarded as righteous in spite of all;
>   For he has the right resolution.[31]

The religion of the heart was a way of reinterpreting in the European and British cultural crises of the seventeenth and eighteenth centuries the Great Commandment given to Israel and taken by Jesus to be the sum of the Law:

> Hear, O Israel: The Lord our God is one Lord; and you shall love the Lord your God with all your heart, and with all your soul, and with all your might (Deuteronomy 6:4).

Notes

Note to Preface

*"St. Luke's Methodist Church," in Rosa Dieu Crenshaw and W. W. Ward, *Cornerstones: A History of Beaumont and Methodism, 1840–1968* (Beaumont, TX: First Methodist Church Historical Committee, 1968), pp. 202–203. Although only my grandfather is credited for the article, my grandmother wrote most of it based on material he had gathered, since he was ill at the time it was due.

Notes to Chapter One

1. The earliest use of the expression of which I am aware is in John Wesley's "Farther Appeal to Men of Reason and Religion, Part II," III:1, "How much more sensible must you be of this if you do not rest on the surface, but inquire into the bottom of religion, the religion of the heart" (in Gerald R. Cragg, ed., *The Appeals to Men of Reason and Religion and Certain Related Open Letters* [Bicentennial Edition of the Works of John Wesley, vol. 11; Oxford: Oxford University Press, 1975], p. 250). The expression seems to have found wider usage, however, in describing various seventeenth and eighteenth century pietistic movements: The *Oxford Dictionary of the Christian Church* refers to Zinzendorf as proclaiming a "religion of the heart" (F. L. Cross and E. A. Livingstone, eds.; Oxford: Oxford University Press, second edition, 1974; s. v. "Zinzendorf") and a contemporary Jewish scholar refers to the Hasidism of eighteenth-century Poland as offering a "religion of the heart" (Bernard D. Weinryb, *The Jews of Poland: A Social and Economic History of the Jewish Community in Poland from 1100 to 1800* [Philadelphia: Jewish Publication Society of America, second edition, 1976], p. 272).
2. New York and Oxford: Oxford University Press.
3. *Ibid.*, pp. v–vi.
4. His work, moreover, is so tainted with overt racism, sexism, and a generally elitist tone, that many contemporary readers can hardly bear to stay with it, despite its brilliant style. In speaking of the Donatist Circumcellions, for example, Knox asked, "can we imagine them, even as natives of that Africa whose remote descendants still furnish the most grotesque examples of American revivalism?" (p. 62); with reference to the women prophets referred to by St. Paul, Knox wrote: "From the Montanist movement onwards, the history of enthusiasm is largely a history of female emancipation, and it is not a reassuring one. Martha Simmonds escorting Nayler into Bristol with cries of Hosanna, Madame Guyon training up her director in the way he should go, the convulsionary priestesses going through the motions of saying Mass at St. Médard—the sturdiest champion of womens' rights will

hardly deny that the unfettered exercise of the prophetic ministry by the more devout sex can threaten the ordinary decencies of ecclesiastical order" (p. 20). Fetters were obviously in order.

5. *Ibid.*, p. 353.

6. Stoeffler, in *The Rise of Evangelical Pietism* (Studies in the History of Religion, no. 9; Leiden: E. J. Brill, 1965), depicts Pietism as arising from "Pietistic Puritanism" (pp. 24–108), Dutch "Precisianism" (pp. 121–62), and northern German Reformed Pietism (pp. 169–79); his "Tradition and Renewal in the Ecclesiology of John Wesley," (in Bernd Jaspert, ed., *Traditio, Krisis, Renovatio als theologischer Sicht: Festschrift Winfried Zeller* [Marburg: Elwert, 1976], pp. 298–316) relates Wesley to continental Pietism; Martin Schmidt, *John Wesley: A Theological Biography* (tr. Norman Goldhawk; Nashville: Abingdon Press, 1963–1973), focuses on the Pietistic influences on the young Wesley (1:138–309); cf. his essay on "Wesley's Place in Church History" (in Kenneth E. Rowe, ed., *The Place of Wesley in the Christian Tradition: Essays Delivered at Drew University in Celebration of the Commencement of the Oxford Edition of the Works of John Wesley* [Metuchen, NJ: The Scarecrow Press, 1976], pp. 67–93); Karl Zehrer, "The Relationship between Pietism in Halle and Early Methodism" (tr. James A. Dwyer; *Methodist History* 17:4 [July 1979]: 211–24; Geoffrey F. Nuttall, "Continental Pietism and the Evangelical Movement in Britain," in J. Van den Berg and J. P. Van Doren, eds., *Pietismus und Reveil: Referate der internationalen Tagung: Der Pietismus in den Niederlanden und seine internationalen Beziehungen* (Leiden: E. J. Brill, 1978), pp. 207–36.

7. Jean Orcibal, "Les Spirituels français et espagnols chez John Wesley et ses Contemporains" (*Revue de l'Histoire des Religions* 139:1 [January–March 1951]: 50–109), and "L'Originalité théologique de John Wesley et les Spiritualités du Continent" (*Revue historique* 222 [1959]: 51–80).

8. Weinryb, pp. 271–73; Joseph P. Schultz, *Judaism and the Gentile Faiths: Comparative Studies in Religion* (Rutherford, NJ: Fairleigh Dickinson University Press, 1981); Alan Lewis Berger, "'Normal' Mysticism and the Social World: A Comparative Study of Quaker and Hasidic Communal Mysticism" (Ph.D. dissertation, Syracuse University, 1976).

9. On recent scholarship on various movements, see the bibliographical notes attached to the first paragraphs of text dealing with the movements. One general (and notable) example of recent publications in English would be the series of *Classics of Western Spirituality* by the Paulist Press.

10. Schultz, p. 250.

11. The methodological approach I follow here is based on that laid out by Frederick J. Streng in *Understanding Religious Life* (Religious Life of Man Series; Wadsworth, CA: Wadsworth Publishing Company, third edition, 1985) and examined further in Streng, Charles L. Lloyd, Jr., and Jay T. Allen, *Ways of Being Religious: Readings for a New Approach to Religion* (Englewood Cliffs, NJ: Prentice-Hall, Inc., 1973). Streng's text on *Understanding Religious Life* (entitled *The Religious Life of Man* in its first edition) is the introductory volume in a series of texts on "The Religious Life of Man" for which he is the editor. Streng's definition of religion as involving "ultimate transformation" is given in *Understanding Religious Life*, pp. 1–9. I have preferred the expression "ultimate values," following the definition laid out by Frederick Ferré in *Basic Modern Philosophy of Religion* (New York: Charles Scribner's Sons, 1967), pp. 30–50, and in his presidential address to the American Academy of Religion on "The Definition of Religion" (*Journal of the American Academy of Religion* 38 [1970]: 3–16). The four categories of religious life laid out below

answer to the "Four Traditional Ways of Being Religious" laid out by Streng (pp. 20–103) and by Streng, Lloyd, and Allen (pp. 23–331).

12. Streng's term for this category is "Creation of Community through Sacred Symbols" (*Understanding Religious Life*, pp. 43–62); cf. Streng, Lloyd, and Allen, whose term is "Creation of Community through Myth and Ritual" (*Ways of Being Religious*, pp. 97–180). I would stress, in comparison with Protestant developments, that the Catholic (and Orthodox) tradition described here placed the emphasis more upon the "ritual" or "sacramental" aspect of this form of religious life than on the "mythical."

13. "Myth" in this respect simply denotes the sacred story (or stories) by which certain religious traditions are constituted; cf. Streng, pp. 49–55.

14. Johann Arndt, *True Christianity*, foreword (in Peter Erb, tr. and ed., *Johann Arndt: True Christianity* [New York, Ramsey, and Toronto: Paulist Press, 1979], p. 23).

15. Streng's category is "Living in Harmony with Cosmic Law" (*Understanding Religious Life*, pp. 63–83); cf. Streng, Lloyd, and Allen, pp. 181–260.

16. Like Luther, Calvin rejected what he perceived as the Pelagianism of the Nominalist theology, and he rejected the casuistry of the *Manuals of Confessors* that had been central for the *Devotio Moderna*. In spite of this, however, he ascribed a prominent role to the community (consistories, congregations and pastors) in disciplining Christians, including an explicit program of rooting out inward and outward sin. Cf. Calvin, *Institutes of the Christian Religion*, 3:3:1–3:4:13 (tr. Ford Lewis Battles; ed. John T. McNeill; Library of Christian Classics, vols. 20 and 21; [Philadelphia: Westminster Press, 1960], 1:592–638).

17. Henricus Denzinger, ed., *Enchiridion Symbolorum, Definitionum, et Declarationum de Rebus Fidei et Morum* (Barcelona: Herder, 32nd edition, 1963), no. 1997 (pp. 443–44); cf. Jean Delumeau, *Catholicism between Luther and Voltaire: A New View of the Counter-Reformation* (London: Burns and Oates, and Philadephia: Westminster Press, 1977), pp. 100–101.

18. Streng, *Understanding Religious Life*, pp. 84–103; Streng, Lloyd, and Allen, pp. 261–331. Scholars of Jewish studies tend to take the broader definition of "mysticism": for them, mysticism denotes a general stress on direct human encounter with God, and in this respect "mysticism" would include both what I have called the "religion of the heart" movements and what Frederick Streng defines as a religious intentionality involving "personal apprehension of a holy presence," and the phenomena of the disciplined meditative life leading up to a mystical union, that is, what I tend to call "mysticism" proper or "ascetic" mysticism: cf. Gershom G. Scholem, *Major Trends in Jewish Mysticism* (New York: Schocken Books, third edition, 1954), pp. 3–4. It is for this reason that scholars in the field of Jewish studies will sometimes distinguish "normal" or "communal" mysticism (more like what I describe as the "religion of the heart") from ascetic or "elitist" mysticism: cf. A. L. Berger, pp. 4–19.

19. Streng, *Understanding Religious Life*, pp. 25–42; Streng, Lloyd, and Allen, pp. 23–95.

20. Cf. Norman Cohn, *The Pursuit of the Millenium: Revolutionary Millenarians and Mystical Anarchists of the Middle Ages* (New York: Oxford University Press, second edition, 1970).

21. On the Thirty Years War, in general, cf. J. V. Polisensky, *War and Society in Europe, 1618–1648* (Cambridge: Cambridge University Press, 1978); on the conventional exaggerations of its effects, see Robert Ergang, *The Myth of the All-Destructive Fury of the Thirty Years' War* (Pocono Pines, PA: The Craftsmen at Pocono Pines, 1956).

22. Polisensky (see above) offers an economic analysis of the conflict, understanding it as a decisive repulsion of the feudal *ancien régime* in Europe. Others have argued that religious, political and economic life were closely bound together in this period, so that religious motives cannot be dismissed: cf. Carl J. Friedrich, *The Age of the Baroque, 1610–1660* (San Francisco: Harper Bros., 1952), pp. 161–63. From a cultural perspective, however, what is most critical is how the conflict was perceived in its own age, namely, as a conflict of Christian doctrinal systems.

23. On the causes of the English Revolution, see Lawrence Stone, *The Causes of the English Revolution, 1529–1642* (New York: Harper and Row, 1972).

24. On the seventeenth century in England, in general, see [John Edward] Christopher Hill, *Century of Revolution, 1603–1714* (Edinburgh: Thomas Nelson and Sons, Ltd., 1961); on the theological and ecclesiastical options, see Henry R. McAdoo, *The Spirit of Anglicanism: A Survey of Anglican Theological Methodology in the Seventeenth Century* (New York: Charles Scribner's Sons, 1965).

25. Anthony F. C. Wallace, "Revitalization Movements," *American Anthropologist* 58 (1956): 269; J. Milton Yinger, *The Scientific Study of Religion* (London: The MacMillan Company, 1970), pp. 415–16.

26. John Wesley, "The Doctrine of Original Sin, according to Scripture, Reason, and Experience" (1757), II:10 (in Thomas Jackson, ed., *The Works of The Reverend John Wesley, A.M.* [14 vols.; London: Wesleyan Conference Office, 1872], 9:221).

27. Ted A. Campbell, "John Wesley's Conceptions and Uses of Christian Antiquity" (Ph.D. dissertation, Southern Methodist University, 1984).

Notes to Chapter Two

1. A general bibliographical note on Jansenism: critical collections of source materials on Jansenism were collected and edited by Lucien Ceyssens (b. 1902), Professor of Ecclesiastical History at the Pontifical Antonian Athenaeum in Rome. Ceyssens' collections of source materials include the following three volumes: *Sources Relatives aux Débuts du Jansénisme et de l'Antijansénisme, 1640–1643* (Bibliothèque de la Revue d'Histoire Ecclésiastique, no. 31; Louvain: Publications Universitaires de Louvain, 1957); *Sources Relatives a l'Histoire du Jansénisme et de l'Antijansénisme des Années 1661–1672* (Bibliothèque de la Revue d'Histoire Ecclésiastique, no. 45; Louvain: Publications Universitaires de Louvain, 1968); and *Sources Relatives a l'Histoire du Jansénisme et de l'Antijansénisme des Années 1677–1679* (Bibliothèque de la Revue d'Histoire Ecclésiastique, no. 59; Louvain: Publications Universitaires de Louvain, 1974). Ceyssens also served as general editor for two series of works devoted to Jansenist studies: *Jansenistica: Studien in Verband met de Geschiedenis van het Jansenisme* (4 vols.; Mechelen: St. Franciscus Drukkerij, 1950–1962); and *Jansenistica Minora* (13 volumes; Mechelen: St. Franciscus Drukkerij, 1950–1979). The most extensive history of Port-Royal was the work of C.-A. Sainte-Beuve, *Port-Royal* (7 vols.; Paris: Librairie Hachette, third edition, 1866). I have found very helpful the extensive article by Michel Dupuy on "Jansénisme" in the *Dictionnaire de Spiritualité* ed. Marcel Viller et al. (Paris: Beauchesne, 1932ff); 8:102–48.

2. In this and the paragraphs that follow, I am indebted to the following general accounts of Jansenism and Port-Royal: Knox, *Enthusiasm*, pp. 176–82; Delumeau, pp. 99–128; and F. Ellen Weaver, *The Evolution of the Reform of Port-Royal: From the Rule of Cîteaux to Jansenism* (Paris: Editions Beauchesne, 1978).

3. On the motives for Richelieu's imprisonment of Saint-Cyran, see Knox, pp. 183–85.

4. Denzinger, *Enchiridion*, nos. 2001–5 (pp. 445–46).

5. Knox, p. 184; Delumeau, p. 107.

6. Blaise Pascal, *Pensées* (tr. A. J. Krailsheimer; London: Penguin Books, 1966), p. 309. On the memorial itself, see the illustration, which is from a book prepared for the tricentennial of the event: Société des Amis de Port-Royal, *Tricentenaire du Mémorial de Blaise Pascal* (n.p.: Presses de l'Imprimerie "La Ruche," 1955).

7. Blaise Pascal, *The Provincial Letters*, letter 2 (tr. A. J. Krailsheimer; London: Penguin Books, 1967), p. 42; cf. Delumeau, p. 103.

8. *Provincial Letters*, Letter 10 (in Krailsheimer edition, pp. 147–62; cf. Delumeau, p. 107.

9. The bull is given in Denzinger, *Enchiridion*, nos. 2010–12 (p. 447), which explicitly attributes the five propositions to Jansen although it does not document the claim. The formulary is in Denzinger, *Enchiridion*, no. 2020 (p. 449).

10. Denzinger, *Enchiridion*, nos. 2400–2502 (pp. 489–98).

11. Knox, pp. 374–81.

12. *Ibid.*, p. 383.

13. Daniel Vidal, *Miracles et Convulsions jansénistes au XVIIIe Siècle: Le Mal et sa Connaissance* (Paris: Presses Universitaires de France, 1987).

14. Cyril B. O'Keefe, *Contemporary Reactions to the Enlightenment (1728–1762): A Study of Three Critical Journals: the Jesuit* **Journal de Trevoux**, *the Jansenist* **Nouvelles Ecclésiastiques**, *and the Secular* **Journal des Savants** (Geneva: Librairie Slatkine, and Paris: Honoré Champion, 1974), pp. 9–11.

15. Timothy Tackett, *Religion, Revolution, and Regional Culture in Eighteenth-Century France: The Ecclesiastical Oath of 1791* (Princeton: Princeton University Press, 1986), pp. 129–33, see especially the maps on pp. 130 and 131; Tackett at this point relies on information from Edmond Préclin, *Les Jansénistes du XVIIIe Siècle et la Constitution civile du Clergé* (Paris, 1929).

16. Weaver, pp. 154–56; cf. Knox, pp. 225–27.

17. Pierre Nicole, *Les Imaginaires et les Visionnaires* (Cologne: Pierre Marteau, 1683), p. 243, where Nicole criticizes the Quakers (*les Trembleurs*) and other "pernicious sects" which he associates with English, Dutch, and German Calvinists (probably referring to Labadists, in the latter case).

18. Dupuy, p. 130.

19. Delumeau, p. 107.

20. Antoine Arnauld, *De la fréquente Communion;* in *Oeuvres de Messire Antoine Arnauld* (Paris: Sigismond d'Arnay, 1779; reprint edition, Brussels: Impression Anastaltique Culture et Civilization, 1967), 27:71–673.

21. *Ibid.*, II:XII (27:382–83).

22. Dupuy, p. 130.

23. The *Guida spirituale* was originally published in Spanish and Italian. English translations were published in 1688 and 1699. The version which I have consulted is of the 1688 English translation, and was edited by Kathleen Lyttelton (London: Methuen and Company, fifth edition 1927).

24. Knox, pp. 311–14.

25. Denzinger, *Enchiridion* nos. 2201–69 (pp. 470–79).

26. A general bibliographical note on Jeanne Marie Guyon: although numerous works were published in her own lifetime, collected editions did not emerge until the middle of the eighteenth century. Her *Lettres chrétiennes* were published in London in five volumes between 1767 and 1768. The bulk of her works were published in 1790 and 1791 in the so-called "Paris edition" by Libraires Associés. The Paris

edition includes the following series: *Discours chrétiens et spirituels* (2 volumes; 1790); *Les Justifications* (3 volumes; 1790); *Opuscules spirituels* (2 volumes; 1790; hereafter cited as *Opuscules spirituels*); *Poesies et Cantiques spirituels* (3 volumes; 1790); and her autobiography, *Vie de Madame J. M. B. de la Mothe–Guyon écrite par elle-même* (3 volumes; 1791). English translations of her works vary considerably: the translations of the New York Congregationalist pastor and scholar, Thomas Upham, were popular in the nineteenth century, but seriously slanted her views to make them appear conformable to Evangelical Protestantism; cf. Knox, pp. 235–38. Both of the English translations cited below show similar tendencies, not only in their shortening the material, but also in their omission of references to traditional catholic institutions and practices (such as spiritual directors).

27. "Indifference," in *Les Torrens spirituels*, Part I, ch. 9, par. 6 (in *Opuscules spirituels* 1:232; English translation by A. W. Marston, *Spiritual Torrents* [London: H. R. Allenson, Ltd., n.d.], p. 108); "annihilation," ibid., part I, ch. 4, section 3, par. 38 (in *Opuscules spirituels* 1:213; Marston, p. 88).

28. This is the conclusion to the *Torrens spirituels*, Part II, ch. 4, par. 12 (in *Opuscules spirituels* 1:272; translation cited is that of Marston, p. 156).

29. *Ibid.*, Part I, ch. 9, par. 4 (in *Opuscules spirituels* 1:230; Marston, p. 107).

30. *Ibid.*, Part I, ch. 1, par. 1 (in *Opuscules spirituels* 1:132; translation cited is that of Marston, p. 1).

31. Chapters 2–4 of Part I of the *Torrens spirituels* lay out these classes of persons (in *Opuscules spirituels* 1:134–66; Marston, pp. 4–34).

32. *Moyen Court*, ch. 1, par. 1 (in *Opuscules spirituels* 1:10; English translation of Thomas Digby Brooke, entitled *A Short and Easy Method of Prayer* [London: Hatchard and Co., 1867], p. 15); the same point—that most should not aspire to the higher contemplative life, is made in the *Torrens spirituels*, Part I, ch. 2, pars. 8–9 (in *Opuscules spirituels* 1:137–38; Marston, pp. 6–8).

33. *Moyen Court*, ch. 9, par. 3 (in *Opuscules spirituels* 1:28; Brooke, p. 44).

34. *Torrens spirituels*, Part I, ch. 2, par. 11 (in *Opuscules spirituels* 1:139; Marston, p. 9; Marston omits all references to spiritual directors in this and other paragraphs).

35. This is the concluding cry of the *Moyen Court*, ch. 24, par. 14 (in *Opuscules spirituels* 1:78; Brooke, p. 118). To it one may compare a similar passage in the second chapter of the *Torrens spirituels* (par. 16; in *Opuscules spirituels* 1:142; Marston, p. 11).

36. Denzinger, *Enchiridion*, nos. 2351–74 (pp. 484–88).

37. Knox, p. 319.

38. A letter from François de Sales to Jeanne Frances de Chantal, dated 10 June 1611; given in Vincent Kerns, tr. and ed., *The Autobiography of Saint Margaret Mary* (Westminster MD: the Newman Press, and London: Darton, Longman, and Todd, 1961), p. ix.

39. The works of Eudes were published in a collected edition between 1906 and 1911 under the title *Oeuvres complètes de bienheureux Jean Eudes, Missionaire apostolique* (vol. 1, Paris: P. Lethielleux, n.d.; vols. 2–12, Paris: G. Beauchesne, 1906–1911; hereafter cited as *Oeuvres complètes*).

40. Eudes, *Le Coeur admirable de très sacrée Mère de Dieu*, Book 12, ch. 11, whose thesis begins, "The sacred heart of Jesus is one with the heart of the Father and the Holy Ghost" (in *Oeuvres complètes* 8:262–69; the English translation is that of Dom. Richard Flower, *The Sacred Heart of Jesus* [New York: P. J. Kenedy and Sons, 1946], pp. 40–45).

41. *Ibid.*, cf. chs. 8–9 (in *Oeuvres complètes* 8:245–58; Flower, pp. 25–35).

42. *Ibid.*, chs. 15–17 (in *Oeuvres complètes*, 1:286–97; Flower, pp. 60–65, 72–76), where Eudes gives devotional readings from Bonaventure, the Carmelite Margaret of Beaune, Lanspergius the Carthusian, and Gertrude the Great.

43. *Ibid.*, fifth meditation, first point (in *Oeuvres complètes* 8:318–19; Flower, pp. 96–97).

44. *Ibid.*, first meditation (in *Oeuvres complètes* 8:309–10; Flower, pp. 85–87).

45. *Ibid.*, cf. the title to ch. 2 (in *Oeuvres complètes* 8:208; Flower, p. 1); the expression "furnace of love" appears in seven of the chapter titles.

46. *Autobiography* (tr. Kerns), pp. 14–15.

47. *Ibid.*, p. 44.

48. *Ibid.*, pp. 77–80.

49. See Henri Béchard, *The Visions of Bernard Francis de Hoyos, S.J.: Apostle of the Sacred Heart in Spain* (New York, Washington, and Hollywood: The Vantage Press, 1959).

50. *New Catholic Encyclopedia*, s.v., "Sacred Heart, Iconography."

51. Thomas M. Gannon and George W. Traub, *The Desert and the City: An Interpretation of the History of Christian Spirituality* (London: The Macmillan Co., and Collier MacMillan, Ltd., 1969), pp. 227–32.

52. On the last point, cf. Martin von Eckhardt aus Kuhdorf, *Die Einfluss der Madame Guyon auf die norddeutsche Laienwelt im 18. Jahrhundert* (Barmen: Staats-Druckerei, 1928).

Notes to Chapter Three

1. In John C. Miller and Robert Halley, eds., *The Works of Thomas Goodwin, D.D., Sometime President of Magdalene College, Oxford* (Nichol's Series of Standard Divines, Puritan Period; 12 vols.; Edinburgh: James Nichol, 1862) 4:93–150; transcription of title page of first edition is given on p. 94. The work is referred to by Kerns, p. xi. Eudes's treatise on the *Coeur admirable de la Mère de Dieu*, which included a chapter on the sacred heart of Jesus, was published in 1670.

2. A general bibliographical note on Puritanism: the literature on English Puritanism (not to mention its North American counterpart) is immense, but a classic study, perhaps still the most comprehensive, is that of William Haller, *The Rise of Puritanism, Or, The Way to the New Jerusalem as Set Forth in Pulpit and Press from Thomas Cartwright to John Lilburne and John Milton, 1570–1643* (New York: Columbia University Press, 1938). Two more recent discussions of the background of Elizabethan Puritanism are those of Patrick Collinson, *The Elizabethan Puritan Movement* (London: Jonathan Cape, 1967) and Peter Lake, *Moderate Puritans and the Elizabethan Church* (Cambridge: Cambridge University Press, 1982). Collinson's *The Religion of Protestants: The Church in English Society 1559–1625* (Oxford: The Clarendon Press, 1982) advances through the reign of James I. F. Ernest Stoeffler discusses the emergence of what he terms "Pietistic Puritanism" in *The Rise of Evangelical Pietism* (Studies in the History of Religion, no. 9; Leiden: E. J. Brill, 1965), pp. 24–108.

3. Haller, pp. 6–16; Collinson, *Elizabethan Puritan Movement*, pp. 101–55 and following; Lake, *passim*. One of the principal contributions of more recent scholarship (Collinson and Lake, in particular) has been to show that Elizabethan Puritanism must be understood not only as a reaction *against* the Elizabethan Settlement, but also (perhaps primarily) as a positive program *for* a national Church Establishment along Protestant lines.

4. M. M. Knappen, *Tudor Puritanism: A Chapter in the History of Idealism* (Chicago and London: University of Chicago Press, 1939), pp. 283–97.
5. Haller, pp. 52–54 and following.
6. Collinson, *Religion of Protestants*, pp. 136–40, 263–73.
7. It was conventionally claimed that the Puritans turned *from* concerns about liturgy and polity *to* concerns about spirituality at this time, but this notion is rejected by more recent interpreters, who maintained that the Puritans' concern for an experiential spirituality was present all along, but simply came to prominence after the defeat of their political and liturgical agenda: this is one of the principal conclusions of Robert Stuart Orkney's study of "The Breaking of the Elizabethan Settlement of Religion: Puritan Spiritual Experience and the Theological Division of the English Church" (Ph.D. dissertation, Yale University, 1976), esp. pp. 59–101.
8. Stoeffler describes what he calls "Pietistic" Puritans, including William Perkins, William Ames, Lewis Bayly, and others: pp. 28–99. In this, Stoeffler follows a well-established pattern of German scholarship that has seen this particular group of Puritans, especially Perkins, as the forerunners of Pietism: Heinrich Heppe, *Geschichte des Pietismus und der Mystik in der reformirte [sic] Kirche, namentlich der Niederlande* (Leiden: E. J. Brill, 1879), pp. 14–52 (Heppe specifically referred to *der puritanische Pietismus Englands*); then August Lang, *Puritanismus und Pietismus: Studien zu ihrer Entwicklung von M. Butzer bis zum Methodismus (Beiträge zur Geschichte und Lehre der reformierten Kirche* series, vol. 6; Neukirchen Kreis Moers: Buchhandlung des Erziehungsvereins, 1941), pp. 101–203. A similar group of Puritans is identified as "Evangelical" by Jerald C. Brauer: "Types of Puritan Piety" (*Church History* 56 [May 1987]: 47–51). Brauer distinguishes the "Evangelical" form of Puritan piety from "Nomistic," "Rationalistic," and "Mystical" forms of Puritan piety. His group largely coincides with those identified as "Pietistic" by the German scholars and Stoeffler, except for the conspicuous and puzzling absence of Perkins and Ames, who in fact are included in none of Brauer's categories.
9. [William Perkins,] *A Golden Chaine, or The Description of Theologie, Containing the Order of the Causes of Salvation and Damnation, according to God's Word* (second edition; Cambridge: John Legate, 1597), p. 7.
10. William Ames, *The Marrow of Theology* (tr. John Dykstra Eusden; The United Church Press, 1968; reprint edition, Durham, NC: The Labyrinth Press, 1983), p. 77.
11. John Calvin, *Institutes of the Christian Religion*, 3:21–23 (tr. Ford Lewis Battles; ed. John T. McNeill; Philadelphia: Westminster Press, 1960), 2:920–64.
12. Ames, pp. 152–56; cf. Eusden's introductory comments, pp. 6–7.
13. The four "degrees" are specifically outlined in Perkins on pages 138, 145, 149 [mislabeled as "145"], and 168; on these stages, more broadly, cf. Haller, pp. 86–92.
14. The five stages are given in Ames, pp. 157–74.
15. Perkins, pp. 138–45; Ames, pp. 157–60.
16. Perkins, p. 145; Ames, p. 162.
17. Perkins, pp. 149–67; Ames, pp. 167–71.
18. Perkins, pp. 168ff.; Ames pp. 171–74.
19. Perkins, p. 144; italics as in text.
20. *Ibid.*, p. 210. On the intent of Perkins's *Golden Chaine* in dealing with the question of knowledge of election, cf. Richard A. Muller, "Perkins' *A Golden Chaine*: Predestinarian System or Schematized *Ordo Salutis?*" (*Sixteenth Century Journal* IX:1

[1978]), pp. 69–81. The theme was obviously central to Perkins: another of his works bears the title "A Treatise Tending unto a Declaration, Whether a Man be in the Estate of Damnation, or in the Estate of Grace" (London: John Porter, 1597).

21. Perkins, *Golden Chaine*, p. 148.

22. Ames, pp. 164–67.

23. *Ibid.*, p. 167.

24. Cf. Muller, p. 80.

25. Perkins, p. 141.

26. Perkins, pp. 140–42; Ames, pp. 158–60, where Ames stressed the "inward" work of the Spirit in bringing about conviction of sin.

27. Perkins (in considerable detail), pp. 149–62; Ames, pp. 167–71.

28. P. 152, mislabeled as "148."

29. Haller, pp. 94–95; excerpts from Goodwin's diary are given in a memoir composed by his son, in Miller and Halley, 2:xlix–lxxv.

30. Miller and Halley, 2:li–lxvii.

31. *Ibid.*, p. lii.

32. *Ibid.*, p. lxi.

33. *Ibid.*, p. lxii.

34. Haller, pp. 95–99.

35. Haller, pp. 102–8.

36. John Bunyan, *The Pilgrim's Progress* (ed. Roger Sharrock; Harmondsworth, Middlesex: Penguin Books, 1965), p. 51.

37. *Ibid.*, pp. 81, 82.

38. Part I ends; Part II of *The Pilgrim's Progress* is a separate narrative.

39. Sayings of Goodwin recorded in a printed broadsheet, now in the British Museum; in Miller and Halley, 12:131.

40. In this section I am indebted to two recent North American studies, both based on the authors' dissertations: Marilyn J. Westerkamp, *The Triumph of the Laity: Scots-Irish Piety and the Great Awakening, 1625–1760* (New York: Oxford University Press, 1988), especially chapters one and two (pp. 15–73); and Leigh Eric Schmidt, *Holy Fairs: Scottish Communions and American Revivals in the Early Modern Period* (Princeton: Princeton University Press, 1989). Both Westerkamp and Schmidt are concerned to relate Scots-Irish revivalism to later North American developments, but Westerkamp focuses on its relationship to the "First Great Awakening" in the Middle Colonies, and Schmidt stresses more its relationship to later revivalism (especially frontier camp meetings) roughly associated with what Americanists refer to as the "Second Great Awakening," i.e., from the last decade of the eighteenth century through the early decades of the nineteenth century. Excerpts from primary sources for Scots-Irish revivalism are given in John Gillies, ed., *Historical Collections relating to Remarkable Periods of the Success of the Gospel* (Title on cover and reprint title page is *Historical Collections of Accounts of Revival;* Kelso: John Rutherford, 1845; Reprint edition, London: Banner of Truth Trust, 1981), pp. 157–208.

41. Schmidt, *Holy Fairs*, discusses the preaching of Robert Bruce and John Welsh as predecessors of the later sacramentalist preachers (pp. 22–25), then the reaction against the Articles of Perth (pp. 25–27).

42. Robert Blair, *The Life of Mr. Robert Blair, Minister of St. Andrews, containing His Autobiography from 1593 to 1636* (Edinburgh: The Woodrow Society, 1848), pp. 19–20; cf. Gillies, pp. 197–98, and especially note 2 on p. 197 where the date of the

188   Notes to Pages 55 to 67

Stewarton revival is discussed; Schmidt, pp. 27–28; and Westerkamp, p. 28. Westerkamp maintains that the revival actually began in Ireland, thus representing the revival in Stewarton (along with that in Shotts) as beginning in 1630.

43. Schmidt, pp. 28–29; several excerpts from Livingston's memoirs concerning the revivals in Scotland are given in Gillies, pp. 198–202.

44. Blair, p. 70.

45. Ibid., pp. 70–71; cf. Gillies, pp. 202–8.

46. Ibid., pp. 84–89; cf. Westerkamp, pp. 23–26, and Schmidt, pp. 29–30.

47. Schmidt, pp. 21–22; Westerkamp, pp. 26–27.

48. The subject of Schmidt's book, in general; cf Westerkamp, pp. 29–34.

49. Westerkamp, pp. 51–68; Schmidt, pp. 32–41.

50. Cf. Westerkamp, chs. 3 and 4, pp. 74–135; Schmidt, p. 50.

51. Cf. Stoeffler, pp. 100–103; or more generally, Christopher Hill, *The World Turned Upside Down: Radical Ideas during the English Revolution* (London: T. Smith, 1972).

52. George Fox, *Journal* for 1644 and 1646; in Douglas V. Steere, ed. *Quaker Spirituality: Selected Writings* (Classics of Western Spirituality series; New York: Paulist Press, 1984), p. 64.

53. Ibid. for 1647; in Steere, p. 65.

54. Ibid. for 1647; in Steere, pp. 65–66.

55. Ibid. for 1647; in Steere, p. 66.

56. Ibid. for 1652; in Steere, p. 79.

57. Isaac Pennington, cited by Steere, p. 11.

58. Robert Barclay, *An Apology for the True Christian Divinity: Being an Explication and Vindication of the Principles and Doctrines of the People called Quakers* (Philadelphia: Friends' Book Store, 1908), p. 13.

59. Ibid., pp. 14–15.

60. 1:33ff.

61. Barclay, p. 85; cf. pp. 81–108 more generally.

62. Ibid., propositions 4–6. In his discussion of these propositions, Barclay explicitly rejects Pelagianism and Socinianism because of their teaching of *natural* human goodness, and warns against "Remonstrant" (i.e., Arminian) teachings because they do not ground their doctrine of a common grace in Christ's work.

63. Ibid., propositions 7–8, p. 18.

64. Ibid., propositions 8–9, pp. 18–19.

65. In Gerald R. Cragg, ed., *The Cambridge Platonists* (A Library of Protestant Thought; New York: Oxford University Press, 1968), p. 76.

66. Cf. Cragg's introduction, pp. 18–19.

67. Ibid., p. 77.

68. In this particular respect, Baxter's program resembles that of the Anglican "Latitudinarians" of his age, such as Edward Stillingfleet, whose *Irenicum* (1659) argued that the ancient church did not have a uniformly episcopal or presbyterian polity.

69. Richard Baxter, *Methodus Theologiae christianae* (London: M. White and T. Snowden, 1681; reprint edition, Ann Arbor: University Microfilms, Wing Collection of Old English Books, reel 53) Part III, pp. 55–61 ("determinations" 16–18). An account of Baxter's thought on election is given in John McClintock and James Strong, *Cyclopedia of Biblical, Theological, and Ecclesiastical Literature* (12 vols.; New York: Harper and Bros., 1891), 1:702–3. Their account is said to be based on the *Methodus Theologiae*, to which it agrees very closely, and Baxter's *Universal Redemption*, to which I have not had access.

70. In fact, the *Methodus Theologiae* utilizes the language of "true faith and repentance" (corresponding to "effectual calling"), then justification, sanctification, and

"glory" very much as Perkins and Ames had done: Part III, p. 55. Cf. also his discussion of these terms (and this sequence) in his *Treatise of Conversion* (in William Orme, ed., *Practical Works of the Rev. Richard Baxter* [23 vols.; London: James Duncan, 1830], 7:18–22).

71. In Orme, 14:i–354; cf. pp. 87–94 in particular on the discernment of spiritual states of parishioners.

72. *A Treatise of Conversion*, in Orme, 7:32; Baxter's elaboration on the change of the will and affections in conversion continues for several pages beyond this point.

73. *The Saints' Everlasting Rest* is given in Orme, vols. 22 and 23. *Appeal to the Unconverted* is another title of a popular Baxter treatise.

74. Richard P. Heitzenrater, "What's in a Name?: The Meaning of 'Methodist,'" in *Mirror and Memory: Reflections on Early Methodism* (Nashville: Kingswood Books, 1989), pp. 23–26.

Notes to Chapter Four

1. A general bibliographical note on Pietism: a general historiographical survey (despite its title) is given in Horst Weigelt, "Interpretations of Pietism in the Research of Contemporary German Church Historians" (*Church History* 39 [June 1970]: 236–41). In English, the standard secondary works are those of F. Ernest Stoeffler of Temple University: *The Rise of Evangelical Pietism* (Studies in the History of Religions, no. 9; Leiden: E. J. Brill, 1965), which chronicles the development of Reformed and Lutheran Pietism up until the time of Spener, and its sequel, *German Pietism during the Eighteenth Century* (Studies in the History of Religions, no. 24; Leiden: E. J. Brill, 1973), which begins with Spener and continues a narrative of Lutheran Pietism through the beginning of the nineteenth century. A somewhat more concise and popular account is given in Dale W. Brown, *Understanding Pietism* (Grand Rapids, MI: William B. Eerdmans, 1978). There is also an English translation of an introductory article by Martin Schmidt, "Pietism" in *Encyclopedia of the Lutheran Church* (ed. Julius Bodensiek; 3 vols.; Minneapolis: Augsburg Publishing House, 1965; 3:1898–1906). A collection of sources has appeared in the Classics of Western Spirituality series: Peter C. Erb, ed., *Pietists: Selected Writings* (New York: Paulist Press, 1983); this work also includes a helpful introduction by the editor (pp. 1–27). The German annual series *Pietismus und Neuzeit* (beginning in 1974) is largely devoted to Pietist studies, and the North American *Covenant Quarterly* frequently carries articles relating to Pietism.

2. See Chapter Three, note 2; German scholars such as Heppe and Lang stressed the role of Perkins and Ames in the development of Pietism; Stoeffler (*Rise of Evangelical Pietism*, pp. 117–21) takes the more cautious approach.

3. Stoeffler, *Rise of Evangelical Pietism*, pp. 117–18; Erb, introduction to *Pietists*, p. 4.

4. On Dutch Pietism, in general, see Martin H. Prozesky, "The Emergence of Dutch Pietism" (*Journal of Ecclesiastical History* 28:1 [January 1977]: 29–37), and Stoeffler's treatment in *The Rise of Evangelical Pietism*, pp. 121–62.

5. See Chapter Three, above; cf. Stoeffler, *Rise of Evangelical Pietism*, pp. 133–41.

6. William [i.e., Willem] Teellinck, *Paul's Complaint against His Natural Corruption, with the Meanes How to be Delivered from the Power of the Same* (London: John Danson, 1621; reprint edition: University Microfilms International, "English Books, 1475–1640" series, reel 1118; p. 35).

7. *Ibid.*, p. 38.

8. *Ibid.*

9. On this may be noted Teellinck's lament, in his epistle to the reader of these published sermons, that although most people would grieve and lament the loss of their worldly possessions, few grieve or lament their sins (pp. A4–A5). See also Stoeffler's notes on Teellinck's Dutch works, *Rise of Evangelical Pietism*, pp. 129–33.

10. "Conventicles" here simply denotes small gatherings of Christians; not illegal or forbidden gatherings, as the term would imply in England; cf. Prozesky, p. 33, note 4.

11. Stoeffler, *Rise of Evangelical Pietism*, p. 142; Prozesky, pp. 35–36.

12. The translation is that of Stoeffler, who also gives an account of the sermons, pp. 146–47.

13. *Ibid.*, pp. 144–45.

14. *Ibid.*, pp. 150–51. According to Prozesky, Ritschl distinguished between an earlier "Precisian" phase and a later "Evangelical" phase of Dutch Pietism, with the transition between the two coming in the 1670s (Prozesky, p. 37, n. 2), although the work of T. G. à Brakel would seem to predate Ritschl's dating of this transition.

15. Stoeffler, *Rise of Evangelical Pietism*, pp. 169–72.

16. *Ibid.*, 172–74.

17. In the following account, I am indebted to the excellent and detailed narrative of Labadie's career provided by T. J. Saxby in *The Quest for the New Jerusalem: Jean de Labadie and the Labadists, 1610–1744* (International Archives of the History of Ideas series; Dordrecht: Martinus Nijhoff Publishers, 1987).

18. *Ibid.*, pp. 1–18.

19. *Ibid.*, pp. 19–40.

20. *Ibid.*, pp. 41–134.

21. Labadie, Jean de, *La Reformation de l'Eglise par le Pastorat* (Middelbourg: Henry Smidt, 1667), letter one, ch. 2, pp. 34–78.

22. *Ibid.*, pp. 131–215; the expression *grace s[e]nsible* as equivalent to *onction divin* is on p. 199.

23. *Ibid.*, letter two, *passim*.

24. *Ibid.*, pp. 135–72.

25. On Comenius and the *Unitas Fratrum*, see the section of this chapter on the Moravians.

26. Saxby, pp. 173–239.

27. *Ibid.*, p. 144. On Sabbatai Tsevi, see Chapter Six, below.

28. *Ibid.*, pp. 208–10.

29. On Arndt: an abridged translation of *True Christianity* has been published recently in the Paulist "Classics of Western Spirituality" series: Peter C. Erb., tr. and ed., *Johann Arndt: True Christianity* (New York: Paulist Press, 1979). See also Eric Lund, "Johann Arndt and the Development of a Lutheran Spiritual Tradition" (Ph.D. dissertation, Yale University, 1979).

30. Oberman, preface to Erb, *Johann Arndt*, p. xiii.

31. Arndt's foreword, in Erb, p. 21.

32. *Ibid.*, pp. 21, 23.

33. Roughly. Arndt himself points to such a schema in the introductions to the second and third books (cf. Erb, pp. 201, 221–22), but it must be noted that within each book there is considerable latitude in the material Arndt included, so that the scheme is only general and does not apply to the actual layout of chapters within the books.

34. See Erb's introduction, in which he compares Arndt's understanding of the *ordo salutis* with that of David Hollatz (pp. 7–8, especially note 22).

35. *Ibid.*, p. 221.

36. See the discussion in Chapter One: this more generalized understanding of "mysticism" holds it to denote any direct divine-human encounter.

37. *Ibid.*, p. 224; cf. the foreword, where Arndt states that "although we cannot, in our present weakness, perfectly imitate the holy and noble life of Christ (which, indeed, is not intended in my book), nevertheless, we ought to love it, and yearn to imitate it . . . ." (Erb, p. 22).

38. One of Lund's principal conclusions, based on his analysis of Arndt's use of Tauler, is that Arndt had utilized mystical sources in a way that was more compatible with conventional Lutheran orthodoxy (pp. 198–211). Cf. also Erb's introduction, where Erb notes that it is only in a broad sense that "mysticism" can be predicated of Arndt (pp. 6–8).

39. The translation is that of Robert S. Bridges, and is cited from *The United Methodist Hymnal: Book of United Methodist Worship* (Nashville: United Methodist Publishing House, 1989), no. 289.

40. The hymn is known to have been based on Bernard of Clairvaux's *Salve caput cruentatum;* the translation is that of James W. Alexander, and is cited from *The United Methodist Hymnal: Book of United Methodist Worship*, no. 286.

41. On Spener, see the biography by K. James Stein, *Philipp Jakob Spener: Pietist Patriarch* (Chicago: Covenant Press, 1986). Stoeffler's *Rise of Evangelical Pietism* discusses Spener (pp. 228–46). The standard (German) edition of his works is that edited by Erich Beyreuther, *Schriften* (4 vols.; Hildesheim and New York: Georg Olms Verlag, 1979–1984). A selection of Spener's works in English translation is given in Erb, *Pietists*, pp. 29–96; on *Pia Desideria*, see below.

42. A sermon quoted in Stein, p. 87; also referred to in Theodore G. Tappert, introduction to Spener's *Pia Desideria* (Philadelphia: Fortress Press, 1964), p. 13.

43. Spener, *Schriften*, ed. Beyreuther, 1:147–218; cf. Tappert, pp. 39–75.

44. *Schriften* 1:218–40; cf. Tappert, pp. 76–86.

45. *Schriften* 1:240–308; cf. Tappert, pp. 87–122.

46. For example, the orthodox theologian Abraham Calovius wrote a letter of support to Spener; cf. Tappert, p. 18.

47. On the Frankfurt ministry in general, cf. Stein, pp. 73–106.

48. Stein, pp. 107–26.

49. In Tappert, p. 24.

50. In 1830, by royal decree, the Lutheran ("Evangelical") and Reformed Churches in Prussia were formally united; on this, see Chapter Seven.

51. On Francke in general, cf. Gary R. Sattler, *God's Glory, Neighbor's Good: A Brief Introduction to the Life and Writings of August Hermann Francke* (Chicago: Covenant Press, 1982), which includes important translations of Francke's sermons and essays; and his earlier article, "August Hermann Francke and Mysticism" (*Covenant Quarterly* 38:4 [November 1980], pp. 3–17). See also the chapters in Stoeffler, *German Pietism during the Eighteenth Century* (chs. 1–2, pp. 1–87). A standard anthology of Francke's works (in German) is that edited by Erhard Peschke, *Werke in Auswahl* (Berlin: Luther-Verlag, 1969). Some of Francke's works are given in English translation in Erb, *Pietists*, pp. 97–166.

52. Sattler, "August Hermann Francke and Mysticism," p. 3. Sattler argues that Francke, along with Luther, Arndt, and Spener, was a "mystic," but defines the

term in the very broad sense as involving "direct experience of the numinous regardless of any metaphysical presuppositions" (p. 3).

53. The translation is that of Sattler, *God's Glory, Neighbor's Good*, p. 31; cf. the version of the same in "August Hermann Francke and Mysticism," p. 12.

54. Francke's own account of the Orphan-House and other institutions, entitled *Die Fussstapfen des noch lebenden Gottes* ("The Footprints of the Yet-Living God") was itself a classic apology. It was printed in English translation in 1727 as *Pietas Hallensis* (Edinburgh: James Davidson, 1727), and was widely influential in the nascent Evangelical movement in the British Isles (see the next chapter).

55. Francke lays out his understanding of the way of salvation in brief in his "Confession of a Christian" (in Sattler, *God's Glory, Neighbor's Good*, pp. 239–41), and his *Scriptural and Basic Introduction to True Christianity* (in Sattler, *God's Glory, Neighbor's Good*, pp. 243–54); Sattler also includes a translation of an "Appendix on Christian Perfection" by Francke (pp. 234–36).

56. On Württemberg Pietism, cf. Stoeffler, *German Pietism during the Eighteenth Century*, ch. 3, pp. 88–130.

57. Despite Luther himself, whose treatise on *The Bondage of the Will* against Erasmus had taught a sternly Augustinian doctrine of predestination.

58. Cf. Arndt, *True Christianity* 1:12 (in Erb, *Johann Arndt*, p. 70), where Arndt asserts the universal scope of the atonement, and 1:38 (in Erb, pp. 170–71), where Arndt states that election and reprobation are grounded in God's foreknowledge of the choice that human beings would make.

59. Arndt, *True Christianity* 1:3 (in Erb, *Johann Arndt*, p. 40) asserts that baptism is the means of regeneration, then in 1:4 (in Erb, p. 45) describes repentance as bringing about "the new creature in Christ and the new birth that alone counts before God." Similarly, cf. Stein's account of Spener's doctrine of baptismal regeneration (pp. 195–97), and Francke's sermon on "The Doctrine of our Lord Jesus Christ concerning Rebirth," part 2 (in Sattler, *God's Glory, Neighbor's Good*, pp. 140–45).

60. So Stein, p. 196 (describing Spener's view that baptismal regeneration was normally lost), and Francke, the sermon on the new birth cited above (in Sattler, p. 143), where Francke reminds his hearers that although they might have been born again in baptism, they could still stand in need of regeneration if they had not been raised in such a way that the gift of grace was faithfully maintained.

61. Francke, a sermon "If and How One May be Certain that One is a Child of God" (1707); in Erb, *Pietists*, p. 147.

62. On Arndt, see the discussion above of his teaching on "union" and the accusations of his mysticism; on Spener, cf. Stein, pp. 165–66, 193–94; Francke expressed his understanding of the goal of Christian life in the "Appendix on Christian Perfection" (in Sattler, *God's Glory, Neighbor's Good*, pp. 234–37), especially sections 9 and 10 (Sattler, pp. 236–37), where Francke explains the sense in which one may, and may not, aspire to perfection in this life.

63. Zinzendorf, sermon "On the Essential Character and Circumstances of the Life of a Christian," in Erb, *Pietists*, p. 312.

64. On Zinzendorf and the early, renewed Moravian community, in general, see John R. Weinlick, *Count Zinzendorf* (New York and Nashville: Abingdon Press, 1956); and A. J. Lewis, *Zinzendorf: The Ecumenical Pioneer: A Study in the Moravian Contribution to Christian Mission and Unity* (Philadelphia: The Westminster Press, 1962). Stoeffler has a chapter on Zinzendorf and the early Moravian community in *German Pietism in the Eighteenth Century*, pp. 131–67. Zinzendorf's *Nine Public Lectures on Important Subjects in Religion*, tr. George W. Forell, are available in English

(Iowa City: University of Iowa Press, 1973), and there is a selection from these and from other writings in Erb, *Pietists*, pp. 289–330. A collected edition of Zinzendorf's writings is that edited by Erich Beyreuther, Gerhard Meyer, and Amedeo Molnár (5 vols.; Hildesheim and New York: Georg Olms Verlag, 1978). See also J. Taylor Hamilton and Kenneth G. Hamilton, *History of the Moravian Church: The Renewed Unitas Fratrum, 1722–1957* (Bethlehem, PA, and Winston-Salem, NC: Interprovincial Board of Christian Education, Moravian Church in America, 1967), part I, pp. 11–159. The *Transactions of the Moravian Historical Society* (1876–1957) dealt mainly with North American Moravian topics but also included articles on the early German communities.

65. Weinlick, pp. 13–22.
66. *Ibid.*, pp. 23–47.
67. *Ibid.*, pp. 48–82.
68. *Ibid.*, pp. 83–92.
69. *Ibid.*, pp. 93–101.
70. *Ibid.*, pp. 114–27.
71. *Ibid.*, pp. 102–13, 128–97.
72. *Ibid.*, pp. 198–234.
73. Zinzendorf, in Erb, *Pietists*, p. 291.
74. Hence Zinzendorf's negative comments on doctrinal and confessional division, cited at the beginning of this section. In the same sermon, Zinzendorf did concede that "the differences in religious denominations are important and venerable concerns, and the distinction of denominations is a divine wisdom" (in Erb, *Pietists*, p. 313). But the value of the distinctions lies solely in the varying gifts that God has given the different churches, not in their claims to being right or wrong in opposition to each other; hence Zinzendorf discourages anyone from "proselytizing" from one denomination to another.
75. *Ibid.*, p. 317.
76. *Ibid.*, pp. 305–8.
77. *Ibid.*, pp. 308–10.
78. The distinction of *fides implicita* and *fides explicita* was indeed utilized in medieval theology, but there it represented the distinction between the faith of the uneducated laity (whose faith is "implicit" so long as they trust what the Church teaches), and the faith of the Church's educated teachers (whose faith must be "explicit").
79. In Erb, *Pietists*, pp. 298–99.
80. Cited in Weinlick, p. 199.
81. In Erb, *Pietists*, p. 302.
82. Weinlick, p. 200.
83. Lewis, pp. 139–60.

Notes to Chapter Five

1. In Cragg, 11:250.
2. The term "Evangelical" is problematic (it can denote fidelity to the Gospel, Protestantism in general, and Lutheranism in particular, in other contexts), but is used here in the sense of "Evangelical Revival" and thus has reference to the British religious revival of the eighteenth century.
3. A useful general history, despite its vehement antireligious prejudices, is that of J. H. Plumb, *England in the Eighteenth Century* (The Pelican History of England,

vol. 7; Harmondsworth, Middlesex: Penguin Books, Ltd.; revised edition, 1963); cf. pp. 77–90 on the Industrial Revolution.

4. The question of the relationship between the early Evangelical societies and the centers of the Industrial Revolution has been vigorously pursued throughout this century. For a fairly recent recap, see John Q. Smith, "Occupational Groups among the Early Methodists of the Keighley Circuit" (*Church History* 57:2 [June 1988], pp. 187–91).

5. A general, now time-honored, text on eighteenth century English philosophy and theology is that of Sir Leslie Stephen, *History of English Thought in the Eighteenth Century* (2 vols; third edition, 1902; reprint edition, New York: Peter Smith, 1949); on Locke and his relevance to the eighteenth century, cf. 1:34–43.

6. A general text on eighteenth-century English religious life is that of Ernest Gordon Rupp, *Religion in England, 1688–1791* (The Oxford History of the Christian Church series, ed. Henry and Owen Chadwick; Oxford: Oxford University Press, 1986); on the development of Deist thought, cf. pp. 257–77. Cf. also Stephen, 1:74–277.

7. Rupp, pp. 278–85. On the development of Moralism through the seventeenth century, see C. F. Allison, *The Rise of Moralism: The Proclamation of the Gospel from Hooker to Baxter* (New York: Seabury Press, 1966).

8. Rupp, pp. 298–322.

9. Rupp, pp. 290–98, 327–30; cf. also John S. Simon, *John Wesley and the Religious Societies* (London: Epworth Press, second edition, 1955), pp. 9–27.

10. Nuttall, pp. 214–15, 217–18. On this point, see also Heitzenrater, *Mirror and Memory*, pp. 33–45.

11. On the question of the origins of the Revival, see the fine essay by John Walsh, "Origins of the Evangelical Revival" (in G. V. Bennett and John D. Walsh, eds., *Essays in Modern English Church History: In Memory of Norman Sykes* [New York: Oxford University Press, 1966], pp. 132–62). For a general description of the Evangelical Revival, see D. W. Bebbington, *Evangelicalism in Modern Britain: A History from the 1730s to the 1980s* (London: Unwin Hyman, 1989), pp. 20–74.

12. And, one might argue, in the British colonies of North America, which were even more removed from the crises of the Industrial Revolution, though not from the cultural challenges of the Enlightenment.

13. Three strands of the Evangelical Revival are often distinguished in recent historiography: the connection of preachers led by George Whitefield and Selina, Countess of Huntingdon (see the next section), the connection of preachers led by John Wesley (see the third section of this chapter), and Anglican parish clergy who carried on their own evangelistic work: cf. Kenneth Hylson-Smith, *Evangelicals in the Church of England, 1734–1984* (Edinburgh: T. and T. Clark, 1988), pp. 10 and 13; Hylson-Smith traces the identification of these three strands to John Walsh's 1956 Cambridge D.Phil. thesis. For the purposes of this chapter, I have elected to deal with the Welsh Revival as a separate unit, despite its close linkage with the "Countess of Huntingdon's Connexion" in England, and I have largely deferred discussion of Evangelicalism among Anglican parish clergy to the next chapter, where it is taken up as a precedent for the institutionalization of the religion of the heart movements.

On the Welsh Revival, in general, see Derec Llwyd Morgan, *The Great Awakening in Wales* (tr. Dyfnallt Morgan; London: Epworth Press, 1988). See also Owain W. Jones, "The Welsh Church in the Eighteenth Century," in David Walker, ed., *A*

History of the Church in Wales (Penarth, S. Glamorganshire: Historical Society of the Church in Wales, 1976), pp. 103–20.

14. Nuttall, pp. 213–17.

15. On Harris, see Richard Bennett, *The Early Life of Howell Harris* (English translation by Gomer M. Roberts; London: Banner of Truth Trust, 1962); also cf. Morgan, pp. 71–85.

16. Bayly's *Practice of Piety* had been available in a Welsh translation since 1685: *Yr Ymarfer o Ddiuwioldeb yn Cyfarwyldo dŷn i Rodio fel y Rhyngo ef Ffod Duw* (1685; reprint edition, University Microfilms International, "Early English Books, 1475–1640" series, reel 1560).

17. Cited in Bennett, p. 26.

18. Cited in Bennett, p. 42.

19. On Rowland, in general, see Eifion Evans, *Daniel Rowland and the Great Evangelical Awakening in Wales* (Carlisle, PA: Banner of Truth Trust, 1985).

20. Cited in Morgan, p. 23.

21. See Chapter Three above.

22. See Chapter Four, above.

23. On George Whitefield, see Stuart C. Henry, *George Whitefield: Wayfaring Witness* (New York and Nashville: Abingdon Press, 1957). A selection of Whitefield's sermons is available, and has been reprinted numerous times: *Select Sermons of George Whitefield, M.A.* (London: Banner of Truth Trust, 1958). Whitefield's *Journals* are available in the edition of William V. Davis, *George Whitefield's Journals* (Gainesville, FL: Scholars' Facsimiles and Reprints, 1969).

24. On the Countess of Huntingdon, see Henrietta Keddie (a.k.a. "Sarah Tytler"), *The Countess of Huntingdon and Her Circle* (London: Sir Isaac Pitman and Sons, Ltd., 1907), [Aaron Seymour,] *The Life and Times of Selina Countess of Huntingdon* (2 vols.; London: William Edward Painter, 1839), and Helen C. Knight, *Lady Huntingdon and Her Friends: Or, the Revival of the Work of God in the Days of Wesley, Whitefield, Romaine, Venn, and Others in the Last Century* (New York: American Tract Society, 1853).

25. Henry, pp. 21–23.

26. Whitefield, *A Short Account of God's Dealings with the Reverend Mr. George Whitefield* (London: 1740), pp. 48–49; cited in Henry, p. 24.

27. Henry, pp. 25–31.

28. Ingham had been a member of John Wesley's Oxford Methodist society and later became an influential Evangelical among the Anglican parish clergy.

29. Knight, p. 13.

30. *Ibid.*, pp. 14–15.

31. Cf. Henry, pp. 25 (on Whitefield's familiarity with Francke) and 32–41 (on the Georgia venture). Whitefield had read Francke's account of the orphanage and other institutions in Halle, which had been published in English translation in 1727 as *Pietas Hallensis;* cf. Nuttall, pp. 209–13.

32. Whitefield's *Journal;* cited in Henry, p. 48.

33. Henry, p. 49.

34. Cited in Albert C. Outler, *Theology in the Wesleyan Spirit* (Nashville: Tidings, 1975), p. 36.

35. In Henry, p. 62.

36. So Henry, p. 131.

37. Cited from *The United Methodist Hymnal: Book of United Methodist Worship* (1989), no. 361.

38. There is an immense bibliography, especially on John Wesley. A helpful biblio-graphical overview is given in Lawrence D. McIntosh, "The Place of John Wesley in the Christian Tradition: A Selected Bibliography," in Kenneth E. Rowe, ed., *The Place of Wesley in the Christian Tradition: Essays Delivered at Drew University in Celebration of the Commencement of the Publication of the Oxford Edition of the Works of John Wesley* (Metuchen, NJ: Scarecrow Press, 1976), pp. 134–59. Two recent biog-raphies of John Wesley are those of Stanley Edward Ayling, *John Wesley* (Nashville: Abingdon Press, 1979), and Henry Rack, *Reasonable Enthusiast: John Wesley and the Rise of Methodism* (London: Epworth, 1989). Also, see Richard P. Heitzenrater, *The Elusive Mr. Wesley* (Nashville: Abingdon Press, 1984), whose two volumes offer a biographical portrait by way of readings from Wesley's own writings and those of others. John Wesley's works have been published in several editions, including those of Pine (1771–1774), Jackson (1829–1831), the so-called "Standard Editions" of the *Journal*, Sermons, and Letters of the 1930s (edited by Nehemiah Curnock, E. H. Sugden, and John Telford, respectively), and most recently the "Bicenten-nial" (formerly "Oxford") edition, which began to appear in 1976 and is still in progress.

39. On Wesley's Oxford period, see Richard P. Heitzenrater, "John Wesley and the Oxford Methodists, 1725–1735" (Ph.D. dissertation, Duke University, 1972); also his *Elusive Mr. Wesley* 1:50–74.

40. Wesley kept careful lists of his readings in this period; these are tabulated in Heitzenrater, "John Wesley and the Oxford Methodists, 1725–1735," pp. 493–526. On the accusations of Origenism, see Campbell, "John Wesley's Conceptions and Uses of Christian Antiquity," pp. 65–66.

41. Campbell, "John Wesley's Conceptions and Uses of Christian Antiquity," pp. 66–75.

42. Frank Baker, *John Wesley and the Church of England* (Nashville and New York: Ab-ingdon Press, 1970), pp. 39–57.

43. Campbell, "John Wesley's Conceptions and Uses of Christian Antiquity," pp. 75–81.

44. Martin Schmidt, *John Wesley: A Theological Biography* (2 vols; tr. Norman Goldhawk; Nashville: Abingdon Press, 1963–1973) is particularly helpful on Wesley's relation-ships with the Pietists in Georgia (1:140–82); and Baker, pp. 49–56.

45. Heitzenrater, *Elusive Mr. Wesley*, 1:78–91. The self-inspection is given in W. Reginald Ward and Richard P. Heitzenrater, eds., *Journals and Diaries* (Bicenten-nial Edition of the Works of John Wesley; Nashville: Abingdon Press, 1988), 1:212–13, n. 95; also in Heitzenrater, *Elusive Mr. Wesley*, 1: 93–96.

46. Franz Hildebrandt and Oliver A. Beckerlegge, eds., *A Collection of Hymns for the Use of the People Called Methodists* (Bicentennial Edition of the Works of John Wes-ley, vol. 7; Nashville: Abingdon Press, 1983), p. 116.

47. Ward and Heitzenrater, 1:249–50.

48. Charles Wesley, *The Journal of the Rev. Charles Wesley, M.A.* (Originally published in 1909; reprint edition, Taylors, South Carolina: Methodist Reprint Society, 1977), p. 153.

49. Schmidt, 1:270–303.

50. Albert C. Outler, ed., *John Wesley* (A Library of Protestant Thought; New York: Oxford University Press, 1964), pp. 121–33.

51. In Ward and Heitzenrater, 1:228; italics as in original.

52. See Albert C. Outler's introduction to this sermon in his edition of Wesley's *Ser-mons* (Bicentennial Edition of the Works of John Wesley; Nashville: Abingdon Press, 1984), 1:109–16, and his note on the date of the sermon, 1:117, n. 1.

53. Nehemiah Curnock, ed., *The Journal of the Rev. John Wesley, A.M., Sometime Fellow of Lincoln College, Oxford* ("Standard Edition" of the Works of John Wesley; 8 vols.; London: Epworth Press, 1906–1919), 2:172–73.

54. "A Plain Account of the People Called Methodists" in John Telford, ed., *Letters of the Rev. John Wesley, A.M.* ["Standard Edition" of the Works of John Wesley; 8 vols; London: Epworth Press, 1931], 2:292–311.

55. The Wesleyan Conference met for the first time in 1744, a year after the first Welsh Conference.

56. Wesley frequently repeated this definition of faith, usually citing Hebrews 11:1, as in the opening paragraphs of his *Earnest Appeal to Men of Reason and Religion* (in Cragg, 11:46–47); a more elaborate explication is given in the sermon "On the Discoveries of Faith" (in Outler, *Sermons*, 4:28–38).

57. On Wesley's oral preaching, see Richard P. Heitzenrater, "Spirit and Life: John Wesley's Preaching," in his *Mirror and Memory*, pp. 162–73.

58. See Hildebrandt and Beckerlegge; the Hymn "Love Divine" is on p. 545; see also J. Ernest Rattenbury, *The Evangelical Doctrines of Charles Wesley's Hymns* (London: Epworth Press, third edition, 1954), where Rattenbury utilizes the imagery of Bunyan's *Pilgrim's Progress* as headings under which he discusses Charles Wesley's proclamation of the way of salvation in the hymns. More recently, cf. Teresa Berger, *Theologie in Hymnen? Zum Verhältnis von Theologie und Doxologie am Beispiel des "Collection of Hymns for the Use of the People Called Methodists" (1780)* (Altenberge: Telos Verlag, 1989).

59. See Bernard G. Holland, *Baptism in Early Methodism* (London: Epworth Press, 1970), especially the conclusion, where Holland reflects on Wesley's inability to overcome this impasse and the subsequent ambiguity that he bequeathed to Methodism on the issue (pp. 140–51).

60. On the Wesleyan "way of salvation" in general, see Outler, *Theology in the Wesleyan Spirit, passim*, and Colin Williams, *John Wesley's Theology Today* (Nashville: Abingdon Press, 1960), pp. 39–73, 98–140, 167–200. On sanctification and Christian perfection in particular, see Harald Lindström, *Wesley and Sanctification: A Study in the Doctrine of Salvation* (London: Epworth Press, 1950).

61. "Directions concerning Pronunciation and Gesture" I:3:(7), in Thomas Jackson, ed., *The Works of the Rev. John Wesley, A.M.* (14 vols.; London: Wesleyan Conference Office, 1872, 13:520).

62. *Ibid.*, IV:7–8 (in Jackson, 13:526).

63. *Ibid.*, IV:6 (in Jackson 13:526).

64. For a recent and detailed analysis of Wesley's categories of religious affections and emotions, cf. Gregory S. Clapper, *John Wesley on Religious Affections: His Views on Experience and Emotion and Their Role in the Christian Life and Theology* (Metuchen, NJ: The Scarecrow Press, 1989).

65. On the influence of the Moravians and Halle Pietists, see the works cited in Chapter One by Stoeffler, Schmidt, Zehrer, and Nuttall; on the influence of the Puritans, see Robert C. Monk, *John Wesley: His Puritan Heritage* (Nashville: Abingdon Press, 1966).

66. John Wesley, ed., *A Christian Library* (50 vols.; Bristol: Felix Farley, 1749–1755); all references to volumes of this series are to this first edition.

67. Orcibal argues that Wesley's distinctive blend of a Protestant stress on justification by faith alone and a more Catholic stress on sanctification and especially Christian perfection came through his study of Continental spiritual writers: "L'Originalité théologique de John Wesley" (*passim*) and "Les Spirituels français et espagnols chez John Wesley et ses Contemporains" (*passim*).

68. The section title is shamelessly borrowed from Knox, who shamelessly borrowed it from Newman.
69. Knox's chapters on "The Parting of Friends" (pp. 459–512) chronicle these divisions.
70. Wesley's *Journal* for the period between 1739 and the early 1740s is dominated by the rift with the Moravians; cf. the fourth fascicle of the *Journal* (Curnock, 2:307–500).
71. Wesley did argue that human beings have "free will" to accept or reject Christ, but the point of agreement is in his consistent rejection of a notion of "natural" (in-born) free will; the tenth (Anglican) Article of Religion had ruled out "natural" free will, maintaining that free will comes only by God's grace "preventing" (preparing) human beings.
72. In Hildebrandt and Beckerlegge, p. 81.
73. On the rift between Arminian and Calvinistic Evangelicals, in general, see Outler, *John Wesley,* pp. 425–91.
74. Given in the so-called "Large Minutes," qu. 77 (in Jackson, 8:337–38).
75. John Wesley, sermon "On the Death of George Whitefield" (in Outler, 2:324–47).
76. The steps by which the Wesleyans became *de facto* separated from the Church of England are chronicled in Baker, *John Wesley and the Church of England,* esp. pp. 218–303.
77. Hylson-Smith, pp. 17–60; cf. G. C. B. Davies, *The Early Cornish Evangelicals, 1735–1760* (London: S.P.C.K., 1951); see Chapter Seven, below, on the institutionalization of the Evangelical Party within the Church of England.
78. See Chapter Seven, below, on both the sectarian and the more institutional groups that emerged from the revival in Great Britain.

Notes to Chapter Six

1. On this, see Ernst Benz, *Die protestantische Thebais: Zur Nachwirkung Makarios des Ägypters im Protestantismus der 16. und 17. Jahrhunderts in Europa und Amerika* (Wiesbaden: Verlag der Akademie der Wissenschaften und der Literatur in Mainz, 1963).
2. On the Non-Jurors and their attempted *liaison* with the Orthodox, see Thomas Lathbury, *A History of the Non-Jurors* (London: William Pickering, 1845), appendix. On the affair of "Bishop Erasmus," cf. Colin Williams, *John Wesley's Theology Today,* pp. 223–25.
3. Constantine Cavarnos, *St. Nicodemos the Hagiorite* (Modern Orthodox Saints; Belmont, MA: Institute for Byzantine and Modern Greek Studies, 1974), pp. 30–35; cf. Robert L. Nichols, "The Orthodox Elders *(Startsy)* of Imperial Russia" (*Modern Greek Studies Yearbook* 1 [1985]), p. 6.
4. Steven Runciman, *The Great Church in Captivity: A Study of the Patriarchate of Constantinople from the Eve of the Turkish Conquest to the Greek War of Independence* (Cambridge: Cambridge University Press, 1968), pp. 238–319.
5. Andrej Shishkin and Boris Uspenskij, "L'influence du Jansénisme en Russie au XVIIIe siècle: Deux Épisodes" (tr. Philippe Frison; *Cahiers du Monde russe et soviétique* 29:3–4 [July–December 1988]), pp. 337–39.
6. *Ibid.,* pp. 339–42.
7. Herbert Patzelt, *Der Pietismus in teschener Schlesien, 1709–1730* (Kirche im Osten series; Gottingen: Vandenhoeck and Ruprecht, 1969); Valdis Mezezers, *The Herrn-*

huterian Pietism in the Baltic and Its Outreach into America and Elsewhere in the World (North Quincy, MA: Christopher Publishing House, 1975); Walter Delius, *Der Protestantismus und die russische-orthodoxe Kirche* (Berlin: Evangelische Verlagsanstalt, 1950), p. 37.

8. A Russian (Slavonic?) translation of *True Christianity* was made by Simeon Todorsky, and was published at Halle in 1735: cf. the *Catalogue général des Livres imprimés de la Bibliothèque Nationale*, 4:421. On Tikhon of Zadonsk's familiarity with Johann Arndt, cf. Nichols, pp. 8–9, who points out that Tikhon had also read the works of Joseph Hall, a moderate Anglican spiritual writer of the early seventeenth century. Hall's *Heaven upon Earth* (1606) was included in John Wesley's *Christian Library.* Cf. Nadejda Gorodetzky, *Saint Tikhon of Zadonsk: Inspirer of Dostoevsky* (Crestwood, NY: St. Vladimir's Seminary Press, 1976), pp. 123, 163–64; Delius, pp. 34–37; Ernst Benz, *Die russische Kirche und das abendländische Christentum* (Munich: Nymphenburger Verlagshandlung, 1966), pp. 31–34; Erich Beyreuther, *August Hermann Francke und die Anfänge der ökumenischen Bewegung* (Hamburg-Bergstedt, Herbert Reich evangelische Verlag, 1957), pp. 54–103.

9. Beyreuther, pp. 54–103; Runciman, pp. 302–3. The Capuchin school at Astrakhan is mentioned in Shishkin and Uspenskij, p. 340.

10. Runciman, pp. 193–205.

11. On the historiography of Russian sectarian movements in general, see J. Eugene Clay, "God's People in the Early Eighteenth Century: The Uglich Affair of 1717" (*Cahiers du Monde russe et soviétique* 26:1 [January–March, 1985]), pp. 73–79. An honored standard is the work of Karl Conrad Grass, *Die russische Sekten* (1907), out of which Grass prepared a short article that is available in English as "Sects (Russian)," in James Hastings, ed., *Encyclopaedia of Religion and Ethics* (13 vols.; Edinburgh: T. and T. Clark, and New York: Charles Scribner's Sons, 1908), 11:334–39. Frederick C. Conybeare's *Russian Dissenters* (Harvard Theological Studies, no. 10; Cambridge, MA: Harvard University Press, 1921) relies largely on Grass. On the current status of the Russian schismatic churches, see "The Russian Old Ritualists" (*Ecumenical Review* 23 [July 1971], pp. 282–302.)

12. Thomas Robbins, "Religious Mass Suicide before Jonestown: The Russian Old Believers" (*Sociological Analysis* 47:1 [Spring 1986]: 1–20.

13. J. Eugene Clay, "The Theological Origins of the Christ-Faith [*Khristovshchina*]" (*Russian History/Histoire russe* 15 [1988]), p. 24.

14. Grass, 11:334–39; Conybeare, pp. 41–150; "The Russian Old Ritualists," pp. 293–94.

15. Conybeare, p. 108; cf. pp. 151–88; "The Russian Old Ritualists," pp. 287–88.

16. Cited in Conybeare, p. 183.

17. Conybeare, pp. 189–213.

18. Clay points out that the "People of God" originated prior to the *Raskol:* "God's People," pp. 80–81.

19. See on the *Doukhobors* below. Clay notes that it was customary for representatives of the Church and civil establishments to identify sectarian groups (such as the "People of God") as "Quakers" or as sharing Western influence: "God's People," p. 73, and "Theological Origins," p. 22. Although it would be nearly impossible to demonstrate Western origins, since the genesis of most of these groups is shrouded in obscurity, it is nevertheless possible (given the evidence in the first section of this chapter) that Western sectarian leaders such as Labadists or Quakers should have made their way to Eastern Europe. Conybeare and later writers consistently deny the possibility of Western influence, although Conybeare noted

that Russians attributed the rise of the "mystical" or "rationalist" groups to Western influences: p. 290, where in relating the origins of the *Molokani*, Conybeare includes their own narrative of the visit of an English merchant to Russia and his bringing Bible learning there. On the other hand, there appears to be very little evidence to see Western Christian movements as a *primary* influence on the Russian sects.

20. Conybeare, pp. 156–72.

21. On the "People of God," in general, see Karl Konrad Grass, "Men of God," in Hastings, 8:544–46; Conybeare, pp. 339–61, although Conybeare's study is based on a longer (German) study by Grass; and the two more recent articles (cited above) by Clay.

22. A hymn cited in Conybeare, pp. 349–50.

23. Clay, "God's People," pp. 87–93.

24. So Conybeare, pp. 343–45.

25. Clay stresses the theological roots of the People of God in the long-standing Orthodox tradition of speaking of *theiosis* as the goal of human existence: "Theological Origins," pp. 25–29.

26. Anton Anastasion Stamouli, "Doukhobors," in Hastings, 4:865; Gary Dean Fry, "The Doukhobors, 1801–1855: The Origins of a Successful Dissident Sect" (Ph.D. Dissertation, The American University, 1976), pp. 38–41, where Fry discusses both the possibilities of "Khlysti" and Quaker (or other Western) origins.

27. A Mennonite account of Kapustin's teachings, translated in Conybeare, p. 277.

28. Conybeare, pp. 273–74.

29. Stamouli, in Hastings, 4:865–67; Conybeare, pp. 267–87, 331–35. The Stundists would later form the basic communities from which modern Russian Baptist Churches developed.

30. Runciman, pp. 347–53; the Confession of Dositheus is given in John Leith, ed., *Creeds of the Churches: A Reader in Christian Doctrine from the Bible to the Present* (Atlanta: John Knox Press, third edition, 1982), pp. 485–517.

31. Cavarnos, *St. Nicodemos the Hagiorite*, pp. 54–55.

32. E. Kadloubovsky and G. E. H. Palmer, trans. and eds., *Writings from the Philokalia on Prayer of the Heart* (London: Faber and Faber, 1941), pp. 24–25, where a treatise of Nicephorus the Solitary (a fourteenth-century monk of Mt. Athos) repeats a story about Anthony of Egypt.

33. *Ibid.*, p. 21, n. 6.

34. *Ibid.*, p. 74.

35. Nichols, pp. 8–9; Gorodetzky, passim.

36. Brenda Meehan-Waters, "Popular Piety, Local Initiative and the Founding of Women's Religious Communities in Russia, 1764–1907" (*St. Vladimir's Theological Quarterly* [1986], pp. 117–42).

37. Nichols, 19–20.

38. The possibility of such an influence is considered (and not ruled out) by Weinryb, pp. 272–73. It is considered at more length by Schultz, pp. 277–79, who suggests that influences from Russian Christian sectarian movements may have come to Hasidism by way of the cult of Sabbatai Tsevi. Schultz, in turn, cites Yaffa Eliach, "The Russian Dissenting Sects and Their Influence on Israel Baal Shem Tov, Founder of Hasidism" (*Proceedings of the American Academy for Jewish Research* 36 [1968]: 57–83), where the argument for indirect influence by way of Sabbataianism is given in more detail.

39. Weinryb, pp. 17–176, and 273, n. 35.

40. *Ibid.*, pp. 181–205.
41. Podolia is now in the western Ukraine.
42. Cited in Weinryb, p. 215.
43. *Ibid.*, pp. 206–35.
44. *Ibid.*, pp. 237–38; cf. Eliach, pp. 60–61.
45. Legends and oral traditions about the Besht were written down from the early nineteenth century, the most famous of these collections being the *Shivhei Habesht* ("Praises of the Besht"), compiled by Baer ben Samuel and published in 1815. An English translation by Dan Ben-Amos and Jerome R. Mintz, *In Praise of the Baal Shem Tov*, was published in 1970 by the University of Indiana Press (reprint edition, New York: Schocken Books, 1984). There is a living tradition of composing and recomposing lives of the Besht based on the *Shivhei Habesht* and other literature; examples of this available in English (though in both cases, translated from German) are the compilations of Salomo Birnbaum, *The Life and Sayings of the Baal Shem* (tr. Irene Birnbaum; New York: Hebrew Publishing Co., 1933), and of Martin Buber, *The Legend of the Baal Shem* (tr. Maurice Friedman; New York: Harper and Brothers, 1955). Unfortunately, neither of these documents gives the sources from which its various sayings and stories are derived.
46. Weinryb, p. 234.
47. Cf. Birnbaum, pp. 1–19.
48. Ben-Amos and Mintz include five variations on the story of the Besht's trembling in prayer; this one is on p. 50, but cf. pp. 50–53; cf. also Birnbaum, pp. 38–39; on the Besht's revelation, cf. Ben-Amos and Mintz, pp. 27–31; Birnbaum, pp. 20–25.
49. Birnbaum, pp. 28–29, 42–44.
50. Although the notion that the Besht "popularized" or "democratized" earlier traditions of Jewish legalism and mysticism is broadly accepted, it is opposed in an important article by Ada Rapoport-Albert, "God and the Zaddik as the Two Focal Points of Hasidic Worship" (*History of Religions* 18 [May 1979]: 296–325). Rapoport-Albert points out that from the time of the Besht the Hasidim conceived of their community in an elitist sense, with the *zaddikim* as a new elite replacing the old elite of rabbis and Kabbalistic adepts. Nevertheless, it must be argued that in the earliest Hasidic communities, entrance into the company of the *zaddikim* was remarkably open.
51. Weinryb, pp. 264–69; cf. Mordecai L. Wilensky, "Testimony against the Hasidim in the Polemical Literature of the Mitnaggedim" (in S. W. Baron, ed., *Yitzhak F. Baer Jubilee Volume* [Jersalem: Israel Historical Society, 1960], pp. 398–498); the article is in Hebrew, and I have had access only to the English abstract [p. xxiv]).
52. Birnbaum, p. 41.
53. Cf. the abstract of the Wilensky article, where charges of the *Mitnaggedim* against the Hasidim are explicitly enumerated.
54. Birnbaum, p. 105.
55. Birnbaum, p. 91.
56. Gerschom Scholem, "Devekut, or Communion with God," in his *The Messianic Idea in Judaism* (New York: Schocken Books, 1971), pp. 203–27.
57. The role of the *zaddikim* in earlier and later Hasidic communities has been a subject of considerable debate in recent years. On the elitism of the *zaddikim*, see the article by Ada Rapoport-Albert cited above. See also Stephen Sharot, "Hasidism and the Routinization of Charisma" (*Journal for the Scientific Study of Religion* 19:4 [1980]: 325–36), and Arthur Green, "The *Zaddiq* as *Axis Mundi* in Later Judaism" (*Journal of the American Academy of Religion* 45:3 [1977]: 327–47, but especially

337–42). On the development of hereditary patterns of leadership among the Hasidim in the nineteenth century, see Chapter Seven below.
58. Sharot, p. 325.
59. Birnbaum, p. 54.
60. Walsh, p. 136.

Notes to Chapter Seven

1. Cited (and translated) in Ward and Heitzenrater, 1:220, n. 25.
2. Yinger, pp. 518–19.
3. *Journal* 1786:04:03 (Jackson 4:329).
4. The first is by William Jones, the second by Joseph Priestley; both are cited in James Hopkins, *A Woman to Deliver Her People: Joanna Southcott and English Millenarianism in an Era of Revolution* (Austin: University of Texas Press, 1982), p. xiv.
5. Cited in Hopkins, p. xiv.
6. Cited in Hopkins, p. 56.
7. Cited in Hopkins, pp. 112–13.
8. Hopkins, p. 114.
9. Hopkins, p. 117.
10. Hopkins, pp. 108–9.
11. Hopkins, pp. 216–17.
12. Elmer T. Clark's *The Small Sects in America* (New York and Nashville: Abingdon Press, second edition, 1949) offers a panorama of various American movements, most of them in one way or another descended from the religion of the heart movements. On the Holiness and Pentecostal movements in North America, cf. Vinson Synan, ed., *Aspects of Pentecostal-Charismatic Origins* (Plainfield, NJ: Logos International, 1975), especially the essays by Donald Dayton (pp. 39–54) and Melvin Dieter (pp. 55–80).
13. Knox, p. v; I do not take seriously Knox's claim (following this quotation) that although this was his original intent, his mind somehow softened during the course of his research and writing.
14. The successive steps by which the Methodist people became separate from the Church of England are carefully detailed by Baker in *John Wesley and the Church of England*.
15. Cf. the works by Hylson-Smith and Davies cited above.
16. Cited from *The United Methodist Hymnal* (1989), no. 378. On Newton, cf. Hylson-Smith, pp. 37–40.
17. Cited from *The United Methodist Hymnal* (1989), no. 622.
18. Wilberforce (eighteenth edition; London: T. Cadell, 1830), p. 248.
19. On the continuing importance of this group, see Gertrude Himmelfarb, "From Clapham to Bloomsbury: A Genealogy of Morals" (*Commentary* 79:2 [February 1985]: 36–45).
20. Both Bosk (pp. 154–66) and Sharot (pp. 333–36) make the point that the transition from "charismatic" to hereditary leadership transitions was not a chronologically uniform process. Sharot also points out that the diversity of forms of leadership transition helped the spread of the movement.
21. The founders of these two schools are contrasted by Bosk (pp. 156–58).
22. Deryck W. Lovegrove, *Established Church, Sectarian People: Itinerancy and the Transformation of English Dissent, 1780–1830* (Cambridge: Cambridge University Press, 1988).

23. Along with the Old Lutheranism and the Oxford Movement, one might also consider the rise of the "Mercersburg Theology" among conservative Reformed Christians in North America.

24. Schleiermacher, *The Christian Faith* Introduction, section 4 (ed. H. R. Mackintosh and J. S. Stewart; Edinburgh: T. and T. Clark, 1928), pp. 12–18.

25. Cf. Nathan O. Hatch, *The Democratization of American Christianity* (New Haven: Yale University Press, 1989).

26. Schultz, p. 250.

27. Knox, p. 20.

28. Similarly, Julian of Norwich and Teresa of Ávila emerged as religious leaders in the context of a form of religious life stressing mystical union where again the sacramental priesthood was closed to them. On women's roles in the early Methodist movement, see Paul Wesley Chilcote, "John Wesley and the Women Preachers of Early Methodism" (Ph.D. dissertation, Duke University, 1984), and Earl Kent Brown, *The Women in Mr. Wesley's Methodism* (New York: Edwin Mellen Press, 1983).

29. D. W. Bebbington, *Evangelicalism in Modern Britain: A History from the 1730s to the 1980s* (London: Unwin Hyman, 1989), p. 19, and ch. 2 in general, pp. 20–74.

30. Peter Gay, *The Enlightenment: An Interpretation*, Volume 1, *The Rise of Modern Paganism* (New York and London: The W. W. Norton Company, 1966), pp. ix–xii.

31. *Bhagavad Gita* 9:30; in Franklin Edgerton, tr., *The Bhagavad Gita* (Cambridge, MA: Harvard University Press, 1972), p. 49.

Bibliography

Primary Sources

Alacoque, Marguerite Marie. *The Autobiography of Saint Margaret Mary.* Translated and edited by Vincent Kerns. Westminster, MD: The Newman Press, and London: Darton, Longman, and Todd, 1961.

Ames, William. *The Marrow of Theology.* Translated by John Dykstra Eusden. The United Church Press, 1968. Reprint edition. Durham, NC: The Labyrinth Press, 1983.

Arnauld, Antoine. *Oeuvres de Messire Antoine Arnauld.* Paris: Sigismond d'Arnay, 1979; reprint edition, Brussels: Impression Anastaltique Culture et Civilization, 1967.

Arndt, Johann. See reference under Erb.

Barclay, Robert. *An Apology for the True Christian Divinity: Being an Explication and Vindication of the Principles and Doctrines of the People called Quakers.* Philadelphia: Friends' Book Store, 1908.

Baxter, Richard. *Methodus Theologiae christianae.* London: M. White and T. Snowden, 1681. Reprint Edition. Ann Arbor: University Microfilms. Wing Collection of Old English Books. Reel 53.

————. See reference under Orme.

Bayly, Lewis. *Yr Ymarfer o Ddiuwioled yn Cyfarwyldo dŷn i Rodio fel y Rhyngo ef Ffod Duw.* 1685; reprint edition, University Microfilms International, "Early English Books, 1475–1640" series. Reel 1560.

Ben-Amos, Dan; and Mintz, Jerome R. *In Praise of the Baal Shem Tov.* University of Indiana Press, 1970; reprint edition, New York: Schocken Books, 1984.

Birnbaum, Salomo. *The Life and Sayings of the Baal Shem.* Translated by Irene Birnbaum. New York: Hebrew Publishing Co., 1933.

Blair, Robert. *The Life of Mr. Robert Blair, Minister of St. Andrews, containing His Autobiography from 1593 to 1636.* Edinburgh: The Woodrow Society, 1848.

Buber, Martin. *The Legend of the Baal Shem.* Translated by Maurice Friedman. New York: Harper and Brothers, 1955.

Bunyan, John. *The Pilgrim's Progress.* Edited by Roger Sharrock. Harmondsworth, Middlesex: Penguin Books, 1965.

Calvin, John. *Institutes of the Christian Religion.* Translated by Lewis Ford Battles. Edited by John T. McNeil. Library of Christian Classics. Vols. 20, 21. Philadelphia: Westminster Press, 1960.

Cragg, Gerald R., ed. *The Appeals to Men of Reason and Religion and Certain Related Open Letters.* Bicentennial Edition of the Works of John Wesley. Vol. 11. Oxford: Oxford University Press, 1975.

————, ed. *The Cambridge Platonists.* A Library of Protestant Thought. New York: Oxford University Press, 1968.

Curnock, Nehemiah, ed. *The Journal of the Rev. John Wesley, A.M., Sometime Fellow of Lincoln College, Oxford.* "Standard Edition" of the Works of John Wesley. 8 vols. London: Epworth Press, 1906–1919.

Davis, William V., ed. *George Whitefield's Journals.* Gainesville, FL: Scholars' Facsimiles and Reprints, 1969.

Denzinger, Henricus, ed. *Enchiridion Symbolorum, Definitionium, et Declaration de Rebus Fidei et Morum.* 32nd edition. Barcelona: Herder, 1963.

Edgerton, Franklin, trans. *The Bhagavad Gita.* Cambridge, MA: Harvard University Press, 1972.

Erb, Peter, trans. and ed. *Johann Arndt: True Christianity.* Classics of Western Spirituality series. New York, Ramsey, and Toronto: Paulist Press, 1979.

————, ed. *Pietists: Selected Writings.* Classics of Western Spirituality series. New York: Paulist Press, 1983.

Eudes, Jean. *Oeuvres complètes de bienheureux Jean Eudes, Missionaire apostolique.* Vol. 1, Paris: P. Lethielleux, n.d.; Vols. 2–12, Paris: G. Beauchesne, 1906–1911.

————. *The Sacred Heart.* Translated by Richard Flower. New York: P. J. Kennedy and Sons, 1946.

Francke, August Hermann. *Pietas Hallensis.* Edinburgh: James Davidson, 1727.

————. *Werke in Auswahl.* Edited by Erhard Peschke, Berlin: Luther-Verlag, 1969.

Gillies, John, ed. *Historical Collections relating to Remarkable Periods of the Success of the Gospel.* Title on Cover and reprint title page is *Historical Collections of Accounts of Revival.* Kelso: John Rutherford, 1845. Reprint edition, London: Banner of Truth Trust, 1981.

Goodwin, Thomas. See reference under Miller.

Guyon, Jeanne Marie de la Mothe. *A Short and Easy Method of Prayer.* Translated by Thomas Digby Brooke. London: Hatchard and Co., 1867.

————. *Spiritual Torrents.* Translated by A. W. Marston. London: H. R. Allenson, Ltd, n.d.

Hildebrandt, Franz; and Beckerlegge, Oliver A., eds. *A Collection of Hymns for the Use of the People Called Methodists.* Bicentennial Edition of The Works of John Wesley. Vol. 7. Nashville: Abingdon Press, 1983.

Jackson, Thomas, ed. *The Works of the Reverend John Wesley, A.M.* 14 vols. London: Wesleyan Conference Office, 1872.

Kadloubovsky, E.; and Palmer, G. E. H., trans. and eds. *Writings from the Philokalia on Prayer of the Heart.* London: Faber and Faber, 1941.

Labadie, Jean de. *La Reformation de l'Eglise par le Pastorat.* Middelbourg: Henry Smidt, 1667.

Leith, John, ed. *Creeds of The Churches: A Reader in Christian Doctrine from the Bible to the Present.* Third edition. Atlanta: John Knox Press, 1982.

Miller, John C.; and Halley, Robert, eds. *The Works of Thomas Goodwin, D.D., Sometime President of Magdalene College, Oxford.* Nichol's Series of Standard Divines, Puritan Period. 12 vols. Edinburgh: James Nichol, 1862. 4:93–150.

Molinos, Miguel de. *Spiritual Guide.* 1688. English translation edited by Kathleen Lyttelton. Fifth Edition. London: Meuthen and Company, 1927.

Nicole, Pierre. *Les Imaginnaires et les Visionnaires.* Cologne: Pierre Marteau, 1683.

Orme, William, ed. *Practical Works of the Rev. Richard Baxter.* 23 vols. London: James Duncan, 1830.

Osborn, George, ed. *The Poetical Works of John and Charles Wesley.* London: Wesleyan Conference Office, 1868.

Outler, Albert C., ed. *John Wesley.* A Library of Protestant Thought. New York: Oxford University Press, 1964.

———. *Sermons.* Bicentennial Edition of the Works of John Wesley. Vols. 1–4. Nashville: Abingdon Press, 1984.

Pascal, Blaise. *Pensées.* Translated by A. J. Krailsheimer. London: Penguin Books, 1966.

———. *The Provincial Letters.* Translated by A. J. Krailsheimer. London: Penguin Books, 1967.

[Perkins, William.] *A Golden Chaine, or The Description of Theologie, Containing the Order of the Causes of Salvation and Damnation, according to God's Word.* Second edition. Cambridge: John Legate, 1597.

Philokalia. See reference under Kadloubovsky.

Schleiermacher, Friedrich. *The Christian Faith.* Edited by H. R. Mackintosh and J. S. Stewart; Edinburgh: T. and T. Clark, 1928.

Spener, Phillip Jacob. *Pia Desideria.* Translated by Theodore G. Tappert. Philadelphia: Fortress Press, 1964.

———. *Schriften.* Edited by Erich Beyreuther. 4 vols. Hildesheim and New York: Georg Olms Verlag, 1979–1984.

Steere, Douglas V., ed. *Quaker Spirituality: Selected Writings.* Classics of Western Spirituality. New York: Paulist Press, 1984.

Telford, John, ed. *Letters of the Rev. John Wesley, A.M.* "Standard Edition" of the Works of John Wesley. 8 vols. London: Epworth Press, 1931.

Teellinck, William [Willem]. *Paul's Complaint against His Natural Corruption, with the Meanes How to be Delivered from the Power of the Same.* London: John Danson, 1621. Reprint edition, University Microfilms International, "English Books, 1475–1640" series. Reel 1118.

The United Methodist Hymnal: Book of United Methodist Worship. Nashville: United Methodist Publishing House, 1989.

Ward, W. Reginald; and Heitzenrater, Richard P., eds. *Journals and Diaries.* Bicentennial Edition of the Works of John Wesley. Nashville: Abingdon Press, 1988.

Wesley, Charles. *The Journal of the Rev. Charles Wesley, M.A.* Originally published in 1909, n.d. Reprint edition. Taylors, SC: Methodist Reprint Society, 1977.

Wesley, John, ed. *A Christian Library.* 50 vols. Bristol: Felix Farley, 1749–1755.

———. See references under Cragg, Curnock, Hildebrandt, Jackson, Osborn, Outler, Telford, and Ward.

Whitefield, George. *Selected Sermons of George Whitefield, M.A.* London: Banner of Truth Trust, 1958.

———. See reference under Davis.

Wilberforce, William. *A Practical View of the Prevailing Religious System of Professed Christians, in the Higher and Middle Classes in this Country, Contrasted with Real Christianity.* Eighteenth edition. London: T. Cadell, 1830.

Zinzendorf, Nicolas Ludwig, Graf von. *Nine Public Lectures on Important Subjects in Religion.* Translated by George W. Forell. Iowa City: University of Iowa Press, 1973.

———. *Werke.* Collected edition. Edited by Erich Beyreuther, Gerhard Meyer, and Amedeo Molnár. 5 vols. Hildesheim and New York: Georg Olms Verlag, 1978.

Secondary Studies

Allison, C. F. *The Rise of Moralism: The Proclamation of the Gospel from Hooker to Baxter.* New York: Seabury Press, 1966.

Ayling, Stanley Edward. *John Wesley.* Nashville: Abingdon Press, 1979.

Baker, Frank. *John Wesley and the Church of England.* Nashville and New York: Abingdon Press, 1970.

Bebbington, D. W. *Evangelicalism in Modern Britain: A History from the 1730s to the 1980s*. London: Unwin Hyman, 1989.

Bechard, Henri. *The Visions of Bernard Francis de Hoyos, S.J.: Apostle of the Sacred Heart in Spain*. New York, Washington, and Hollywood: The Vantage Press, 1959.

Bennett, Richard, *The Early Life of Howell Harris*. Translated by Gomer M. Roberts. London: Banner of Truth Trust, 1962.

Benz, Ernst, *Die Ostkirche im Lichte der protestantischen Gesichtsschreibung von der Reformation bis zur Gegenwart*. Munich: Verlag Karl Albert Freiburg, 1952.

————. *Die protestantische Thebais: Zur Nachwirkung Makarios de Ägypters im Protestantismus der 16. und 17. Jahrhunderts in Europa und Amerika*. Wiesbaden: Verlag der Akademie der Wissenschaften und der Literatur in Mainz, 1963.

————. *Die russische Kirche and das abendländische Christentum*. Munich: Nymphenburger Verlagshandlung, 1966.

Berger, Alan Lewis. " 'Normal' Mysticism and the Social World: A Comparative Study of Quaker and Hasidic Communal Mysticism." Ph.D. dissertation, Syracuse University, 1976.

Berger, Teresa. *Theologie in Hymnen? Zum Verhältnis von Theologie und Doxologie am Beispiel des "Collection of Hymns for the Use of the People Called Methodists" (1780)*. Altenberge: Telos Verlag, 1989.

Beyreuther, Erich, *August Hermann Francke und die Anfänge der ökumenischen Bewegung*. Hamburg-Bergstedt: Herbert Reich Evangelisches Verlag, 1957.

Bosk, Charles L. "The Routinization of Charisma: The Case of the Zaddik." *Sociological Inquiry* 49:2–3 (1979): 150–67.

Brauer, Jerald C. "Types of Puritan Piety." *Church History* 56 (May 1987): 47–51.

Brown, Dale W. *Understanding Pietism*. Grand Rapids: William B. Eerdmans, 1978.

Brown, Earl Kent. *The Women in Mr. Wesley's Methodism*. New York: Edwin Mellen Press, 1983.

Campbell, Ted A. "John Wesley's Conceptions and Uses of Christian Antiquity." Ph.D. dissertation, Southern Methodist University, 1984.

Cavarnos, Constantine. *St. Nicodemus the Hagiorite*. Modern Orthodox Saints. Belmont, MA: Institute for Byzantine and Modern Greek Studies, 1974.

Chilcote, Paul Wesley. "John Wesley and the Women Preachers of Early Methodism." Ph.D. dissertation, Duke University, 1984.

Clapper, Gregory S. *John Wesley on Religious Affections: His Views on Experience and Emotion and Their Role in the Christian Life and Theology*. Metuchen, NJ: The Scarecrow Press, 1989.

Clark, Elmer T. *The Small Sects in America*. Second edition. New York and Nashville: Abingdon Press, 1949.

Clay, J. Eugene. "God's People in the Early Eighteenth Century: The Uglich Affair of 1717." *Cahiers du Monde russe et soviétiqe* 26:1 (January–March 1985): 69–101.

————. "The Theological Origins of the Christ-Faith [*Khristovshchina*]." *Russian History/Histoire russe* 15 (1988): 21–41.

Cohn, Norman. *The Pursuit of the Millennium: Revolutionary Millennarians and Mystical Anarchists of the Middle Ages*. Second Edition. New York: Oxford University Press, 1970.

Collinson, Patrick. *The Elizabethan Puritan Movement*. London: Jonathan Cape, 1967.

————. *The Religion of Protestants: The Church in English Society 1559–1625*. Oxford: The Clarendon Press, 1982.

Conybeare, Frederick C. *Russian Dissenters*. Harvard Theological Studies, no. 10. Cambridge, MA: Harvard University Press, 1921.

Cross, F. L.; and E. A. Livingstone, eds. *The Oxford Dictionary of the Christian Church*. Second Edition. Oxford: Oxford University Press, 1974.

Davies, G. C. B. *The Early Cornish Evangelicals, 1735–1760*. London: S.P.C.K., 1951.

Delius, Walter. *Der Protestantismus und die russisch-orthodoxe Kirche*. Berlin: Evangelische Verlagsanstalt, 1950.

Delumeau, Jean. *Catholicism between Luther and Voltaire: A New View of the Counter-Reformation*. London: Burns and Oates; Philadelphia: Westminster Press, 1977.

Dupuy, Michel. "Jansénisme." In Marcel Viller, et al. eds., *Dictionnaire de Spiritualité*. Paris: Beauchesne, 1932ff. 8:102–48.

Eckhardt, Martin von. *Die Einfluss der Madame Guyon auf der norddeutsche Laienwelt im 18. Jahrhundert*. Barmen: Staats-Druckerei, 1928.

Eliach, Yaffa. "The Russian Dissenting Sects and Their Influence on Israel Baal Shem Tov, Founder of Hasidism." *Proceedings of the American Academy for Jewish Research* 36 (1968): 57–83.

Ergang, Robert. *The Myth of the All-Destructive Fury of the Thirty Years War*. Pocono Pines, PA: The Craftsmen at Pocono Pines, 1956.

Evans, Eifion. *Daniel Rowland and the Great Evangelical Awakening in Wales*. Carlisle, PA: Banner of Truth Trust, 1985.

Ferré, Frederick. *Basic Modern Philosophy of Religion*. New York: Charles Scribner's Sons, 1967.

———. "The Definition of Religion." *Journal of the American Academy of Religion* 38 (1970): 3–16.

Friedrich, Carl J. *The Age of the Baroque*. San Francisco: Harper Bros., 1952.

Fry, Gary Dean. "The Doukhobors, 1801–1855: The Origins of a Successful Dissident Sect." Ph.D. dissertation, The American University, 1976.

Gannon, Thomas M.; and Traub, George W. *The Desert and the City: An Interpretation of the History of Christian Spirituality*. London: The MacMillan Co., and Collier MacMillan, Ltd., 1969.

Gay, Peter. *The Enlightenment: An Interpretation*. Volume 1, *The Rise of Modern Paganism*. New York and London: The W. W. Norton Company, 1966.

Gorodetzky, Nadejda. *Saint Tikhon of Zadonsk: Inspirer of Dostoevsky*. Crestwood, NY: St. Vladimir's Seminary Press, 1976.

Grass, Karl Conrad. "Men of God." In James Hastings, ed. *Encyclopaedia of Religion and Ethics*. 13 vols. Edinburgh: T. and T. Clark; and New York: Charles Scribner's Sons, 1908. 8:544–46.

———. "Sects (Russian)." In James Hastings, ed. *Encyclopaedia of Religion and Ethics*. 13 vols. Edinburgh: T. and T. Clark; and New York: Charles Scribner's Sons, 1908. 11:334–39.

Green, Arthur. "*The Zaddiq* as *Axis Mundi* in Later Judaism." *Journal of the American Academy of Religion* 45 (September 1977): 327–47.

Haller, William. *The Rise of Puritanism, Or, The Way to the New Jerusalem as Set Forth in Pulpit and Press from Thomas Cartwright to John Lilburne and John Milton, 1570–1643*. New York: Columbia University Press, 1938.

Hamilton, J. Taylor and Hamilton, Kenneth G. *History of the Moravian Church: The Renewed Unitas Fratrum, 1722–1957*. Bethlehem, PA, and Winston-Salem, NC: Interprovincial Board of Christian Education, Moravian Church in America, 1967.

Hatch, Nathan O. *The Democratization of American Christianity*. New Haven: Yale University Press, 1989.

Heitzenrater, Richard P. *The Elusive Mr. Wesley*. 2 vols. Nashville: Abingdon Press, 1984.

———. "John Wesley and the Oxford Methodists, 1725–1735." Ph.D. dissertation, Duke University, 1972.

———. *Mirror and Memory: Reflections on Early Methodism.* Nashville: Kingswood Books, 1989.

Henry, Stuart, *George Whitefield: Wayfaring Witness.* Nashville: Abingdon Press, 1957.

Heppe, Heinrich. *Geschichte des Pietismus und der Mystik in der reformirte Kirche, namentlich der Niederlande.* Leiden: E. J. Brill, 1879.

Hill, Christopher. *Century of Revolution, 1603–1714.* Edinburgh: Thomas Nelson and Sons, Ltd., 1961.

———. *The World Turned Upside Down: Radical Ideas during the English Revolution.* London: T. Smith, 1972.

Himmelfarb, Gertrude. "From Clapham to Bloomsbury: A Genealogy of Morals." *Commentary* 79:2 (February 1985): 36–45.

Holland, Bernard G. *Baptism in Early Methodism.* London: Epworth Press, 1970.

Hopkins, James. *A Woman to Deliver Her People: Joanna Southcott and English Millenarianism in an Era of Revolution.* Austin: University of Texas Press, 1982.

Hylson-Smith, Kenneth. *Evangelicals in the Church of England, 1734–1984.* Edinburgh: T. and T. Clark, 1988.

Jones, Oswain W. "The Welsh Church in the Eighteenth Century." In David Walker, ed. *A History of the Church in Wales.* Penarth, S. Glamorganshire: Historical Society of the Church in Wales, 1976.

Keddie, Henrietta, a.k.a. "Sarah Tytler". *The Countess of Huntingdon and Her Circle.* London: Sir Isaac Pitman and Sons, Ltd., 1907.

Knappen, M. M. *Tudor Puritanism: A Chapter in the History of Idealism.* Chicago and London: University of Chicago Press, 1939.

Knight, Helen C., *Lady Huntingdon and Her Friends: Or, The Revival of the Work of God in the Days of Wesley, Whitefield, Romaine, Venn, and Others in the Last Century.* New York: American Tract Society, 1853.

Knox, R. A. *Enthusiasm: A Chapter in the History of Religion with Special Reference to the Seventeenth and Eighteenth Centuries.* New York and Oxford: Oxford University Press, 1950.

Lake, Peter. *Moderate Puritans and the Elizabethan Church.* Cambridge: Cambridge University Press, 1982.

Lang, August. *Puritanismus und Pietismus: Studien zu ihrer Entwicklung von M. Butzer bis zum Methodismus.* Beiträge zur Geschichte und Lehre der reformierten Kirche series, vol. 6. Neukirchen Kreis Moers: Buchhandlung des Erziehungsvereins, 1941.

Lathbury, Thomas. *A History of the Non-Jurors.* London: William Pickering, 1845.

Lewis, A. J. *Zinzendorf: The Ecumenical Pioneer: A Study in the Moravian Contribution to Christian Mission and Unity.* Philadelphia: The Westminster Press, 1962.

Lindström, Harald. *Wesley and Sanctification: A Study in the Doctrine of Salvation.* London: Epworth Press, 1950.

Lovegrove, Deryck W. *Established Church, Sectarian People: Itinerary and the Transformation of English Dissent, 1780–1830.* Cambridge: Cambridge University Press, 1988.

Lund, Eric. "Johann Arndt and the Development of a Lutheran Spiritual Tradition." Ph.D. dissertation, Yale University, 1979.

McAdoo, Henry R. *The Spirit of Anglicanism: A Survey of Anglican Theological Methodology in the Seventeenth Century.* New York: Charles Scribner's Sons, 1965.

McClintock, John; and Strong, James. *Cyclopedia of Biblical, Theological, and Ecclesiastical Literature.* 12 vols. New York: Harper and Bros., 1891.

McIntosh, Lawrence D. "The Place of John Wesley in the Christian Tradition: A Selected Bibliography." In Kenneth E. Rowe, ed. *The Place of Wesley in the Christian Tradition: Essays Delivered at Drew University in Celebration of the Commencement of the Publication of the Oxford Edition of the Works of John Wesley.* Metuchen, NJ: Scarecrow Press, 1976. 134–59.

Meehan-Waters, Brenda. "Popular Piety, Local Initiative and the Founding of Women's Religious Communities in Russia, 1764–1907." *St. Vladimir's Theological Quarterly* (1986): 117–42.

Mezezers, Valdis. *The Herrnhuterian Pietism in the Baltic and its Outreach into America and Elsewhere in the World.* North Quincy, MA: Christopher Publishing House, 1975.

Monk, Robert C. *John Wesley: His Puritan Heritage.* Nashville: Abingdon Press, 1966.

Morgan, Derec Llwyd. *The Great Awakening in Wales.* Translated by Dyfnallt Morgan. London: Epworth Press, 1988.

Muller, Richard A. "Perkins' *A Golden Chaine:* Predestinarian System or Schematized *Ordo Salutis?*" *Sixteenth Century Journal* 9:1 (1978): 69–81.

Nichols, Robert L. "The Orthodox Elders [*Startsy*] of Imperial Russia." *Modern Greek Studies Yearbook* 1 (1985): 1–30.

Nuttall, Geoffrey F. "Continental Pietism and the Evangelical Movement in Britain." In van den Berg, J.; and van Dooren, J. P., eds. *Pietismus und Reveil.* Leiden: E. J. Brill, 1978. 207–36.

O'Keefe, Cyril B. *Contemporary Reactions to the Enlightenment (1728–1762): A Study of Three Critical Journals: The Jesuit* Journal de Trevoux, *the Jansenist* Nouvelles Ecclésiastiques, *and the Secular* Journal de Savants. Geneva: Librairie Slatkine; and Paris: Honoré Champion, 1974.

Orcibal, Jean. "L'Originalité théologique de John Wesley et les Spiritualités du Continent." *Revue historique* 222 (1959): 51–80.

Outler, Albert C. *Theology in the Wesleyan Spirit.* Nashville: Tidings, 1975.

————. "Les Spirituels français et espagnols chez John Wesley et ses Contemporains." *Revue de l'Histoire des Religions* 139:1 (January–March 1951): 50–109.

Plumb, J. H. *England in the Eighteenth Century* The Pelican History of England, vol. 7. Harmondsworth, Middlesex: Penguin Books, Ltd., revised edition, 1963.

Patzelt, Herbert, *Der Pietismus in teschener Schlesien, 1709–1730.* Kirche im Osten series. Göttingen: Vandenhoeck und Ruprecht, 1969.

Polisenky, J. V. *War and Society in Europe, 1618–1648.* Cambridge: Cambridge University Press, 1978.

Prozesky, Martin H. "The Emergence of Dutch Pietism." *Journal of Ecclesiastical History* 28:1 (January 1977): 29–37.

Rack, Henry D. *Reasonable Enthusiast: John Wesley and the Rise of Methodism.* London: Epworth, 1989.

Rapoport-Albert, Ada. "God and the Zaddik as the Two Focal Points of Hasidic Worship." *History of Religions* 18 (May 1979): 296–325.

Rattenbury, J. Ernest. *The Evangelical Doctrines of Charles Wesley's Hymns.* Third edition. London: Epworth Press, 1954.

Robbins, Thomas. "Religious Mass Suicide Before Jonestown: The Russian Old Believers." *Sociologocal Analysis* 47:1 (Spring 1986): 1–20.

Runciman, Steven. *The Great Church in Captivity: A Study of the Patriarchate of Constantinople from the Eve of the Turkish Conquest to the Greek War of Independence.* Cambridge: Cambridge University Press, 1968.

Rupp, Ernest Gordon. *Religion in England, 1688–1791.* The Oxford History of the Christian Church series, edited by Henry and Owen Chadwick. Oxford: Oxford University Press, 1986.

"The Russian Old Ritualists." *Ecumenical Review* 23 (July 1971): 282–302.

Sattler, Gary R. "August Hermann Francke and Mysticism." *Covenant Quarterly* 38:4 (November 1980): 3–17.

——— . *God's Glory, Neighbor's Good: A Brief Introduction to the Life and Writings of August Hermann Francke.* Chicago: Covenant Press, 1982.

Saxby, T. J. *The Quest for the New Jerusalem: Jean de Labadie and the Labadists, 1610–1744.* International Archives of the History of Ideas series. Dordrecht: Martinus Nijhoff Publishers, 1987.

Schmidt, Leigh Eric. *Holy Fairs: Scottish Communions and American Revivals in the Early Modern Period.* Princeton, NJ: Princeton University Press, 1989.

Schmidt, Martin. *John Wesley: A Theological Biography.* Translated by Norman Goldhawk. Nashville: Abingdon Press, 1963–1973.

——— . "Pietism." In Julius Bodensiek, ed. *Encyclopedia of the Lutheran Church.* 3 vols. Minneapolis: Augsburg Publishing House, 1965. 3:1898–1906.

——— . "Wesley's Place in Church History." In *The Place of Wesley in the Christian Tradition: Essays Delivered at Drew University in Celebration of the Commencement of the Oxford Edition of the Work of John Wesley.* Edited by Kenneth E. Rowe. Metuchen, NJ: The Scarecrow Press, 1976. Pp. 67–93.

Scholem, Gershom G. "Devekut, or Communion with God." In *The Messianic Idea of Judaism.* New York: Schocken Books, 1971.

——— . *Major Trends in Jewish Mysticism.* Third Edition. New York: Schocken Books, 1954.

Schultz, Joseph P. *Judaism and the Gentile Faiths: Comparative Studies in Religion.* Rutherford, NJ: Farleigh Dickinson University Press, 1981.

[Seymour, Aaron.] *The Life and Times of Selina Countess of Huntingdon.* 2 vols. London: William Edward Painter, 1839.

Sharot, Stephen. "Hasidism and the Routinization of Charisma." *Journal for the Scientific Study of Religion* 19:4 (December 1980): 325–36.

Shishkin, Andrej; and Uspenskij, Boris. "L'influence du Jansénisme en Russie au XVIIIe siècle: Deux Épisodes." Translated by Phillippe Frison. *Cahiers du Monde russe et soviétique* 29:3–4 (July–December 1988): 337–42.

Simon, John S. *John Wesley and the Religious Societies.* Second edition. London: Epworth Press, 1955.

Smith, John Q. "Occupational Groups among the Early Methodists of the Keighley Circuit." *Church History* 57:2 (June 1988): 187–96.

Stamouli, Anton Anastasion. "Doukhobors." In James Hastings, ed. *Encyclopaedia of Religion and Ethics.* 13 vols. Edinburgh: T. and T. Clark; and New York: Charles Scribner's Sons, 1908. 4:865.

Stein, K. James. *Philipp Jakob Spener: Pietist Patriarch.* Chicago: Covenant Press, 1986.

Stephen, Leslie. *History of English Thought in the Eighteenth Century.* 2 vols. Third edition, 1902. Reprint edition, New York: Peter Smith, 1949.

Stoeffler, F. Ernest. *German Pietism during the Eighteenth Century.* Studies in the History of Religions, no. 24. Leiden: E. J. Brill, 1973.

——— . "Religious Roots of Early Moravian and Methodist Movements." *Methodist History* 24:2 (1986 April): 132–40.

——— . *The Rise of Evangelical Pietism.* Studies in the History of Religion, no. 9. Leiden: E. J. Brill, 1965.

——— . "Tradition and Renewal in the Ecclesiology of John Wesley." In *Traditio, Krisis, Renovatio als theologischer Sicht: Festschrift Winfried Zeller.* Edited by Bernd Jaspert. Marburg: Elwert, 1976. Pp. 298–316.

Stone, Lawrence. *The Causes of the English Revolution, 1529–1642*. New York: Harper and Row, 1972.

Streng, Frederick J.; Charles Lloyd, Jr.; and Jay T. Allen. *Ways of Being Religious: Readings for a New Approach to Religion*. Englewood Cliffs, NJ: Prentice-Hall, Inc., 1973.

Streng, Frederick J. *Understanding Religious Life*. Third edition. Wadsworth, CA: Wadsworth Publishing Company, 1985.

Stuart, Robert Orkney. "The Breaking of the Elizabethan Settlement of Religion: Puritan Spiritual Experience and the Theological Division of the English Church." Ph.D. dissertation, Yale University, 1976. Reprint edition: Ann Arbor, MI: Xerox University Microfilms, 1978.

Synan, Vinson, ed. *Aspects of Pentecostal-Charismatic Origins*. Plainfield, NJ: Logos International, 1975.

Tackett, Timothy. *Religion, Revolution, and Regional Culture in Eighteenth-Century France: The Ecclesiastical Oath of 1791*. Princeton: Princeton University Press, 1986.

Vidal, Daniel. *Miracles et Convulsions jansénistes au XVIIIe Siècle: Le Mal et sa Connaissance*. Paris: Presses Universitaires de France, 1987.

Wallace, Anthony F. C. "Revitalization Movements," *American Anthropologist* 58 (1956): 264–81.

Walsh, John. "Origins of the Evangelical Revival." In G. V. Bennett and John D. Walsh, eds. *Essays in Modern English Church History: In Memory of Norman Sykes*. New York: Oxford University Press, 1966.

Weaver, F. Ellen. *The Evolution of the Reform of Port-Royal: From the Rule of Cîteaux to Jansenism*. Paris: Editions Beauchesne, 1978.

Weigelt, Horst. "Interpretations of Pietism in the Research of Contemporary German Church Historians." *Church History* 39 (June 1970): 236–41.

Weinlick, John R. *Count Zinzendorf*. New York and Nashville: Abingdon Press, 1956.

Weinryb, Bernard D. *The Jews of Poland: A Social and Economic History of the Jewish Community in Poland from 1100 to 1800*. Second edition. Philadelphia: Jewish Publication Society of America, 1976.

Westerkamp, Marilyn J. *The Triumph of the Laity: Scots-Irish Piety and the Great Awakening, 1625–1760*. New York: Oxford University Press, 1988.

Wilensky, Mordecai L. "Testimony against the Hasidim in the Polemical Literature of the Mitnaggedim." In S. W. Baron, ed. *Yitzhak F. Baer Jubilee Volume*. Jerusalem: Israel Historical Society, 1960. Pp. xxiv, 398–498.

Williams, Colin. *John Wesley's Theology Today*. Nashville: Abingdon Press, 1960.

Yinger, J. Milton. *The Scientific Study of Religion*. London: The MacMillan Company, 1970.

Zehrer, Karl. "The Relationship between Pietism in Halle and Early Methodism." *Methodist History* 17:4 (July 1979): 211–24.

Index

À Brakel, Theodore and Willem, 74
Acceptants, 26
Adoption. *See* Assurance of salvation
Affections, affective devotion, 27, 28, 47–48, 52, 53, 68, 74, 96–97, 148–49
À Kempis, Thomas. *See* Thomas à Kempis
Alacoque, Marguerite Marie, 39–40, 96
Aldersgate, 119
Alleine, Joseph, 102, 124
Alumbrados, 11, 30, 75
America, 94, 95, 98, 109, 117, 128, 158, 172
Ames, William, 14, 46–48, 70, 71
Anti-intellectualism, 34–35
Apocalyptic teachings, 12, 154, 156–57, 174
Appellants, 26
Arminius and Arminianism, 46, 52, 65–67, 70, 123, 125–27, 141, 188n.62, 198n.71
Arnauld, Antoine, 22–23, 28–29
Arnauld, Jacqueline (Angélique), 18–20, 174
Arndt, Johann, 8, 79–82, 84, 87, 124, 130, 143, 190n.29
Assurance of salvation, 47–48, 52, 72, 95, 114, 118–19, 120
Attrition, 21
Augustine of Hippo, 21, 29, 46
Ávila, Teresa of. *See* Teresa of Ávila

Baal Shem Tov, 146–49, 150, 201n.45
Baer, Dov, of Mezerich, 149
Baptism, 90, 117, 139, 192n.59, 197n.59
Baptists, 58, 70
Barclay, Robert, 61–63, 77
Baroque, 40
Baxter, Richard, 65–68, 124
Bayly, Lewis, 84, 103, 195n.16
Bebbington, D. W., 175
Belgium. *See* Spanish Netherlands

Bengel, Johann Albrecht, 88
Berger, Alan Lewis, 4, 181n.18
Berger, Teresa, 197n.58
Besht. *See* Baal Shem Tov
Bezpopovtsy, 136–37, 140
Bible, 62, 88, 100, 102, 164
Blair, Robert, 55, 105
Blake, William, 156, 157
Bohemian Brethren, 92
Böhme, Jakob, 11
Booth, Catherine and William, 158
Bossuet, Jacques, 32–34, 35
Bourignon, Antoinette, 30–31, 77, 124
Brauer, Jerald C., 186n.8
Buber, Martin, 171
Buddhism, 7, 10, 12, 178
Bunyan, John, 50–52, 102, 124

Calvin, John, 9, 44, 46, 76, 181n.16
Cambridge Platonists, 64–65
Camisards, 154–55
Capuchins, 13, 20, 134
Carmelites, 11, 30
Chantal, Jeanne Frances de, 37
Chilcote, Paul Wesley, 203n.28
Christ, 96–97, 106, 139, 155
Church Missionary Society, 164
Church of England, 7, 15, 120, 128, 161–65
Circulating Schools, 103
Clapham Sect, 162–65
Clapper, Gregory S., 197n.64
Clarke, Samuel, 50
Collegia pietatis, 84, 101, 167
Collinson, Patrick, 185nn.2, 3
Comenius, Jan Amos, 77, 94
Communalism, 106
Conference, 106, 111, 121, 127
Congregationalists, 57
Contrition, 21–22, 28
Conventicles and societies, 56, 73, 77, 84, 87, 92, 101, 109, 115, 121, 167